CHANGE LEADERSHIP
IN HIGHER EDUCATION

CHANGE LEADERSHIP IN HIGHER EDUCATION

A Practical Guide to Academic Transformation

Jeffrey L. Buller

A Wiley Brand

Cover design by Wiley
Cover image: © MACIEJ NOSKOWSKI | Getty

Published by Jossey-Bass
A Wiley Brand
One Montgomery Street, Suite 1200, San Francisco, CA 94104-4594—
www.josseybass.com

Jossey-Bass books and products are available through most bookstores. To contact Jossey-Bass directly call our Customer Care Department within the U.S. at 800-956-7739, outside the U.S. at 317-572-3986, or fax 317-572-4002.

Wiley publishes in a variety of print and electronic formats and by print-on-demand. Some material included with standard print versions of this book may not be included in e-books or in print-on-demand. If this book refers to media such as a CD or DVD that is not included in the version you purchased, you may download this material at http://booksupport.wiley.com. For more information about Wiley products, visit www.wiley.com.

Library of Congress Cataloging-in-Publication Data has been applied for and is on file with the Library of Congress.

ISBN 9781118762035 (hardcover); ISBN 9781118762233 (ebk.);
ISBN 9781118762127 (ebk.)

Printed in the United States of America
FIRST EDITION
HB Printing   10 9 8 7 6 5 4 3 2 1

THE JOSSEY-BASS HIGHER AND ADULT EDUCATION SERIES

CONTENTS

For Dr. Khalid Al-Anqari and Dr. Khaled Al-Sultan,
my wise mentors, role models, and friends

ABOUT THE AUTHOR

Jeffrey L. Buller has served in administrative positions ranging from department chair to vice president for academic affairs at a diverse group of institutions: Loras College, Georgia Southern University, Mary Baldwin College, and Florida Atlantic University. He is the author of *The Essential Department Chair: A Comprehensive Desk Reference; Academic Leadership Day by Day: Small Steps That Lead to Great Success; The Essential College Professor: A Practical Guide to an Academic Career; The Essential Academic Dean: A Practical Guide to College Leadership; Best Practices in Faculty Evaluation: A Practical Guide for Academic Leaders;* and *Positive Academic Leadership: How to Stop Putting Out Fires and Start Making a Difference.* He has also written more than two hundred articles on Greek and Latin literature, nineteenth- and twentieth-century opera, and college administration. From 2003 to 2005, he served as the principal English-language lecturer at the International Wagner Festival in Bayreuth, Germany. More recently, he has been active as a consultant to the Ministry of Higher Education in Saudi Arabia, where he is assisting with the creation of a kingdom-wide Academic Leadership Center. Along with Robert E. Cipriano, Buller is a senior partner in ATLAS: Academic Training, Leadership, and Assessment Services, through which he has presented numerous training workshops on change leadership in higher education.

INTRODUCTION

WHENEVER YOU TALK ABOUT change in higher education, someone will inevitably express one or both of two common sentiments. The first is that it's a little bit odd to regard change in higher education as a topic in and of itself because higher education by its very nature is constantly changing. With new technologies, increased competition for students and resources, shifting social attitudes about the very purpose of higher education, the continual emergence of new disciplines or fields of inquiry, changing demographic patterns that alter who goes to college and when, and similar developments throughout society, no one actually needs to initiate change in higher education. It's already there. The second cliché someone will invariably introduce at some point in the conversation is that despite all the changes it's going through, higher education doesn't handle change particularly well.

In many ways, even though I hear this second remark all the time, it's far more surprising than the first: Why should the very institutions that exist to develop innovative ideas and question traditional ways of doing things be so resistant to change that they often stifle it? As every academic leader knows only too well, many strategic planning processes either collapse entirely or fail to produce even a small fraction of what they promised. The result of these two commonly cited truisms is that (1) colleges and universities are perennially in a process that (2) they don't handle well and that produce few tangible results. Change processes in higher education usually mean missed opportunities and a resulting waste of resources.

In that context, what can yet another book about change in higher education bring to the discussion that is new and helpful? Certainly the very topic of change in higher education today has become almost a cottage industry. As we'll see in chapter 1, there's no shortage of books arguing that higher education is undergoing, should undergo, or must undergo radical change. Many of these books are also rather prescriptive about the type of change colleges need. "More distance learning is the answer!" "No, emphasizing job skills is the answer!" "Wait. That's not right. Active learning is the answer!" "To the contrary, cutting costs is the answer!"

"Seriously now, a focus on the STEM disciplines is the answer!" "Abolishing tenure is the answer!" "Greater competition is the answer!" Every six months a new "answer" appears, and yet the question is never really answered, and the problem is never really solved. The contribution that I'd like to make to this ongoing conversation is that *effective change leadership in higher education is rarely if ever about imposing specific answers; it's about asking the right questions.* For this reason, the change leaders we'll meet in this book (particularly in chapters 7 through 9) who have brought about sustained and meaningful change at their institutions—as opposed to change that is merely trendy or designed to look as though the school is moving in a new direction while it basically continues along its current path—are those who devote their energy to changing the culture, not mandating a new vision. As we'll see, genuine change leaders are almost never voices crying in the wilderness that this idea or that idea is the wave of the future. They're the ones who become catalysts for change.

Despite what we read in newspapers and see on television, lasting change in higher education usually isn't the product of a billionaire who pours resources into academic models that initially seem impressive but ultimately prove to be unsustainable. It's surprising how often today's "next big thing" quickly becomes yesterday's fad of questionable value. I've witnessed that pattern often enough to conclude that the last thing the world needs is yet another book designed to tell you what to change at your college or university. Instead what I think we need is a guide to leading the change process, an exploration of what works best within the very distinctive organizational culture of higher education. And that's what *Change Leadership in Higher Education* is all about. It's not about the next big thing. It's about how we as presidents, provosts, deans, chairs, and faculty members can work together constructively to produce an academic culture that responds well to each new challenge or opportunity, capitalize on evolving possibilities when times are good, and demonstrate resilience when times are bad.

I don't want to leave anyone with the impression that there has never been a useful guide to change leadership in higher education before. In fact, you will find the most informative of these earlier works—Peter Eckel, Barbara Hill, Madeleine Green, and Bill Mallon's American Council on Education report *On Change* (1999)—cited a number of times in the pages that follow. The American Council on Education report provided a framework that has effectively guided many institutions through their own change processes for well over a decade. But the landscape that produced *On Change* is very different from the landscape we find today. It's different largely because the recommendations it provided were so beneficial. But it dates from a time before massive open online courses (MOOCs) had appeared on the scene and at a time when the competition between for-profit and nonprofit institutions was just getting under way. In 1999, distance education was still largely done by broadcast or closed video networks; it was only a few years later that online courses replaced broadcast courses almost entirely. The year 1999 was also when the tragedy at Columbine occurred and long before similar shootings at Virginia Tech and Sandy Hook raised fundamental questions about campus safety and whether physical campuses, where large numbers of people are necessarily gathered within a confined space, are truly desirable or even necessary. Although there were a few activist legislatures and governing boards before the twenty-first century began, there wasn't as strong a sense among legislatures and governing boards that they knew more about what higher education should be doing than did the educators themselves. In brief, change itself has changed quite a bit over the past decade and a half, and it's high time to look at this process with fresh eyes.

One unavoidable factor that colors current discussions about change in higher education is the widening gulf between legislatures, governing boards, and upper administrators on the one hand and faculty, deans, and chairs on the other about why we have colleges and universities in the first place and how we can best and most affordably achieve that purpose. A recent study by the Chronicle of Higher Education, *Attitudes on Innovation* (2013), suggests that while university presidents tend to be highly positive about the current direction of higher education, the view of faculty members is far bleaker. Only 32 percent of the faculty members surveyed felt that higher education is moving in the right direction, as opposed to 64 percent of presidents. While 35 percent of presidents described the American system of higher education as the best in the world, only 17 percent of their faculty members concurred, and only 7 percent of the faculty believed that it would remain so over the next ten years. Nevertheless, these two groups generally agreed about the need for change in higher education. Only 1 percent of university presidents and 3 percent of their faculty thought that higher education in the United States was doing just fine and didn't really need to change very much. In a similar way, only 11 percent of presidents and 10 percent of faculty members thought that the current pace of change in higher education was too slow. So if all this change is already occurring at our colleges and universities anyway, how can we best lead it so that it can be as positive as possible, not merely as disruptive and costly as possible? This question guides the discussion that appears in this book, with the hope that readers will come away from it with some concrete ideas about what they can do in order to lead positive change at whatever level of the institution or system they happen to be.

Many people were extremely generous in contributing thoughts and ideas to this book as it developed. In particular, I thank:

- Gil Brady for his insights into scenario planning
- Khalid Al-Anqari and Mohammad Al-Ohali for their many hours of conversation about the challenges and prospects of change throughout higher education in the Kingdom of Saudi Arabia
- Harvey Perlman for introducing me to the concept of the strategic compass and for explaining how this approach worked at the University of Nebraska–Lincoln
- Michael Tanner for his perspectives on the iron triangle
- Edwin Massey and Christina (Tina) Hart for their generosity in showing me firsthand how substantive change was taking place at Indian River State College
- Dana Babbs for designing figures 1.1, 1.2, 1.3, and 2.2 and giving me permission to use them in this book
- Sandy Ogden and Megan Geiger for research assistance, editorial support, and general good-natured tolerance of my idiosyncrasies
- Magna Publications for allowing me to adapt and reuse in chapter 3 some material that originally appeared in *Academic Leader*. (Reprint permission was granted by Magna Publications and *Academic Leader*.)

I hope you'll find the argument I present provocative and interesting no matter whether you see change as beneficial in and of itself since it shakes things up and causes us to challenge our common assumptions, a threat that all too often ends up throwing out some very attractive babies with some not particularly dirty bathwater, a tool that can be harnessed for productive growth, or something else entirely. The one thing that we never seem to avoid about change is talking about it. So if we're going to discuss change anyway, let's at least have a stimulating and constructive conversation.

JEFFREY L. BULLER
Atlantic University

September, 2014
Jupiter, Florida

REFERENCES

Chronicle of Higher Education. (2013). *Attitudes on innovation: How college leaders and faculty see the key issues facing higher education.* Washington, DC: Chronicle of Higher Education. Retrieved from results.chronicle.com/InnovationSurvey2013_Adobe

Eckel, P., Hill, B., Green, M., & Mallon, B. (1999). *On change.* Washington, DC: American Council on Education.

CHANGE LEADERSHIP
IN HIGHER EDUCATION

THE ONLY THING WE HAVE TO CHANGE IS—CHANGE ITSELF

IT SHOULD COME AS no surprise to anyone that change is rampant in higher education today. One of the most widely read magazines about postsecondary learning is simply called *Change*. If you enter a bookstore (anywhere that bookstores still exist), you'll find book after book in the higher education section that has the word *change* in its title. Witness the following.

- *Change.edu: Rebooting for the New Talent Economy* (2013) by Andrew S. Rosen
- *Checklist for Change: Making American Higher Education a Sustainable Enterprise* (2013) by Robert Zemsky
- *Women, Universities, and Change: Gender Equality in the European Union and the United States* (2012) by Mary Ann Danowitz Sagaria
- *The Innovative University: Changing the DNA of Higher Education from the Inside Out* (2011) by Clayton M. Christensen and Henry J. Eyring
- *Community College Leadership: A Multidimensional Model for Leading Change* (2010) by Pamela Lynn Eddy and George R. Boggs
- *Driving Change through Diversity and Globalization: Transformative Leadership in the Academy* (2008) by James A. Anderson
- *Sustaining Change in Universities* (2007) by Burton R. Clark
- *Transformational Change in Higher Education: Positioning Colleges and Universities for Future Success* (2007) by Madeleine B. D'Ambrosio and Ronald G. Ehrenberg
- *Reclaiming the Ivory Tower: Organizing Adjuncts to Change Higher Education* (2005) by Joe Berry

- *Public Funding of Higher Education: Changing Contexts and New Rationales* (2004) by Edward P. St. John and Michael D. Parsons
- *Strategic Change in Colleges and Universities: Planning to Survive and Prosper* (2001) by Daniel James Rowley, Herman D. Lujan, and Michael G. Dolence
- *From Strategy to Change: Implementing the Plan in Higher Education* (2001) by Daniel James Rowley and Herbert Sherman
- *Understanding and Facilitating Organizational Change in the 21st Century: Recent Research and Conceptualizations* (2001) by Adrianna Kezar

And those are just the works published since the turn of the century. Moreover, if you go to workshops and conferences on higher education, you'll almost always find a panel or even an entire day devoted to the topic of strategic change. Then consider all the articles on the need for change in higher education, how we ought to change higher education, or what we can do to respond to all the changes in higher education that regularly appear in the *Chronicle of Higher Education, Insight Higher Ed, Faculty Focus, Academe*, and the *Journal of Higher Education*. There's even a website with *change* in it: www.changinghighereducation.com. The topic is almost inescapable.

So in light of all the attention that's been paid to change in higher education, I have to ask a rather uncomfortable question: *Why do those of us who devote our lives to teaching and research handle change so poorly?*

If you've been involved in higher education for any time at all, you know exactly what I mean: visionary strategic plans that somehow never get realized; curricular reforms that stall halfway through; changes in institutional direction that are deemed absolutely essential by the administration but then are blocked by the faculty at every turn. It's both frustrating and confusing. Why is it that in a field of endeavor that prides itself on new ideas and cutting-edge innovations, we so frequently resist, undermine, or obstruct change? It's not the case, of course, that colleges and universities are the only entities we know that seem averse to change.

All organizations resist change. After all, that's their job. The whole purpose of any organization is to act in ways that are regular, consistent, and predictable. And regularity, consistency, and predictability are natural enemies of change.

Yet despite how often change is resisted in the world at large, colleges and universities seem particularly resistant to even modest change. In a comment attributed to various figures, including former governor Zell Miller of Georgia, chancellor of the University System of Georgia Stephen Portch, and the headmaster of Ohio's Lawrence School Lou Salza, "It's easier to change the course of history than it is to change a history course." But does it have to be that way?

In order for us to answer these questions, it may be helpful to begin with a look at three common models of change and a discussion of why these models aren't particularly helpful when it comes to higher education. Although there are many more change models we could consider (I introduce several in later chapters), the three that I'll examine here provide a good, general introduction to the way in which change is often perceived. Besides, these three models are particularly easy to remember because they all begin with the letter *K*.

The Kübler-Ross Model of Change Management

Elisabeth Kübler-Ross introduced what's become known as the five-step model of change in her 1969 book, *On Death and Dying*. As that title implies, her focus in the book was the five-step process many people go through when they learn that they have a terminal illness:

1. Denial
2. Anger
3. Bargaining
4. Depression
5. Acceptance

In most cases, a dying person progresses through these steps in the exact order listed, although exceptions certainly occur. Some people regress temporarily from a later to an earlier stage, and others skip certain stages entirely. Grief counselors can assist people as they move through this process, but the steps themselves are regarded as natural and almost inevitable. It does little good to try to reason with someone in the denial stage when a person's reaction is almost entirely emotional, and it's futile to try to cheer someone up in the depression stage when he or she is yielding temporarily to grief. Kübler-Ross's process is simply the way in which most people adjust to the idea of their own mortality. While some people spend more time at one step than another, these steps all appear to be vital components that have an important role to play in comprehending and acknowledging the finality of death.

It wasn't long after Kübler-Ross first presented her five-step model that organizational theorists began to realize that death isn't the only event that can trigger this type of progression. P. David Elrod and Donald Tippett (2002) outlined how Kübler-Ross's basic concept ultimately developed—through such intermediaries as Walter Menninger's change curve model, John D. Adams's theory of transition, and Dottie Perlman and George Takacs's ten stages of change—into Thomas Harvey's recognition that responses to change mimic almost precisely those that people have when faced with the loss of a loved one or their own impending death: "It is crucial to remember that for every change proposed or achieved, someone loses something" (Harvey and Wehmeyer, 1990, 6).

Many of the change models based on Kübler-Ross's five stages of grief represent the process graphically as a series of active and passive responses over time. (See figure 1.1.) Because of the shape of this curve, the five-step model is sometimes also called the *rollercoaster model of change*. By understanding this natural progression, it is argued, effective change managers can respond in an appropriate way to what those experiencing the change are feeling.

○ During the denial stage, change managers can keep their message consistent, emphasizing why the change is both necessary and desirable.

Figure 1.1 Kübler-Ross Model of Change

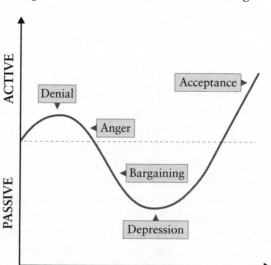

o During the anger stage, they can remember not to take resistance and rejection personally, calming stakeholders with a positive, forward-looking message.

o During the bargaining stage, they can resist the urge to make concessions that may initially seem minor but ultimately will be detrimental to their overall vision.

o During the depression stage, they can emphasize improvements and accomplishments that are already being made along the way, thus helping people see that what they have lost is more than compensated for by what they have gained.

o During the acceptance stage, they can use the energy of those who have come to support the change vision to begin making more rapid progress and moving more systematically toward their ultimate goal.

Perhaps the most important contribution of the Kübler-Ross model to the field of change management is its theory of why people so often resist change: they perceive each break with the past as like a little death. Leaders who attempt to ignore the need for healing that must occur during every change process thus run the risk of deepening resistance to the new vision and undermining the entire process.

The Krüger Model of Change Management

Until his retirement in 2008, Wilfried Krüger served as a professor of management and organization at Justus Liebig University in Giessen, Germany. In articles like "Implementation: The Core Task of Change Management" (1996) and essays like those appearing in *Excellence in Change*, Krüger posited a theory of change that has become commonly known as the iceberg model. His idea was that change, like an iceberg, is a phenomenon for which most of the danger lies below the surface. Krüger believed that most people involved in organizational change tend to engage only in issues management—the facts and figures that result from the process. They devote their time to such factors as cost, the time that will be required to complete the change, input and output metrics, and the desire to improve quality. But these issues are rarely what cause the real problems for a change process. More frequently difficulties arise because of less immediately visible factors, like power relationships, politics, beliefs, biases, and perceptions. The successful change manager, Krüger argued, is the person who takes time to address these hidden elements of any organization, which he believed could constitute as much as 90 percent of an initiative's success or failure (figure 1.2).

Change managers deal with these invisible factors by making sure that the human element of the process isn't overlooked in their desire to get matters of cost, time, and quality right. They know their organizations well enough to understand who is likely to oppose the change and whether that opposition will probably be due to a resistance to all change or just a distaste for this particular change. They also know who the opportunists are who might outwardly support the process in order to curry favor with their supervisors, while passive-aggressively working to make sure that the change never actually takes place. But it's not just awareness of where opposition will arise that's important. Change managers also need to know who their likely supporters are going to be. They thus spend time persuading those with open minds to become advocates for the new

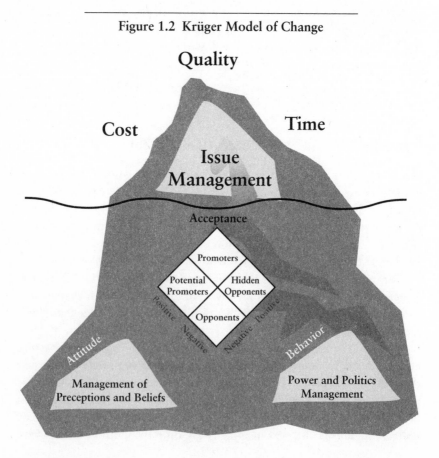

Figure 1.2 Krüger Model of Change

initiative and to rally others to the cause. They balance their task orientation (getting the job done) with a people orientation (getting everyone onboard), recognizing that changes succeed or fail because of what stakeholders believe, accept, and trust.

The Krüger model implies that effective change management requires leaders to adopt a systems approach. That is, those in charge of the process have to understand the political environment and power dynamics of the organization in which they work. In addition to those who openly support or oppose the initiative, there may be others whose actions are more covert: potential supporters who are afraid to speak their minds because they believe that those opposed to the change will retaliate against them and secret critics of the change who pretend to support the idea in public but then do nothing to advance or undermine it (at least in any open manner). By pursuing strategies that cause potential supporters to become active advocates, change managers counter the threat posed by the opportunists and passive-aggressive opponents. Failing to address these often invisible aspects of perceptions, beliefs, office politics, and power relationships can sometimes produce a change that initially appears to be successful but is actually superficial and unlikely to be truly transformative. We might think of these managers as people who are so fixated on the surface issues of cost, time, and quality that their change processes run aground or capsize once they strike the unseen elements of the Krüger iceberg.

The Kotter Model of Change Management

Perhaps the most influential approach to change management today was developed by John P. Kotter, the Konosuke Matsushita Emeritus Professor of Leadership at Harvard and founder of his own consulting firm that assists corporations with issues of change. In such books as *Leading Change* (2012), *A Sense of Urgency* (2008), and (coincidentally in light of the Krüger model) *Our Iceberg Is Melting* (Kotter and Rathgeber, 2006), Kotter describes successful change processes as having eight significant steps (and is thus sometimes also known as the eight-step model of change management; see figure 1.3):

1. *Establish a sense of urgency.* Change processes fail, Kotter argues, when members of an organization don't fully comprehend the need for the change and thus don't buy into it. The basic rule of thumb is this: until the pain of doing nothing becomes greater than the pain of doing something, most people will continue to do nothing. Inertia resists change.

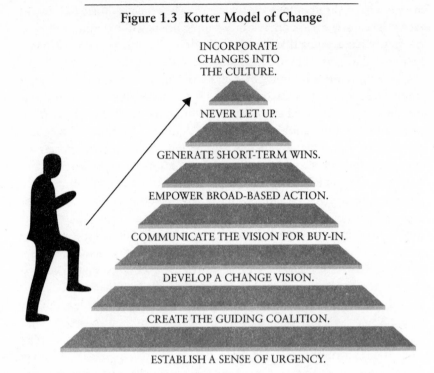

Figure 1.3 Kotter Model of Change

INCORPORATE
CHANGES INTO
THE CULTURE.

NEVER LET UP.

GENERATE SHORT-TERM WINS.

EMPOWER BROAD-BASED ACTION.

COMMUNICATE THE VISION FOR BUY-IN.

DEVELOP A CHANGE VISION.

CREATE THE GUIDING COALITION.

ESTABLISH A SENSE OF URGENCY.

It therefore becomes important for managers to identify the threats that the organization faces and communicate these dangers to stakeholders in a compelling enough manner that a consensus in favor of change begins to emerge.

2. *Create the guiding coalition.* Managers can't guide a successful change process by themselves. They must rely on the help, advice, and support they receive from their leadership team. In addition to those whose authority is a function of the positions they hold—what Peter Northouse (2012), professor of communication in the School of Communication at Western Michigan University, calls assigned leadership—this guiding coalition should be expanded to include early adopters, opinion leaders, and those whose authority stems from the respect they receive from their peers—what Northouse calls emergent leadership. The best type of guiding coalition is one that includes wide representation from stakeholders both vertically (from different levels of the institutional hierarchy) and horizontally (from different departments or specialties on the organizational chart).

3. *Develop a change vision.* The manager should next develop a clear and easily remembered mental image of the desired end state after the

change. He or she should ask how the threat described in step 1 will be avoided and how the organization's stakeholders will be better off after the change has occurred. In this way, the change manager's vision becomes rather similar to Stephen Covey's second habit of highly effective people: "Begin with the end in mind" (Covey, 1989). In other terms, the change vision is the destination at which the organization will arrive after its journey through the change process. Although it's not essential for every aspect of this future state to be specified in advance, the goal should be clear enough for it to be quickly comprehended by as many people as possible and desirable enough to make the inevitable setbacks along the way seem endurable.

4. *Communicate the vision for buy-in.* Once the desired change has been identified, it needs to be described to larger and larger circles of stakeholders in a manner that will cause them to embrace it. Managers should explain to others why the new vision benefits them and why current practices are no longer acceptable. These explanations should occur often, maintain a consistent focus, and be supported by the data that were used to generate the vision in the first place. For example, if a competing institution is planning to launch a new program with scholarships and travel opportunities far beyond what you're able to offer, describe what you know about this potential competitor and indicate how your vision can counter that threat. Discuss the vision whenever you get a chance. Run the risk of sounding like a broken record. It's this repeated, consistent type of communication that increases awareness that change is truly inevitable and that you have a clear idea of where the organization is going. If people have concerns, address them openly and candidly, but don't let the inevitable complaining about the discomfort of change interfere with the progress of the project. Enlist the support of early adopters to help you overcome the resistance of those opposed to the idea.

5. *Empower broad-based action.* As you enter the implementation phase of the change process, you'll inevitably encounter barriers along the way. Additional funding may be needed. Staff training may be required. Procedures may have to be updated. By empowering others to accomplish these tasks, you achieve two goals simultaneously. First, you reduce your own workload by delegating key responsibilities to others. Second, you encourage even more buy-in by expanding yet again the circle of those directly participating in the change process. As an added benefit, opponents of the change may see obstacles that they regarded as insurmountable effectively cleared away and thus come to accept the change that you're implementing.

6. *Generate short-term wins.* Any truly transformational change requires a great deal of time. Along the way, some supporters may

lose interest, while others may become disillusioned by the inevitable frustrations and setbacks that occur. To maintain momentum, change managers make a priority of celebrating small victories as they occur. Rather than waiting to see whether a major grant proposal is funded, for example, they celebrate each phase of the proposal's completion. Rather than waiting for enrollment to increase dramatically, they celebrate when rates of attrition decline, retention holds steady, and even a slight rise in applications occurs. People become more enthusiastic about a change if they begin to see tangible, positive results, and effective change managers identify these short-term gains as a way of keeping stakeholders engaged in the process.

7. *Never let up.* Taking time to celebrate these minor victories doesn't mean that managers mistake milestones for the ultimate goal. They redouble their efforts and use each small success as a basis for further achievement. The way in which faculty members are hired, developed, and evaluated may need to change. For example, if the proposed change involves shifting the institution's priority from teaching alone to a combination of teaching and research, search announcements may need to be written in such a way that they attract candidates who are highly productive in research. Criteria for promotion and tenure may need to be revised. The center for teaching and learning may need to be paired with a new center for research development. Although the ultimate aim may already be in sight, effective managers don't change their rhetoric, and they don't move on to the next big idea before the current big idea has come to fruition.

8. *Incorporate changes into the culture.* The biggest mistake change managers make is assuming that once a new initiative is well under way, they don't need to attend to it anymore. In fact, they need to incorporate the change into the institution's culture by making it part of the orientation for new employees and, if appropriate, including references to it in the mission statement of the institution or unit. Kotter notes that truly substantial changes may lead to the loss of some personnel who can't adjust to the new initiative. But these departures are a useful component of developing a new institutional culture since it leaves the organization with a more solid base of employees who will support the endeavor. In time, people will stop regarding the initiative as a change and start seeing it as "the new normal." But that process can't be rushed, and managers shouldn't assume that it will simply occur on its own.

The goal of the Kotter change model is thus to provide a consistent level of emphasis on the process regardless of how long it takes. Unlike other models that deal only with the implementation of the change itself, the Kotter model includes the vital steps that need to occur before the process is launched and the equally vital steps that must occur after the process is complete in order to make the change permanent. (For a similar model, but somewhat expanded to include twelve steps instead of eight, see Mento, Jones, and Dimdorfer, 2002.)

The Role of Organizational Culture in Change Processes

All three of these change management approaches provide significant insights for college administrators. I'll repeatedly use the lessons learned from the three models just explored, as well as other attempts to describe organizational change processes, in examining how change tends to occur in higher education. But it's also important to realize at the beginning of this study that in order to incorporate change into the culture in the way that Kotter recommends, we first have to understand what that culture is. And when we do, what we discover is that change models that were designed to describe other environments, such as corporate change or general changes in a person's life, have only limited applicability to higher education. Here's why.

We can think of an organization as a structured system in which individuals come together as a group in order to achieve a common goal. As a structured system, organizations develop ways of assigning power, authority, and responsibility for the sake of making decisions. If they didn't, no decision would ever be final: no person or subgroup would be authorized to render a final judgment. But not every organization is structured the same way. The different ways in which decisions are made and power, authority, and responsibility are allocated affect more than just the shape of the organizational chart. They also affect what Edgar Schein, emeritus professor of management at MIT, calls the group's organizational culture. The type of culture that Schein has in mind is somewhat different from the type of culture that anthropologists and sociologists are talking about when they define culture as the beliefs, artifacts, symbols, and practices that distinguish one group of human beings from others:

> The culture of a group can … be defined as a pattern of shared basic assumptions learned by a group as it solved its problems of external adaptation and internal integration, which has worked well enough to be considered valid and, therefore, to be taught to new members as the correct way to perceive, think, and feel in relation to those problems. (Schein, 2010, 18)

In other words, organizational culture embodies what the members of an organization:

○ Take for granted—their *assumptions*
○ Use to solve problems—their *strategies*
○ Rely on to understand their place in the organization—their *roles*
○ Pass on to new members of the organization—their *legacy*

With this definition of organizational culture in mind, let's consider the three most familiar ways in which groups might structure themselves in order to allocate decision-making power.

Hierarchical Organizations

Allocating power hierarchically is probably the most common, as well as the oldest, way of structuring an organization. Hierarchical organizations can be pictured as a social pyramid in which power rises at each level as you go up the organizational structure and in which numbers of employees increase at each level as you go down the structure (figure 1.4). It's the same type of organizational structure we find in ancient Mesopotamia, Shang dynasty China, medieval Europe, armies throughout all of human history—and most modern corporations. Hierarchical organizations have certain advantages. They can respond to situations quickly because decisions can be made at the highest level without necessarily consulting (or even informing) lower levels. Responsibilities and expectations are clear at every level in the hierarchy. If you're a warrior, merchant, liege lord, or vice president of marketing, you have a predetermined "job description" from which you and everyone else in the social pyramid know exactly where your responsibilities begin and where they end. As Kim Cameron and Robert Quinn note in *Diagnosing and Changing Organizational Culture* (2011), hierarchical organizations are

> characterized by a formalized and structured place to work. Procedures govern what people do. Effective leaders are good coordinators and organizers. Maintaining a smoothly running organization is important. The long-term concerns of the organization are stability, predictability, and efficiency. Formal rules and policies hold the organization together ... Large organizations and government agencies are generally dominated by a hierarchy culture, as evidenced by large numbers of standardized procedures, multiple hierarchical levels (Ford has seventeen levels of management), and an emphasis on rule reinforcement. (42)

Figure 1.4 Hierarchical Organizations

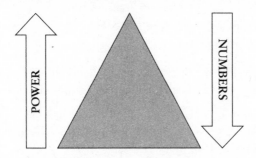

But social pyramids also have several disadvantages. Since lower levels of the structure aren't always consulted about major decisions and not expected to have much insight into the big picture, their talents aren't fully used, and the upper levels of the structure don't receive the full benefit of their knowledge and experience. In addition, members of the organization can feel as though they're locked in their current status. In certain societies, that feeling derives from a rigid caste system that actually prevents upward mobility. In rigidly hierarchical societies and in much of the corporate and military worlds, promotion to another level may be possible, but a certain us-versus-them identity at each stage in the hierarchy sometimes prevents people from even trying to rise in the organization. For example, it may technically be possible for a mail clerk one day to become president of the company, but low-level employees often begin to see themselves as culturally different from "the people on the tenth floor" and thus never pursue opportunities beyond their immediate sphere. The anthropologist Chie Nakane (1967) uses the term *tate shakai* (vertical society) to refer to this type of social hierarchy in which each rank or level has its own habits and protocols for dealing with all other ranks or levels and where styles of dress, manners of speech, and forms of recreation cue insiders as to each person's place in the pecking order. *Tate shakai* sacrifices social equality for order, speed in making decisions, and clear lines of authority.

Moreover, even when promotion from within the social pyramid does occur, members of the organization soon encounter another reality of the hierarchical structure: each social pyramid isn't a single, monolithic pyramid but rather a triangle-shaped scaffolding that consists of many smaller pyramids (figure 1.5). In other words, if employees think, "If only I become a manager, I can finally make decisions by myself," they're deluding themselves. Being at the top of the employee pyramid

Figure 1.5 Hierarchical Organizations, Detailed Configuration

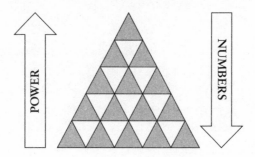

is essentially the same as being at the bottom of the manager pyramid. Likewise, managers who climb to the top of the manager pyramid suddenly find themselves at the bottom of the vice president pyramid. That pattern is repeated throughout the entire hierarchy, so it's not merely that lower levels of the organization have less decision-making authority than do the upper levels; it's also that their decision-making process is more prolonged and tentative. Anything decided at a low level can be countermanded at an upper level, and so there's an actual disincentive for those who are at the bottom of the organizational chart to be innovative when it comes to promoting substantive change. Proposals are too easy to be vetoed as they go up the hierarchy, and the employee's initiative may backfire ("I pay you to work. I don't pay you to think. Who asked you to come up with this lame-brained idea?"). As a result, change processes tend to be initiated by a relatively small number of stakeholders. In the most extreme situation, they can begin in the mind of only one person: the king or CEO.

Decentralized Organizations

At the opposite end of the organizational spectrum, there are what we might call *decentralized organizations*. The operating principle of this type of structure is democracy, or one-person, one-vote decision making. In this type of hierarchy, every member of the organization is equidistant from power (figure 1.6). No one is authorized to make a final decision alone. Instead, decisions can be made only in clusters: by consensus, majority rule, or some other system that assigns equal weight to the view of each individual.

In the academic world, we're most familiar with decentralized organizations when we work on committees. And if you've ever worked on a

Figure 1.6 Decentralized Organizations

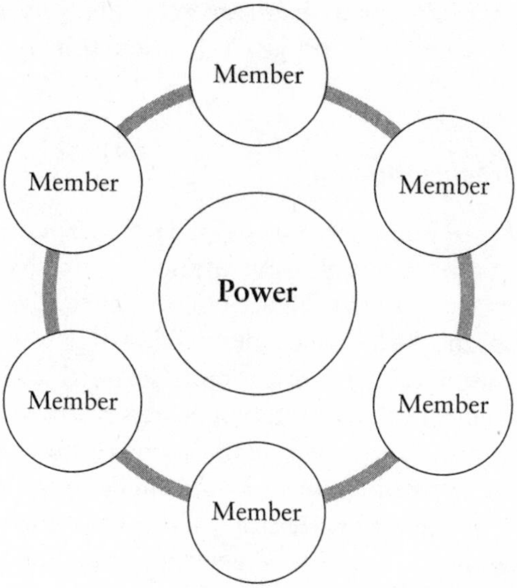

committee, you immediately recognize both the strengths and weaknesses of decentralized decision making. On the one hand, they're extremely fair. No one's opinion counts more than anyone else's. A multitude of views is regularly expressed, and members of the organization have perfect freedom to be persuaded by whichever case they find most convincing. On the other hand, decentralized groups can take an incredibly long time to make decisions. Even then, decisions may not be "final" because those who are on the losing side of the debate have the right to argue that their case wasn't given a fair hearing or that relevant issues remain to be discussed. So if the advantage of the decentralized organization is that every voice gets to be heard, the disadvantage is that *every* voice gets to be heard—even if people become tired of hearing it.

For this reason, both hierarchical and decentralized organizations have a valid place in decision making. For issues where sufficient time is available, decentralized organizations provide an opportunity for groups to get a broader perspective, anticipate possible deficiencies in an idea, and build buy-in for the change. For issues where a crisis is pending, hierarchical organizations provide a clear understanding of who's in charge and allow a swifter response to the problem at hand. Most university faculties wouldn't tolerate having the curriculum dictated to them by a president, provost, or dean, but at the same time, university faculties don't expect people to wait for the recommendation of the fire evacuation task force when the building is burning down. The choice of which type of organizational structure groups adopt frequently comes down to which of two factors is more desirable in a given situation: broad-based consensus or speed.

Distributed Organizations

Distributed organizations occur when power is shared among various individuals or groups within the organization. Unlike hierarchical organizations, it's not the case that higher ranks in the institution possess all the power of the ranks below them plus additional powers resulting from additional responsibilities. Unlike decentralized organizations, it's not the case that each member of the institution possesses power equal to that of every other member. Distributed organizations retain at least some sort of loose or honorary hierarchical structure, but decision making is shared through the twin processes of delegation (the assignment of responsibility to others) and empowerment (the assignment of authority to others). In many cases, upper ranks preserve the right to veto the decisions made by lower or parallel ranks, but not to initiate or modify the actions of those ranks when it comes to matters that have been entrusted to them.

Perhaps the best way of understanding how distributed organizations work is to examine the balance of power established by the US Constitution for the executive, legislative, and judicial branches of government (figure 1.7). The legislative branch makes the laws, the judicial branch interprets the laws, and the executive branch enforces the laws. The executive branch can veto decisions of the legislative branch, and the judicial branch can declare them unconstitutional, but while presidents may recommend new laws, neither they nor the judiciary can create them. That power has been entirely delegated to Congress. Moreover, even though the executive branch is traditionally thought of as the highest of the three branches because of its role in national defense and foreign policy, there actually are distinct spheres of influence among the three branches, and none of them can truly be said to outrank the other two.

While most people think of higher education as composed of hierarchical organizations—and organization charts are usually constructed to depict them that way—colleges and universities share many features with distributed organizations. For example, the concept of shared governance is essential to the way in which most Western universities work. The governing board retains fiduciary responsibility and sets basic policies. The administration implements those policies and is responsible for the

Figure 1.7 The US Constitution as an Example of a Distributed Organization

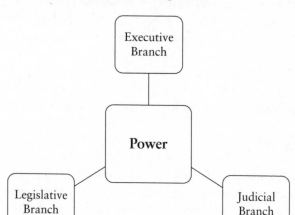

day-to-day operation of the institution. The faculty is responsible for the curriculum of the school, the provost is responsible for academic personnel, and the students are responsible for the allocation of student activity funds. (That distribution is merely an example; there's a great variety in how institutions allocate power and responsibility.) Adriana Kezar (2014) describes this type of culture:

> Higher education is a professional bureaucracy, a unique type of institution with a distinctive structure and culture that is different than what is found in businesses or government. Professional bureaucracies are characterized by dual power and authority systems. Professionals (e.g. faculty and sometimes staff) are considered to be autonomous workers who are involved in their own evaluation, develop policies governing their working conditions, and plan and coordinate much of their work on their own. They are given a high degree of authority and autonomy with the understanding that they will be accountable to one another and will engage in self-policing and peer review. (93)

Furthermore, the concept of academic freedom has both a legal and a traditional meaning in higher education. As a legal term, it relates to the right of colleges and universities to set their own curricula, standards, and policies without external interference. In this sense, the courts sometimes speak of institutional academic freedom. But as the term *academic freedom* is used traditionally by those who work in higher education, it refers to the rights of faculty members, as professionals in their academic areas, to teach their approved syllabi in the manner they deem most appropriate. In this context, the expression *individual academic freedom* is sometimes used. (For example, see www.aaup.org/report/1940-statement-principles-academic-freedom-and -tenure.) For this reason, administrators and faculty members in higher education retain a great deal of autonomy within their own spheres of influence, thus producing an organizational structure in which power is widely distributed and collegiality among constituents is highly prized.

The IKEA Effect

Because colleges and universities are structured as distributed organizations, most approaches to change management aren't particularly effective for them. And it should come as no surprise why: those strategies were developed for corporations, the military, and other types of hierarchical organizations. In a culture of shared governance, faculty members don't view change just as an issue affecting the university; they view it as an issue affecting *them*. In fact, they often view it as an *indictment* of them. In hierarchical cultures, most people can distinguish between themselves and the organization. Workaholics and William Whyte's Organization Man, the archetype of the employee whose life is dedicated entirely to "the company," are notable precisely because they're viewed as aberrations. For the vast majority of employees, a job is what they do; it isn't who they are. Even though it's common for Americans to define themselves largely in terms of their jobs—"Good to meet you. I'm Taylor, an accountant with Wilder and Roundtree"—they still usually view their jobs as a means to an end, not an end in itself. When they win the lottery or receive a large inheritance, few people have any compunction about walking away from their jobs. Even in the military where identification with one's own squad, platoon, or company tends to be strong, soldiers often joke with one another about the absurdities of "the Army" as though it were something foreign to themselves and not an integral part of who they are.

In a distributed culture like a university, it's much more difficult to say, "Don't ask me. I just work here," because the faculty members often are the very people who developed the policies or designed the program. For this reason, change management in higher education runs counter to a phenomenon known as the *IKEA effect*. As conceived and validated by Michael Norton, Daniel Mochon, and Dan Ariely (2012), the IKEA effect states that we tend to overvalue products that we ourselves participate in creating when compared to similar prefabricated items.

In other words, most people place a higher dollar value on a table they themselves assembled out of an IKEA kit, a toy they themselves designed at a Build-a-Bear Workshop, or strawberries they themselves picked at a local farm over identical (or even superior) items they played no part in creating. In addition to their own controlled experiments, Norton, Mochon, and Ariely cite earlier findings—such as the discovery in the 1950s that consumers preferred cake mixes to which they had to add an egg over those to which they just added water and Leon Festinger's 1957 discovery that people value an activity more when they have to put more effort into it—suggesting a strong correlation between personal engagement and assigned value. Labor leads to love, they conclude, and the more of ourselves we put into something, the more perfect we regard it as being. Some social psychologists call this tendency *effort justification* (see Alessandri, Darcheville, and Zentall, 2008; Singer and Zentall, 2011; Lydall, Gilmour, and Dwyer, 2010), and it's a tendency that's rampant in higher education because of the type of institutional culture it involves.

In distributed organizations, many of the policies and procedures that govern the way in which an institution operates were developed by the members themselves. Declaring that change is necessary is tantamount to concluding that the members of the organization "got it wrong" when they first set those policies and procedures. At a university, for example, when an administrator states that the general education program needs to be revised, his or her audience is likely to include many people who designed that program in the first place. Because they helped build it, they overvalue its quality. Moreover, they interpret the claim that it needs to be changed as an accusation that they're stupid, incompetent, or short-sighted for not getting that initiative right the first time. While members of all organizations tend to resist change because it promises uncertainty and discomfort (at least temporarily), members of distributed organizations tend to resist change most strongly because they view what's being discarded as a part of themselves. It's no wonder that so many faculty members take proposals for change personally. They view the status quo as a key ingredient in their own identities in a way that people who "just work here" never do.

Why Change Must Change

If changes need to occur in higher education because we see important shifts in our academic and economic environments, then it's clear we can't rely on traditional change management models and approaches to effect those innovations. For one thing, as active participants in a distributed organization, faculty members at a university don't really see themselves as employees who are subject to being "managed" by administrators, many of whom are far less qualified in the faculty members' areas of specialty than are the faculty members themselves. They view themselves as independent contractors, subject perhaps to the ultimate approval of their chairs and deans, but preserving a great deal of autonomy over their research, the way they teach their courses, and their opinions about how the institution is being run. The reason that so many academic leaders describe their jobs as "herding cats" is due to this degree of independence that is integral to the nature of faculty work. Professors, it may be said, are literally unmanageable because they actively resist the types of management that traditionally succeed in more hierarchical environments.

Viewing higher education through the lens of organizational behavior makes it clear why so many approaches to change management have been ineffective in higher education:

o *They relied on a dichotomy between decision makers and decision implementers that doesn't really apply to the role faculty members have.* For example, the Kübler-Ross or rollercoaster model of change management implies the existence of an outside observer, or "control agent," that is utterly alien to how higher education works. It suggests that someone is present to observe and respond to the onset of denial, anger, bargaining, and so on, adjusting his or her responses to the emotional responses of the employees. But in a distributed organization, the manager and the managed are often the same. Or perhaps, to put it more accurately, the very concept of management doesn't apply to an environment where shared governance means that faculty members are empowered to make their own decisions in certain spheres of their responsibilities. Moreover, the metaphor on which the Kübler-Ross change model relies is singularly unfortunate in a system where people identify so closely with the organization. Specifically, in an environment where faculty members are accustomed to saying things like, "We *are* the university," presenting change as akin to a type of death and the universal reaction to change as a type of mourning is likely to cause faculty members to become apoplectic. If you view yourself as intimately related to the entity that's being changed, you're more likely to respond positively if the process is envisioned as a type of growth and renewal, not as a form of hospice care or as a funeral director's well-intentioned effort to comfort the survivors.

o *By suggesting that change is being imposed from the outside rather than growing organically from within, they produced a type of learning anxiety that's antithetical to smooth transitions.* In the Krüger or ice-berg model of change management, for instance, there's an assumption that managers need to be aware of a vast number of hidden factors that employees are unlikely to see. Edgar Schein (2010) posits that change frequently results in five types of learning anxiety that can make the smooth transition to a new paradigm far more difficult:

1. *Fear of loss of power or position.* As the frequently cited witticism states, "Turf wars are particularly intense in higher education because the stakes are so small." Curricular changes could result in "my course" no longer being required as part of the major. Structural changes could result in "my committee" no longer being relevant. If a proposed change appears to threaten the perceived basis of faculty status or power, it's likely to be met with strong resistance.

2. *Fear of temporary incompetence.* Schein (2010) cites the common phenomenon of people who resist buying a new computer, adopting a new program, or switching to a new operating system—even if the change will bring many advantages with it—because they don't want to deal with the learning curve required. In higher education, faculty members often see a direct connection between their level of knowledge and the amount of control they have over their environment. If an externally mandated change occurs, they will enter a situation in which they are temporarily at a loss because they don't know the ground rules. As a result, they will see the change as a threat to their self-image and thus resist it.

3. *Fear of punishment for incompetence.* Despite all the changes occurring in higher education, it's still a publish-or-perish world. If adapting to a change will be time intensive, it could reduce the amount of time faculty members have for refereed publications, writing and submitting grant proposals, updating courses, and maintaining currency in the discipline. Since promotions and merit raises are frequently based on productivity in these areas, any activity that's seen as a distraction from them will meet with strong opposition.

4. *Fear of loss of personal identity.* We've already seen that college faculty members often have an image of themselves as singularly well-educated and competent people. Any change that disrupts that sense of self, even temporarily, is likely to be regarded as a significant threat. But there are also other ways in which change can threaten personal identity. As Schein (2010) says, "We may not want to be the kind of people that the new way of working would require us to be" (304). For example, a president who proposes that a campus

become more "student friendly" may expect faculty members to assist students when they move into the residence halls each fall. If a faculty member's personal identity is that he or she is a scholar and expert who maintains a lofty distance from students and would never think of filling this type of "servant's role," the proposed change may appear to be a severe threat that needs to be resisted.

5. *Fear of loss of group membership.* Since, as we've seen, cultures distinguish themselves from other cultures through their assumptions, strategies, roles, and legacy, anything that's viewed as altering those distinctive features can be interpreted as a hostile act. For example, if a faculty defines itself as distinctly different from staff, a governing board that proposes eliminating that distinction will be seen as a threat. Even worse, if the proposal includes the abolition of tenure, then anyone whose self-image is that of "a tenured faculty member" will oppose this change for all five of Schein's reasons.

While these problems may arise in any type of change, they're particularly troublesome in the context of higher education where stakeholders regard themselves as competent, well educated, and quick to master new information. Any change process that challenges this self-image is likely to meet with strong resistance. Any change process that conveys the impression that a great deal of information is being concealed from them (since it is "below the surface") is likely to be dismissed as a lack of transparency. Moreover, Kruger's metaphor of the organization (in our case, the college or university) as a ship headed for an iceberg is only slightly less fortunate than the Kübler-Ross image of change as death.

o *They described the change process in a manner that most faculty members would have regarded as manipulative.* For example, in the Kotter or eight-step model of change management, the order in which processes occur runs strongly counter to a system of shared governance. Communication of the process outside the guiding coalition and the empowerment of major constituencies don't even occur until halfway through the process. The entire model begins with the change manager's manufacturing a sense of urgency long before major stakeholders are even given their first opportunity to weigh in on whether the situation is truly as urgent as it is presented. The vision for change is expected to derive from the manager, an occurrence that may work well in hierarchical organizations but runs counter to the culture of decentralized or distributed organizations. In short, change management, as it commonly occurs in higher education, feeds the faculty's suspicion that the initiative has been undertaken more to build an administrator's résumé than to address a genuine need. And in that suspicion, faculty members have too often been right.

For all these reasons, it's clear that if change is to occur successfully throughout higher education, it must be undertaken in a manner different from what we see in traditional change management models. In short, it must proceed in a manner that fits the organizational culture of the modern college or university.

What about Other Stakeholders?

So far in this discussion of academic change, I've been assuming that the change manager is an administrator or member of the governing board and the group of constituents who either embrace or resist the change consists of the faculty. It's a fair question to ask whether that's an accurate assessment of university life today. What about the other stakeholders who are affected by major changes at a college or university? And what about change processes that begin elsewhere than among the administration?

Certainly it's true that other segments of a university population may be concerned about what happened when an institution they care deeply about seems to be undergoing a radical transformation. Alumni may be worried that they soon won't be able to recognize "their" school any-more. Current students (and their parents) may wonder whether proposed changes could delay their progress toward their degrees. Staff could be anxious as to whether their jobs might be in jeopardy or their work-load might increase. Donors may keep a watchful eye on whether their investment might be compromised. In other words, change processes in higher education are never simply about the faculty and administration. Other constituencies can play a part and even end up on opposite sides of an issue. Parents of current students might applaud a radical reduc-tion in staffing if they think it will keep personnel costs under control, while members of the faculty and staff may resist these cuts as hitting a bit too close to home. Yet as we'll see in some of the actual cases of significant change that we'll encounter in later chapters, while other stake-holders may play a role in change processes, the key players are almost always the faculty, administration, and governing board. They're the ones who possess genuine decision-making authority in the shared governance of most universities. Students, staff, alumni, donors, parents, and mem-bers of the community may raise their voices to support or scuttle an innovation—and are able to affect policy indirectly by withholding finan-cial support or moving to another institution—but they usually don't have sufficient power to initiate or forestall a change themselves. They work instead by trying to influence one or more of the groups that actually do possess decision-making responsibility.

The second major issue we haven't yet addressed, changes that are initiated by the faculty and opposed by the administration or governing board (or both), are also outliers in higher education. While friction among these groups is not uncommon, the changes that capture the attention of the national and global press aren't usually those that involve issues of most concern to the faculty: compensation, reward structures, working conditions, class size, and the like. Even issues like academic freedom and tenure that are more visible to the public tend not to occur because faculty members are attempting to initiate a change. Rather, these matters become noticed by the national media because faculty members are usually trying to preserve a right they feel they have, not bring about a change in the institution that most people would regard as truly transformative. Certainly there are exceptions to this general rule, but the fact remains that the type of change that causes the greatest turmoil at colleges and universities is that which originates from the administration or governing board but is resisted by the faculty. Those are the change processes that require the most careful handling and the greatest amount of care.

Conclusion

The way in which change is approached at an institution is significantly affected by organizational culture. In a distributed organization like a college or university, many strategies of change management that are effective in corporate or military environments have only limited application in higher education. In fact, the very concept of *change management* is a misnomer when it comes to a college or university.

Change isn't something that academic leaders manage. It's something that they lead, initiate, guide, and occasionally capture.

If we're to deal with the degree of change that most people agree is occurring in higher education today, we need to find more successful ways to initiate, guide, and capture that change. In order to be truly transformative in our approach, we must change our entire way of thinking about change and move from trying to manage it to leading it. It's to that process that we turn in the next several chapters.

REFERENCES

Alessandri, J., Darcheville, J. C., & Zentall, T. R. (2008). Cognitive dissonance in children: Justification of effort or contrast? *Psychonomic Bulletin and Review, 15*(3), 673–677.

Anderson, J. A. (2008). *Driving change through diversity and globalization: Transformative leadership in the academy.* Sterling, VA: Stylus.

Berry, J. (2005). *Reclaiming the ivory tower: Organizing adjuncts to change higher education.* New York, NY: Monthly Review Press.

Cameron, K. S., & Quinn, R. E. (2011). *Diagnosing and changing organizational culture: Based on the competing values framework* (3rd ed.). San Francisco, CA: Jossey-Bass.

Christensen, C. M., & Eyring, H. J. (2011). *The innovative university: Changing the DNA of higher education from the inside out.* San Francisco, CA: Jossey-Bass.

Clark, B. R. (2007). *Sustaining change in universities.* Maidenhead: McGraw-Hill International.

Covey, S. R. (1989). *The seven habits of highly effective people: Restoring the character ethic.* New York, NY: Simon & Schuster.

D'Ambrosio, M., & Ehrenberg, R. G. (2007). *Transformational change in higher education: Positioning colleges and universities for future success.* Cheltenham, UK: Edward Elgar.

Eddy, P. L., & Boggs, G. R. (2010). *Community college leadership: A multidimensional model for leading change.* Sterling, VA: Stylus.

Elrod, P.D.E., & Tippett, D. D. (2002). The "death valley" of change. *Journal of Organizational Change Management, 15*(3), 273–291.

Festinger, L. (1965). *A theory of cognitive dissonance.* Stanford, CA: Stanford University Press.

Harvey, T. R., & Wehmeyer, L. B. (1990). *Checklist for change: A pragmatic approach to creating and controlling change.* Boston, MA: Allyn and Bacon.

Kezar, A. J. (2001). *Understanding and facilitating organizational change in the 21st century: Recent research and conceptualizations.* San Francisco, CA: Jossey-Bass.

Kezar, A. J. (2014). *How colleges change: Understanding, leading, and enacting change.* New York, NY: Routledge.

Kotter, J. P. (2008). *A sense of urgency.* Boston, MA: Harvard Business Press.

Kotter, J. P. (2012). *Leading change.* Boston, MA: Harvard Business Review Press.

Kotter, J. P., & Rathgeber, H. (2006). *Our iceberg is melting: Changing and succeeding under any conditions.* New York, NY: St. Martin's Press.

Krüger, W. (1996). Implementation: The core task of change management. *CEMS Business Review, 1,* 77–96.

Krüger, W. (2009). *Excellence in Change: Wege zur strategischen Erneuerung.* Wiesbaden: Gabler/GWV: Wiesbaden, Germany.

Kübler-Ross, E. (1969). *On death and dying.* New York, NY: Macmillan.

Lydall, E. S., Gilmour, G., & Dwyer, D. M. (2010, November). Rats place greater value on rewards produced by high effort: An animal analogue of the "effort justification" effect. *Journal of Experimental Social Psychology, 46*(6), 1134–1137.

Mento, A. J., Jones, R. M., & Dimdorfer, W. (2002). A change management process: Grounded in both theory and practice. *Journal of Change Management, 3*(1), 45–60.

Nakane, C. (1967). *Tate shakai no ningen kankei.* Tokyo, Japan: Kodansha.

Northouse, P. (2012). *Leadership: Theory and practice.* Thousand Oaks, CA: Sage.

Norton, M. I., Mochon, D., & Ariely, D. (2012). The IKEA effect: When labor leads to love. *Journal of Consumer Psychology, 22*(3), 453–460.

Rosen, A. (2013). *Change.edu: Rebooting for the new talent economy.* New York, NY. Kaplan/Simon & Schuster.

Rowley, D. J., Lujan, H. D., & Dolence, M. G. (2001). *Strategic change in colleges and universities: Planning to survive and prosper.* San Francisco, CA: Jossey-Bass.

Rowley, D. J., & Sherman, H. (2001). *From strategy to change: Implementing the plan in higher education.* San Francisco, CA: Jossey-Bass.

Sagaria, M.A.D. (2012). *Women, universities, and change: Gender equality in the European Union and the United States.* Basingstoke, England: Palgrave Macmillan.

Schein, E. H. (2010). *Organizational culture and leadership* (4th ed.). San Francisco, CA: Jossey-Bass.

Singer, R. A., & Zentall, T. R. (2011). Preference for the outcome that follows a relatively aversive event: Contrast or delay reduction? *Learning and Motivation, 42*(3), 255–271.

St. John, E. P., & Parsons, M. D. (2004). *Public funding of higher education: Changing contexts and new rationales.* Baltimore, MD: Johns Hopkins University Press.

Whyte, W. H. (1956). *The organization man.* New York, NY: Simon & Schuster.

Zemsky, R. (2013). *Checklist for change: Making American higher education a sustainable enterprise.* New Brunswick, NJ: Rutgers University Press.

RESOURCES

Bastedo, M. N. (2012). *The organization of higher education: Managing colleges for a new era*. Baltimore, MD: Johns Hopkins University Press.

Bowen, W. G. (2013). *Higher education in the digital age*. Princeton, NJ: Princeton University Press.

Bremer, M. (2012). *Organizational culture change: Unleash your organizations potential in circles of 10*. Zwolle, Netherlands: Kikker Groep.

Cameron, E., & Green, M. (2012). *Making sense of change management: A complete guide to the models, tools, and techniques of organizational change* (3rd ed.). London: Kogan Page.

Hiatt, J., & Creasey, T. J. (2012). *Change management: The people side of change*. Loveland, CO: Prosci Learning Center Publications.

Thornton, P. H., Ocasio, W., & Lounsbury, M. (2012). *The institutional logics perspective: A new approach to culture, structure, and process*. New York: Oxford University Press.

Tierney, W. G. (2008). *The impact of culture on organizational decision-making: Theory and practice in higher education*. Sterling, VA: Stylus.

REFRAMING CHANGE

IF, AS WE'VE SEEN, the organizational structure and culture of higher education means that colleges and universities are not well served by the change management strategies developed for corporate and military environments, what works better? Everyone knows there are plenty of changes already occurring throughout higher education today: globalization, the flipped classroom, increased competition, rapidly diminished resources, continually changing technology, and all the other factors that can be placed in the category I'll call *received change*. To these we can add all the changes we'd like to see in our programs: more creative teaching and active learning, higher levels of student success, more innovative research, progress in efficiency and effectiveness, higher levels of satisfaction, and all the other goals that we might call *intentional change*.

Different Ways of Viewing Change

With so much change going on all around us, how can academic leaders approach their challenges and opportunities in ways that will most benefit the programs they supervise? Let's begin to answer this question by understanding that there are several different ways to look at change and that the perspective we take profoundly affects the way we lead others through a change process.

The Common View of Change

If you were to go up to people on the street and ask them to define the word *change*, most of them would probably say it's about "making something different from what it was." In other words, it was A before; it's B now. A has "changed into" B. This common view of change is what frequently makes people uncomfortable with the prospect of change: it suggests that you're always losing something. To use the Kübler-Ross model, it's like the old state we were in has died. "But what if I really liked A or at least liked key elements of A?" people might ask. "How do I know I'll like B better? And if A no longer exists and we realize that the change was a mistake, will it be possible to go back? Will we be giving up more than we will gain? Maybe the devil we know is better than the devil we don't?" We might call this common view of change the *replacement view of change*. At colleges and universities, due to the IKEA effect (see chapter 1), this reaction tends to become even more pronounced than it would be in other situations—for example: "This idea of changing to B makes me uncomfortable. Doing things differently always means a lot more work and the loss of things that I'm perfectly happy with right now. Besides, I was one of the people who developed A. We put a great deal of thought into it and did a good job. Why would we discard all that just to try something unproven? Don't you think we knew what we were doing when we developed A in the first place?"

> People don't really fear change. They fear loss.

A fundamental problem with many change processes in higher education is that they let the replacement view of change frame the discourse. When a single, very common model is introduced during a discussion and no one challenges it, it starts to seem like a fact after a while, not a metaphor or merely one possible paradigm among many others we could adopt. As we'll see, however, there are many other ways of thinking about change than regarding it as replacement for or loss of what we have right now. In addition, the replacement view of change frequently merges with a phenomenon known as the sunk cost fallacy—the mistaken belief that past expenditure of either money or labor (what is known as the retrospective or sunk cost) has a bearing on the value of something in the present. We engage in the sunk cost fallacy when we refuse to sell a stock because its price has declined far lower than what we paid for it (even if we have good reasons to believe that its price will continue to decline), won't walk away from a slot machine because we want to win back all the money we've "invested" in it, stick with a research project that's clearly taking us down a blind alley because we've already spent so much time on it—or change a curriculum, procedure, or organizational structure at our school because we put so much effort into developing it in the first place. The real question must always be, "Of what value is A to us now, and what value is it likely to have in the future?" not, "How strongly should we be committed to A based on how much we've invested in it in the past?" The replacement view of change fears "losing" A because we've paid so dearly for it.

Challenging the replacement view of change and sunk cost fallacy head-on can be emotionally satisfying at times, but that direct approach rarely changes anyone's mind. It's a natural human tendency to dig in your heels when someone openly questions your reasoning process, and that tendency is all the more common at academic institutions where we pride ourselves on our analytical abilities and have a hard time imagining ourselves committing a fallacy. The more effective way of introducing an understanding of these concepts into a change process is through a suggestion such as, "We've been looking at this issue only in terms of what we'd be giving up. Let's also look at it in terms of what we stand to gain," or, "I think there's another way for us to approach this question. So far, we've been talking about replacing A with B. Perhaps it's more useful to look at what we're doing a little differently"—and then describe one of the other change models that we'll examine in this chapter. In fact, since the word *change* itself is likely to be seen by many people as a synonym for the *replacement view of change*, the best thing may be to avoid the word entirely and adopt one of the other ways of describing the proposed initiatives that I outlined in *Positive Academic Leadership* (Buller, 2013, 78):

- ○ An opportunity to build on our solid foundations
- ○ A chance to take full advantage of our past successes
- ○ A natural development from the solid foundations this program has laid
- ○ The next logical step in our ongoing progress
- ○ An occasion to grow that's been made possible by our program's established strengths
- ○ Carrying the plans we've made together to the next stage

The basic idea here is to reframe the discussion not as replacing A with B, but continuing A to its next, most appropriate stage of evolution: A'. In their book *Switch: How to Change Things When Change Is Hard* (2010), Chip and Dan Heath call this approach "shrinking the change." Rather than frightening people with how revolutionary and innovative the new approach will be, the goal becomes to calm people by reassuring them how minor and painless the process will be.

The Classical View of Change

The observation that there are serious flaws in the belief that change involves completely replacing one thing with another is hardly new. As early as the mid-fourth century BCE, Aristotle argued in the *Physics* that what we've called the replacement view of change was unsatisfactory. One way of understanding Aristotle's objection is to consider what that model is really saying: "It was A before. It's B now." But if that's the case, what is "It"? In other words, the replacement view of change suggests that A utterly ceases to exist when B comes into existence. But that's not really change; it's substitution. In order to declare that an actual change has occurred, something has to remain that is still somehow recognizable as A. To account for this "continuation despite modification," Aristotle posits that everything in the physical world has two distinct components: matter (the stuff that remains) and form (the shape that changes). We can think of the classical view of change in terms of a potter who's creating a vase. She first makes a pitcher, then finds that result unsatisfactory and, before placing the soft clay into the kiln, reshapes it into a bowl. Believing that she already has too many bowls, she changes her mind again and flattens the clay into a plate. Throughout this entire process, the matter (the clay) has remained the same; its chemical composition hasn't been altered in the slightest. But its form (the shape the clay assumes) has been modified. That, Aristotle says, is what all change is about: giving matter a different form from the one it possessed previously. To revert to our earlier terminology, he saw change as far more similar to A → A' than to A → B. In this system of annotation, A represents the matter; the presence or absence of the apostrophe (') represents the modification in form.

> "The art of progress is to preserve change amid order and preserve order amid change."—Alfred North Whitehead (Whitehead, Griffin, and Sherburne, 1929/1978, 339).

The point of introducing Aristotle's theory of change here isn't simply to indicate that there's more than one way to understand what change is (although that's certainly a valuable by-product), but rather to see how we need to reframe the discussion when we start seeing stakeholders interpreting change in higher education as loss rather than gain. In the change processes that occur in higher education, we do have something that persists along the lines of Aristotle's concept of matter: our core values. What the classical view of change reminds us is that it's important to prevent discussions of desirable change from being hijacked by the assumption that change is identical to replacement and loss. Rather, we can reframe the discussion so as to make the following equation clearer:

$$\text{Change} = \text{Replacement} + \text{resilience}$$

In this equation, I'm using the term *resilience* as it's been defined by Andrew Zolli, the executive director of the global community of innovators known as Pop! Tech: "the capacity of a system, enterprise, or a person to maintain its core purpose and integrity in the face of dramatically changed circumstances" (Zolli and Healy, 2012, 7). In other words, our core purpose (our mission) and our integrity (the values and guiding principles that we hold dear) are the basis of who we are. They're the institutional equivalent of Aristotle's matter: the factors that persist even as change goes on all around them. What changes, we might say, is merely external form: procedures, terminology, and the means to achieve specific ends, not the ends themselves.

The classical view of change holds that the true essence of something remains unaffected by what we might call "the next logical step in our ongoing progress." We can imagine an academic leader dispelling the fear of those who feel threatened by the change by saying:

> Who we are isn't going to change, but how we operate is going to have to change in light of how higher education is evolving. We may need to do things a little differently, but our values will remain intact. They're what defines who we are and where we want to go in the future. New practices and new technologies may make our outward appearance look a bit different. But those practices and technologies will merely help us better embody our unchanging values and more effectively reach our long-standing goals.

The View of Continual Change

As ancient as Aristotle's classical view of change was, it was by no means the first view of change proposed by Western philosophers, and it is not the only model that can help us better understand faculty resistance to change. More than a century before Aristotle, another Greek philosopher, Heraclitus of Ephesus, was fascinated by the idea that even things that seem most permanent to us eventually change. In Plato's *Cratylus* (402 a 8), Heraclitus's views are summarized with the words *panta chorei* (everything changes), often misquoted as *panta rhei* (everything flows). Heraclitus's basic idea was that the only constant in existence is change and that everything around us is changing all the time (figure 2.1). In this way, he paralleled a view that was being developed by the early Buddhists

Figure 2.1 The View of Continual Change

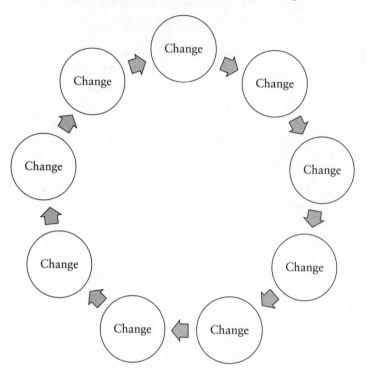

in India at roughly the same time. Even mountains are gradually worn away, coastlines shift, and rivers change their course. Since change is necessarily continual, there's no reason to fear it. It's a natural phenomenon that we can embrace, and sometimes take advantage of, not an intrusion into a normally static universe.

Of course, many observers other than Heraclitus have noticed the universality of change. The impermanence of all things is a fundamental concept in most schools of Zen and provides an important theme to works as diverse as Lucretius's *On the Nature of Things* and Wagner's *Twilight of the Gods*. Permanence is an illusion, these authors tell us, and those who seek to build structures designed to last forever, no matter whether they're Valhalla, statues of Ozymandias, or curricular plans, are doomed to failure:

> Change is not an event, with a beginning, middle, and comfortable end point. Rather it is an ongoing, organic process in which one change triggers another, often in unexpected places, and through which an interrelationship of the component parts leads to an unending cycle of reassessment and renewal. (Eckel, Hill, Green, and Mallon, 1999, 2)

As Paul Gaston, Trustees Professor and former provost at Kent State University, has often observed, revising a university's general education program isn't like building a pyramid—something stable and monumental that's intended to last forever; it's more like building a better felucca, the swift-moving boats commonly seen on the Nile. In fact, what you really want is something that, like a felucca, can respond almost instantaneously to changes in the environment even as they occur. (See, e.g., www.laregentsarchive.com/Academic/Agendas/2003/06/8.pdf; P. Gaston, personal communication, June 12, 2013.) In terms of sheer expediency, the more flexible one's mind-set is, the more palatable the entire idea of change tends to be:

> There is less pressure to build a curriculum if the task is seen as one of building for a period of time, rather than "for all time." It is enough to create a sound program that continues to grow and evolve. (Gaston and Gaff, 2009, 21)

Since everyone knows that there will inevitably be changes in demographics, technology, social values and priorities, opportunities for funding, and institutional leadership, it's foolish to assume that the decisions we make today won't be reevaluated tomorrow. Failure to build bridges or tall buildings that can flex when necessary is often a recipe for disaster. The same principle applies to the innovations we pursue as academic leaders: unless our plans can adapt to changing conditions, they'll end up being torn apart as the inevitable pressure against them builds.

Another common metaphor used to describe the continual view of change is that of a journey or voyage of discovery. As is frequently the case in travel narratives, the destination of a trip can be far less important than the adventures occurring along the way. The journey thus becomes a microcosm of life itself. If you don't pay attention to each experience as it unfolds, you'll have nothing but regrets at the end. In certain situations, that's not a bad way to look at many processes at colleges and universities. We're never completely finished revising curricula, introducing new forms of pedagogy, exploring different approaches in research, structuring committees, and responding to the need for change. A strategic planning process can be less threatening if an institution regards itself as in a constant process of planning and improvement. It's not that the university is exchanging something new and unfamiliar for something old and cherished (the replacement view of change) or even that it's modifying something old and cherished so that it takes on a wholly different form (the classical view of change). Rather, what's occurring is that the university is constantly in a state of evolution and growth. Everything is just a draft; nothing should ever be regarded as the final, published version.

The Intentional View of Change

I can imagine some people arguing, "That's all fine in theory, but a journey without a destination isn't really a journey. It's just meandering. And a change process with no particular goal in mind doesn't reflect sound strategic planning. It's simply an abdication of leadership." In other words, the metaphor of the institution's journey can itself assume several forms. If the type of journey we've already considered might be called *change as journey* or *voyage of discovery,* an alternative way to view it is to see it in terms of *change as pilgrimage.* Although in a pilgrimage, it may be true that the experiences along the way are at least as valuable as the destination itself, the focus of the traveler is always on that destination: it provides the underlying reason for the journey, and people set out on the road with the understanding that something important will occur when the pilgrimage site is finally reached. The intentional view of change lies behind Alice's often cited (and just as often misquoted) exchange with the Cheshire Cat:

> "Would you tell me, please, which way I ought to go from here?"
> "That depends a good deal on where you want to get to," said the Cat.
> "I don't much care where—" said Alice.
> "Then it doesn't matter which way you go," said the Cat.
> "—so long as I get SOMEWHERE," Alice added as an explanation.
> "Oh, you're sure to do that," said the Cat, "if you only walk long enough." (Carroll, 1994, 64–65)

Simply having a destination in mind doesn't mean that you'll always remain at that destination once you get there. In fact, the end of each journey may simply be the start of another, with each destination merely serving as a waypoint along the road (figure 2.2). But the journey is still always a matter of getting somewhere, as Alice said, rather than wandering blindly: those on this path are pilgrims, after all, not vagrants.

Ken Blanchard, the author of *The One Minute Manager* (Blanchard and Johnson, 1982) and *Who Killed Change?* (Blanchard, 2009) frequently notes that we should think of change as a journey, not a destination, and that we should thus devote more of our energy to "managing the journey than announcing the destination" (Blanchard and Ridge, 2009, 15). That's a good lesson to keep in mind as we work to bring about meaningful change in higher education. Too often we miscommunicate with our stakeholders about why they should support

Figure 2.2 The Intentional View of Change

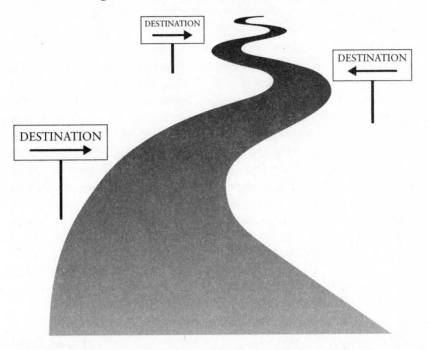

an idea or proposal. After all, from our perspective as academic leaders, change journeys can seem pretty exciting at times. They're the way we move forward, make new discoveries, and measure our progress. But from the perspective of our often-unwilling fellow travelers, the journey isn't so much a matter of reaching new destinations as of leaving familiar places behind. They may have a sense that "we keep reaching our goal, but we never really arrive. There's barely time to reap the fruits of the old strategic plan before we head off in another direction established by a new strategic plan." So what seems to us like a fascinating adventure strikes them as involving a lot of packing up, saying good-bye to valued friends, and beginning yet another forced march toward an indistinct horizon. That's why, when we try to win faculty members and donors over with the argument that the journey ahead will be exciting, our message so often falls on deaf ears. We'd be far better off to take people's fears about leaving the comforts of "home" seriously and speak about the continuity of our path, not merely the new direction we're going to be heading in.

The Visionary View of Change

The last view of change we'll explore in this chapter is quite different from the first four. Rather than suggesting that change is something a person passively endures or occasionally co-opts, it describes change as a process that people should seek out, embrace, and cultivate. In the words of the computer scientist Alan Kay, "The best way to predict the future is to invent it" (www.ecotopia.com/webpress/futures.htm). As we'll see in chapter 4, this approach requires making a transition from change management to change leadership. But in light of what we've already discovered about the distinctive organizational structure of colleges and universities, that leadership has to be demonstrated in a way that's appropriate to the culture. Even if you do everything that Ken Blanchard suggests—continually manage the change after you've announced the destination—you'll still encounter significant resistance from many of your stakeholders. Faculty members *hate* being managed; it makes them feel that they are problems that need to be solved rather than as valued partners in our journey. And that reaction is perfectly justified. In a system of shared governance, the role of the faculty isn't that of employees who merely carry out the orders they receive from "management." College professors are highly trained professionals whose insights and expertise are needed in order for any meaningful change to occur. Even the word *leadership* troubles them at times. No one is fond of being treated as a sheep that needs to be led. But at least we can describe this process in terms of more enlightened models of leadership—such as servant leadership, lateral leadership, centrifugal leadership, and positive leadership (see Buller, 2013)—that better reflect the relationship between faculty and administration than the corporate or military forms of leadership that immediately spring to mind.

Our mental image of the person who invents the future and guides the process of change in higher education shouldn't be a Thomas Edison, laboring alone in his lab and finding those proverbial "10,000 ways that won't work." That's a nineteenth- or twentieth-century image of what inventors do. Today's visionary leaders are more like Steve Jobs who might have followed the words of the old Apple commercial, "Think Different," but who also worked as part of a creative team. In much the same way that Jobs worked with Steve Wozniak and a few others to develop the Apple 1, each member of the team needs all the others. Each person brings different talents, resources, and experiences to the project to create the synergy that produces something "insanely great," in Jobs's famous phrase. Without the technician, the product wouldn't be user friendly. Without the visionary, it wouldn't be groundbreaking. Without the entrepreneur, it would never reach the market. It's that type of teamwork that's required for innovative change to occur in higher education. Faculty, administration, staff, students, donors—in fact, all of an institution's constituencies—have to be part of a group effort working collaboratively to make a positive difference.

Bolman and Deal's Four-Frame Model

If leading effective change in higher education means that we must reexamine the very way we look at both change and organizational culture in higher education, it's also incumbent on us to reexamine what it is we do as academic leaders. Perhaps the most familiar way of describing this process of reexamination is Lee Bolman and Terry Deal's notion that we can think of organizations as having four complementary frames (table 2.1):

1. The *structural frame*, which includes institutional policies and procedures, the organizational chart, and the strategic plan
2. The *human resources frame*, which includes agendas (both open and hidden), individual motivations, and fundamental human needs
3. The *political frame*, which includes alliances, coalitions, and conflicts
4. The *symbolic frame*, which includes organizational culture and traditions, institutional memory, and "the way we do things around here" (Bolman and Deal, 2013)

In higher education, change processes can run aground in any of these four frames. For example, a proposed change might not follow logically from the strategic plan (structural frame), conflict with the priorities of key constituents (human resources frame), require the ongoing cooperation of two habitually hostile groups (political frame), or require the demolition of a building long seen by alumni as the heart of the institution (symbolic frame).

One effective way of exploring how best to implement a proposed change is to examine it through each of Bolman and Deal's four frames in terms of where potential resistance is most likely to occur. For example, change processes that range anywhere from slight program modifications to complete realignments of institutional mission, can avoid many of what Paul Gaston and Jerry Gaff have dubbed the "potholes" of

Table 2.1. Bolman and Deal's Four-Frame Model

	Frame			
	Structural	Human Resources	Political	Symbolic
Metaphor for organization	Factory or machine	Family	Jungle	Carnival, temple, theater
Central concepts	Rules, roles, goals, policies, technology, environment	Needs, skills, relationships	Power, conflict, competition, organizational politics	Culture, meaning, metaphor, ritual, ceremony, stories, heroes
Image of leadership	Social architecture	Empowerment	Advocacy	Inspiration
Basic leadership challenge	Attune structure to task, technology, environment	Align organizational and human needs	Develop agenda and power base	Create faith, beauty, meaning

Source: Adapted from Bolman and Deal (1998, 15).

academic change (Gaston and Gaff, 2009) by asking such questions as the following:

STRUCTURAL FRAME

1. Do we have the resources to carry this initiative through to its full implementation?

2. Does the initiative follow logically from who we are right now and who we want to become?

3. Which existing groups, such as councils and committees, will be integral to the success of this initiative?

4. What groups may need to be created in order for this initiative to be a success?

5. Is this initiative something that we can accomplish by means of existing structures and procedures, or would it require a radically new operating procedure?

HUMAN RESOURCES FRAME

1. Have we paid adequate attention to the responsibility assignment matrix (often known as RAM or RACI)? In other words, have we thoroughly considered who among the various stakeholder groups falls into each of the following categories?

   - *Responsible:* Those whose active involvement is necessary for the initiative's success
   - *Accountable:* Those who are involved in a decision-making or supervisory capacity
   - *Consulted:* Those whose opinions matter as the initiative proceeds
   - *Informed:* Those who must be kept in the loop as the process continues

2. What is the likely reaction to this initiative going to be from each stakeholder group?

3. How can the need for this change be phrased in such a way that each stakeholder group understands its benefit to them?

4. Have we laid the appropriate groundwork so that stakeholders' response to this initiative will be based on its merits and not on the quality of our relationship with them?

5. Which of our stakeholders might have motives that could complicate or derail this process?

POLITICAL FRAME

1. Whose support for this initiative can we count on because they trust us or are early adopters in most change processes?

2. Whose resistance to this initiative should we expect because they don't trust us or tend to oppose change for its own sake?

3. Whose toes might be stepped on by this change if we don't bring them onboard?

4. Who are the opinion leaders on campus or in the community whose importance goes far beyond their titles and positions?

5. Who are the people who are likely to feel that they own what we're changing?

SYMBOLIC FRAME

1. How might the proposed change be perceived by some as a loss or departure from values and ideas that are essential to what we stand for?

2. How will the institution emerge from this process recognizably better off but also still true to its core values and beliefs?

3. What are the key events and ceremonies that can be used to get the word out about the importance of this initiative?

4. How might the change message be interpreted differently based on the spokesperson chosen to deliver that message?

5. What metaphor shall we use to describe the type of change we have in mind? A rebirth? A reboot? A natural growth process? A leap into the future? A metamorphosis?

While all four frames are important in order to understand any organizational culture, the symbolic frame is particularly important at colleges and universities during a time of profound change:

> Academic administrators who bring the imagination to envision new possibilities and the skills to convey a compelling picture of the future enable others to feel positive and hopeful about their work, their institution, and its leadership. Certain roles, like president, chancellor, dean, and director, are by their nature heavily and visibly symbolic. The dean represents the school, the president the college, the director his or her program or center, and so on. Occupants of such roles preside over more ceremonies and get more opportunities to take center stage and to play the role of public leader with gravitas and flair than those who lead informally or without executive titles. (Bolman and Gallos, 2011, 111)

One of the factors that dooms many academic change processes is that administrators forget this lesson. They spend so much time trying to get the vision and the decisions right that they overlook getting the symbols and motivation right. (Recall Krüger's iceberg from chapter 1.) But symbols and traditions are the very things that give people a sense of engaging in a cause that's part of a higher purpose. If you make a good decision but trample on something that people regard as sacred or that helps them feel their contributions are important, you're likely to end up creating a far greater problem than the one you just "solved."

As an antidote to this problem, the questions I associated with Bolman and Deal's four frames help academic leaders understand how a change process feels different to different stakeholders at the university. Moreover, it reminds us that in higher education, we can't define stakeholders only in terms of their position on the organization chart. In *The Department Chair*

Primer, Don Chu (2012) distinguishes between a closed-system perspective and an open-system perspective. In a closed system, we limit our view to stakeholders who are clearly inside that system. For example, if we speak to members of a typical academic department and ask them to identify their primary stakeholders, we're likely to receive an answer similar to the following.

Constituents (Whose needs do we serve?): Students

Engine (Who does the work?): Faculty

Leadership (Who guides the work?): The department chair

But this approach overlooks the very people—like alumni, parents of current students, and donors—who are likely to feel blindsided by a change because we didn't inform them about it before implementing it. A better approach is to view the system in which we work as a flexible and frequently shifting set of stakeholders, an open system that includes constituents both inside and outside the institution (figure 2.3). After all, if you inadvertently overlook someone who should have appeared on your RACI matrix, you'll delay and possibly destroy any chance for success you may have had.

De Bono's Six Thinking Hats

Bolman and Deal's four-frame model is currently the system most academic leaders use to incorporate multiple perspectives into any decision, but it's not the only model of its kind. For example, six years before the first edition of *Reframing Organizations* appeared, Edward de Bono, the polymath who also coined the term *lateral thinking* (which we'll discuss in chapter 6), proposed that people use what he called six thinking hats in order to adopt different perspectives toward various problems and challenges (see table 2.2). Perhaps the best way of seeing how de Bono's six thinking hats can work to expand Bolman and Deal's four-frame model is to consider what both might tell us about an actual process of academic change.

Let's imagine that we're dealing with the following situation: a new president at a university proposes moving the institution away from its traditional emphasis on teaching toward a new focus on externally funded research. Here's what might result from using Bolman and Deal's four frames combined with de Bono's six thinking hats:

Figure 2.3 An Open Academic System

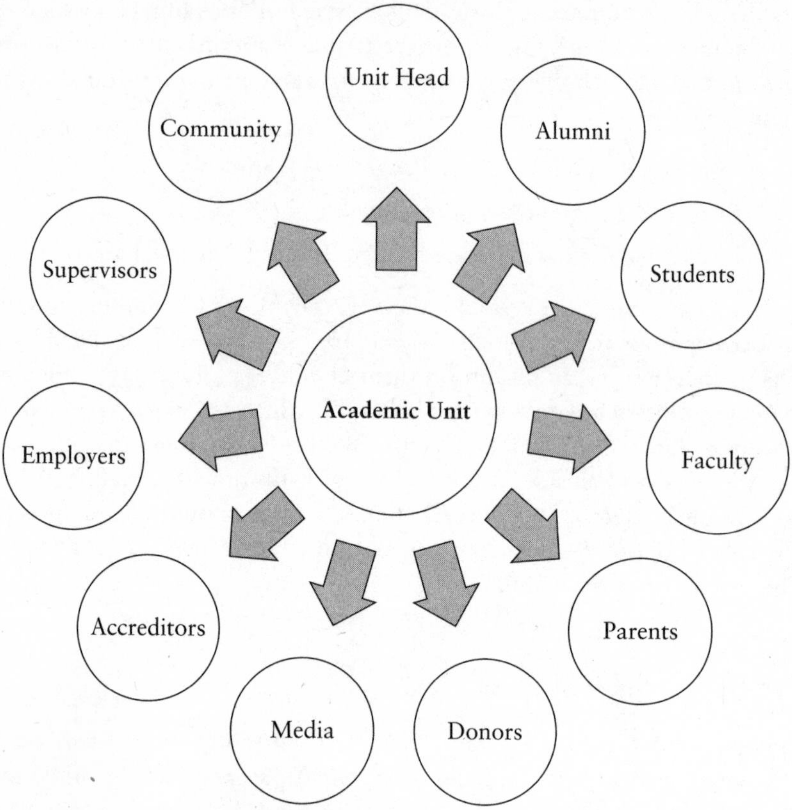

Four-frame model	Structural frame	We're taking a serious gamble here because we're hoping that the proposed change will bring us the resources we need, but we haven't yet identified the resources it will take to implement this change. For example, we'll need to expand staffing in our division of research significantly. The university's current strategic plan, with four years left to run, did not address this type of change, and so we haven't been developing the kind of infrastructure it will take to make this change a success.

Human resources frame	In addition to the new president, early support for this proposal is coming from the governing board and certain segments of the faculty. The student body, alumni, parents of students, donor base, community members, state regulatory body, and main sources of transfer students are less supportive. In order for the initiative to be successful, we'll have to find a way to meet the objections of these key groups.
Political frame	The new president is currently still enjoying a fairly strong honeymoon phase, and so certain key constituencies (most important, the faculty senate and graduate council) are likely to support the proposal, at least in principle. However, leaders of the faculty union were alienated by the former president, and those attitudes of distrust remain unchanged under the current administration. We should thus expect strong resistance from the union to any initiative proposed by the upper administration and not by the faculty itself.
Symbolic frame	For many years, the university has used the expressions "Teaching First" and "Where Education Really Matters" in all its publicity materials. Certain stakeholders are likely to perceive the new president's proposal as an abandonment of the institution's traditional values. It will be important, therefore, for the role that an expanded emphasis on research can have on improving teaching and enriching education to become a key part of our communications with all constituencies.

Six think-
ing hats

White hat

In terms of potential benefits that we can document, research institutions in our state are funded at a 22 percent higher rate than institutions like ours where the mission is focused primarily on teaching. In addition, an emphasis on research would bring the university much-needed overhead from federal grants. In terms of potential costs that we can expect, hired consultants recently estimated that the president's plan will require an initial investment of at least $560,000 of continuing funding (for staff salaries and operating budgets) plus at least $14 million in one-time funding (for infrastructure and facility upgrades) in order for the university to become even minimally competitive for the level of federal grants envisioned by the president.

Red hat

There is a great deal of excitement and prestige associated with a move toward greater research productivity. The president and board have been very successful in promoting this initiative among existing donors. Many faculty members remain anxious, however, because they're uncertain of the effect this initiative will have on the university's standards for tenure and promotion. Many students have expressed opposition because they fear that resources will be drained from scholarships and educational enrichment in order to fund the initiative. Other constituencies appear to have adopted a wait-and-see attitude.

Black hat   If the initiative is not successful in
                 obtaining access to the level of expanded
                 resources envisioned by the president, the
                 university could actually be worse off
                 financially because of the size of the
                 initial investment. The reputation of the
                 university would suffer due to a
                 perception that it tried to become
                 something it wasn't suited for. The state
                 regulatory body, which has taken a
                 strong stance against mission creep, could
                 punish the university in future funding
                 decisions. The president's leadership
                 authority would be compromised by a
                 significant failure.

Yellow hat   If the institution is successful in launching
                 this initiative, the increase in revenue
                 obtained from grants would more than
                 offset the initial investment. This
                 additional funding could then be used to
                 improve other areas of the university,
                 including those related to its educational
                 mission. Expanded media attention
                 resulting from cutting-edge research
                 could lead to higher enrollments, which
                 would bring in additional tuition dollars.
                 Faculty and staff morale would increase
                 as a result of being identified with an
                 exciting new enterprise. A larger number
                 of high-ability students, as well as faculty
                 members with more impressive
                 credentials, might be attracted to the
                 university.

Green hat   What if we shift the focus of the proposal
                 slightly to promoting undergraduate
                 research, thereby forging a distinctive
                 institutional mission and avoiding direct
                 competition with the four other large
                 research universities already in our state?
                 What if we expand research only in the
                 one or two areas for which the university

	is already well known and that don't require as large an initial investment? Are we making a false assumption that federal grants are the only potential source of significantly reduced income or that this funding source will remain secure for the future?
Blue hat	Because the likelihood and impact of the potential problems so far outweigh the likelihood and impact of the proposal's potential benefits, it is recommended that the university not proceed as planned. Instead, it is recommended that the initiative be modified as follows: (1) In the short term, emphasis will be given to the university's distinctive role in promoting undergraduate research, particularly in key areas of proven success. (2) A foundation will be prepared with key stakeholder groups to illustrate the ways in which an expanded research mission will actually enhance the university's teaching mission. (3) Donors will be sought for naming opportunities that will provide the necessary infrastructure for an expanded research mission. (4) If these preliminary efforts are successful, the proposal will be reconsidered in four years as the university prepares its next long-term strategic plan.

Of course, not all applications of this approach will result in a recommendation not to proceed with the proposed change as occurred in our hypothetical example. It's far more likely that the institution will come away from this reframing process with a decision to continue the initiative, but with a better understanding of the challenges that lie ahead. Even more important, the application of analyzing proposed initiatives through Bolman and Deal's four frames and de Bono's six thinking hats is likely to result in a much more realistic road map for the future. Academic leaders will gain from this exercise an understanding of which stakeholder groups they need to win over, which arguments are most likely to resonate with

Table 2.2. De Bono's Six Thinking Hats

Hat	Color Association	Focus	Relevant Questions
White hat	Purity	Objectivity	What are the facts? What is indisputable? What do the data indicate?
Red hat	Fire, anger	Emotionality	What's our gut reaction? How do the facts make us feel? How might other stakeholders feel about it?
Black hat	Devil's advocate	Negativity	What could go wrong? What's the worst-case scenario? What problems might we encounter along the way?
Yellow hat	Sunny optimism	Positivity	What could work out unexpectedly well? What's the best-case scenario? What benefits might occur because of this idea?
Green hat	Vegetation	Fertility, creativity	How can we be creative and think about this idea differently? What unnecessary assumptions have we made? Have we considered all imaginable "What if?" scenarios?
Blue hat	The sky	"The 30,000 feet view"	If we put the previous five perspectives together, now what? How do all the details fit together into an overall pattern? Based on what we know and feel, shall we proceed? If so, how?

each group, which strategies may cause people to see the change in terms of loss instead of improvement and growth, which aspects of the initiative must be emphasized immediately, and which rhetorical approaches are likely to backfire and bring the proposal to a prompt and inglorious demise. Reframing change helps academic leaders see the way forward, not just as they themselves see it, but as it might be viewed throughout the open system that is essential to the initiative's success.

Ten Analytical Lenses

Despite all the advantages of the four frames and six thinking hats, they do have limitations. They're designed for general use in any type of organization, not just for the unique organizational culture of higher education that we explored in chapter 1. As I suggested in *Positive Academic Leadership* (2013), Bolman and Deal's four-frame model simply doesn't go far enough in helping academic leaders see the full context of their decision. It doesn't help them as well as it could to identify their options in light of the mission and vision of their units, all the stakeholders who compose their open system, the strict practicalities of working within a system of shared governance, or the idealism and dreams that often guide academics in their work. De Bono's six thinking hats, which were revolutionary in 1985, seem rather dated today. With our current level of multicultural awareness, I've seen faculty members and students angrily refuse to consider any approach that, even unintentionally, equates perspective with specific colors. (Think about it for a moment: How is a multicultural audience likely to respond to a system that identifies white with purity and black with negativity? How is a politically liberal audience likely to regard a system that identifies red with letting our emotions run wild?) For all these reasons, academic leaders need a way to reframe proposals for change in higher education with an approach that borrows from the best of the Bolman and Deal and de Bono models while avoiding their limitations. I call the resulting approach *ten analytical lenses* through which to examine academic change (table 2.3). These ten analytical lenses bring multiple perspectives into focus.

○ The *20/20 lens* is similar to de Bono's white hat thinking. It consists of seeing a proposed change objectively and clearly, assessing what is known about our situation, and interpreting documented evidence without subjectivity or prejudice.

○ The *concave lens* causes us to pull back a bit and try to see an issue in its entirety. It represents a conscious effort to avoid getting so caught up in details that we overlook the overall impact of what we're proposing.

○ The *convex lens* allows us to take the opposite view. Rather than permitting us to be swept away by the excitement of our hopes and dreams, it causes us to look at relevant details and ask what steps would need to be taken, in what order, and at what likely cost.

○ The *telephoto lens* gives us a chance to glimpse the distant future. It urges us to look at trends, demographics, and our own strategic goals in order to determine the best way to journey from where we are to where we want to be. This lens also includes the creative elements found in de Bono's green hat thinking because it causes us to realize that there may be more than one way to get from one point to another; there may even be a more desirable destination that we haven't yet identified.

○ The *bifocal lens* allows us to see more clearly what's right in front of our eyes. It urges us not to ignore existing infrastructure and resources, no matter whether those are pieces of equipment, facilities, sources of funding, or people. This lens cause us to take Bolman and Deal's structural frame into account, but it also includes elements of their symbolic frame. In other words, by using our bifocal lens, we're paying attention to everything that affects our current environment: things, people, ideas, and cultural context.

○ The *rose-colored glasses* are similar to de Bono's yellow hat thinking. They involve taking an optimistic view and exploring the benefits that would accrue if everything goes well.

○ The *sunglasses* are similar to de Bono's black hat thinking. They involve taking a pessimistic view and asking about the damage that would be done if things go poorly.

○ The *rearview mirror* helps us avoid forgetting where we came from. In administrative terms, it helps us keep our mission, vision, and core values in mind. It also prevents us from losing sight of any competitors who are speeding up behind us and helps us avoid being blindsided by external threats and pressures.

○ The *contact lenses* are similar to Bolman and Deal's human resources and political frames. We might conceptualize this approach as follows: most people wear contact lenses not because they receive any medical benefit they wouldn't get from ordinary glasses; rather, they think these lenses make them look better and improve their social interactions. In the context of a change process, we might be said to be using our analytical contact lenses when we scan our system to look for those who might be affected by a proposed change and consider how we should interact with them to make them understand why this action is necessary.

○ The *wide-angle lens* is similar to de Bono's blue hat thinking. It involves putting each of the first nine perspectives together into a single broad picture and drawing conclusions from what we see.

These ten analytical lenses thus offer a technique to understand the full complexity of a proposed change before we get so far into the process that we cause irreparable harm. They alert us to questions we still need to ask, the feelings of constituents we need to consider, and the important groundwork we need to prepare. They help us compensate for our own

Table 2.3. Ten Analytical Lenses

Lens	Focus	Relevant Questions
20/20 lens	Provide clarity and objectivity	What are the facts? What is indisputable? What do the data indicate?
Concave lens	Correct for myopia	How can we see the forest, not just the trees? What is the big picture? How might we get too caught up in petty details?
Convex lens	Correct for hyperopia	How can we see the trees, not just the forest? What details do we need to see before we can proceed? How might we get too carried away by remote possibilities?
Telephoto lens	Scan distant horizons	What is far off in the distance? What is the territory like between here and there? How can we sharpen our view of what lies ahead of us?
Bifocal lens	Permit close analysis	What has been right in front of our faces all along? What resources and assets do we see around us? What information do we need to see clearly before we proceed?
Rose-colored glasses	Take an optimistic view	What could work out unexpectedly well? What's the best-case scenario? What benefits might occur because of this idea?
Sunglasses	Take a dim view	What could go wrong? What's the worst-case scenario? What problems might we encounter along the way?
Rearview mirror	Bring the unseen into view	Where have we come from? What is looming behind us? What might we be overlooking?
Contact lenses	Enhance social interactions	Who are the people around us? What do they want and need from us? What do we want and need from them?
Wide-angle lens	Take in the whole picture	How do all these views fit together? How do we feel about the overall landscape? Based on what we see, should we proceed?

individual limitations as academic leaders. Some of us are vision people who can find the idea of a new initiative so exciting that we fail to take care of all the details necessary to be successful. Others of us are detail people who can become so fixated on the day-to-day steps in implementing a plan that we ignore the big picture that excites donors, prospective students, and funding agencies. Like the four-frame model and the six thinking hats, the ten analytical lenses help us decide whether to proceed with a change process and, if we choose to proceed, what actions are needed to increase the likelihood of our success.

Conclusion

Since the organizational culture of higher education is different from that of other institutions, academic leaders can't effectively promote change without viewing their proposals from certain key perspectives, most notably that of their wide range of stakeholders. In hierarchical structures, change can flow more easily from the top to the bottom. A brilliant corporate leader—such as a Jeff Bezos, Estee Lauder, or Elon Musk, the cofounder of PayPal, SpaceX, and Tesla Motors—can transform an industry through effective top-down management. (As we'll see in chapter 8, however, there's usually a lot more going on even in those cultures than just the vision of a brilliant visionary leader.) But since colleges and universities have organizational structures that aren't the same as those found in businesses, armies, and committees, the lessons corporate leaders teach us about change management don't always apply to a university setting. In higher education, academic leaders have to work within a much more open system and examine proposed changes through a larger set of lenses than are needed elsewhere. What ten analytical lenses can reveal to us is whether an innovation is likely to succeed or fail, which approaches are best adopted when exploring the idea with each stakeholder group, and even whether there's a valid need for change. It's the last of these topics—the validity of the need—that we turn to in the next chapter.

REFERENCES

Blanchard, K. H. (2009). *Who killed change? Solving the mystery of leading people through change.* New York, NY: Morrow/HarperCollins.
Blanchard, K. H., & Johnson, S. (1982). *The one minute manager.* New York, NY: Morrow.

Blanchard, K. H., & Ridge, G. (2009). *Helping people win at work: A business philosophy called "Don't mark my paper, help me get an A."* Upper Saddle River, NJ: FT Press.

Bolman, L. G., & Deal, T. E. (2013). *Reframing organizations: Artistry, choice, and leadership* (5th ed.). San Francisco, CA: Jossey-Bass.

Bolman, L. G., & Gallos, J. V. (2011). *Reframing academic leadership.* San Francisco, CA: Jossey-Bass.

Buller, J. L. (2013). *Positive academic leadership: How to stop putting out fires and start making a difference.* San Francisco, CA: Jossey-Bass, 2013.

Carroll, L. (1994). *The complete works of Lewis Carroll.* New York, NY: Barnes & Noble.

Chu, D. (2012). *The department chair primer: Leading and managing academic departments* (2nd ed.). San Francisco, CA: Jossey-Bass.

De Bono, E. (1985). *Six thinking hats.* Boston, MA: Little, Brown.

Eckel, P., Hill, B., Green, M., & Mallon, B. (1999). *On change.* Washington, DC: American Council on Education.

Gaston, P. L., & Gaff, J. G. (2009). *Revising general education—and avoiding the potholes.* Washington, DC: Association of American Colleges and Universities.

Heath, C., & Heath, D. (2010). *Switch: How to change things when change is hard.* New York, NY: Broadway Books.

Whitehead, A. N., Griffin, D. R., & Sherburne, D. W. (1929/1978). *Process and reality: An essay in cosmology.* New York, NY: Free Press.

Zolli, A., & Healy, A. M. (2012). *Resilience: Why things bounce back.* New York, NY: Free Press.

RESOURCES

Jones, B. B., & Brazzel, M. (Eds.). (2006). *The NTL handbook of organization development and change: Principles, practices, and perspectives.* San Francisco, CA: Jossey-Bass/Pfeiffer.

Kezar, A. (2014). How colleges change: Proven tools for academic leaders to successfully lead change. *Academic Leader, 30*(2), 5–6.

Metcalf, M., & Palmer, M. (2011). *Innovative leadership fieldbook: Field-tested integral approaches to developing leaders, transforming organizations and creating sustainability.* Tucson, AZ: Integral Publishers.

Palmer, I., Dunford, R., & Akin, G. (2009). *Managing organizational change: A multiple perspectives approach.* Boston: McGraw-Hill Irwin.

3

DETERMINING THE NEED
FOR CHANGE

IT SEEMS REASONABLE TO ASK, "How can we as academic leaders determine whether our colleges and universities need change?" But that's really the wrong question. The choice in higher education today isn't *whether* we should change but *how*. As we'll see later in this chapter, there are so many drivers of change affecting everything we do that the ways in which we teach, learn, and conduct research seem to be in a constant state of flux. Advanced learning is no longer the exclusive domain of traditional colleges and universities but can be acquired through massive open online courses (MOOCs), for-profit institutions, iTunes U, businesses like the Teaching Company and Rosetta Stone, and any number of podcasts. Even the most provincial school is under pressure to participate with other schools globally in an increasingly complex academic marketplace. The very purpose of a college education is regularly debated, with many governors and legislatures arguing that higher education exists primarily for job preparation, particularly in the science, technology, engineering, and mathematics disciplines, while the American Academy for the Arts and Sciences in its 2013 publication, *The Heart of the Matter* (available at www.amacad.org) countered that an increased emphasis on the arts, humanities, and social sciences is necessary in order to prepare future generations of informed citizens, not merely employed workers.

Change is already here. The issue is what we're going to do about it and what type of change we want for our colleges and universities.

Is All Change Good for Higher Education?

Since change is inevitable in higher education, does all change have to be good? Some would argue that it is; change by its very existence helps higher education from becoming stale. As Winston Churchill once remarked during a debate about taxes on silk and sugar, "To improve is to change; to be perfect is to change often." (See hansard.millbanksystems.com/commons/1925/jun/23/finance-bill-1# S5CV0185P0_19250623_HOC_339). Administrators have been known to quote these words in the belief that any institution that remains the same for too long will lose its edge as the faculty become complacent and the curriculum obsolete. To avoid such a fate, so the argument goes, academic leaders must promote constant change in order to keep pedagogy, research, and the institution's attractiveness to donors and potential students up to date. The best faculty members, it's said, are those who always challenge their own ideas. That challenge then becomes a catalyst for change.

There's some truth to this belief. We've all been approached by trustees, donors, and legislators who ask, "What's new in your area?" (For years, my stock reply was, "Well, my area is ancient history. So, by definition—nothing.") It's an uncomfortable feeling to find yourself unable to answer this question in a way that indicates your program is growing and expanding into new areas so as to remain ahead of your peers. Proponents of continual change argue that since colleges and universities must constantly adapt to new developments in higher education anyway, it's far better to be a cause of that change than simply to respond to it. Besides, change causes us to challenge our assumptions. It's rather like moving from one home to another. As difficult as packing and relocating may be, good things inevitably come from it: you have to discard things that aren't useful any longer, rearrange things so that they fit into a new space, and develop new ways of getting wherever you need to go from your new location. That's what change in higher education is like. It forces us to reexamine policies we might not reexamine otherwise, defend those decisions that remain useful, and abandon efforts that no longer serve a useful purpose. Besides, our environment is always changing. Each year another group of students passes through our courses, studios, and laboratories. They have different needs and interests from the students who graduated only a few years before, and we have to change in order to meet those needs and address those interests. Change is thus a key factor in keeping us creative, innovative, and engaged.

Is All Change Bad for Higher Education?

The opposing point of view argues that although certain of the changes imposed on us by external forces may indeed be inevitable, institutions harm themselves and their students by making a fetish out of change.

Many policies and structures at universities exist for a very good reason, and as the saying goes, "If it ain't broke, don't fix it." By pursuing unwarranted changes in curriculum, organization, pedagogy, and procedures, institutions cause faculty members to divert precious time from their primary responsibilities of teaching, research, and service, accomplishing little of value in the process. In addition, faculty members often believe (at times justifiably) that administrators are trying to initiate a change not because they really believe there's a significant problem to be solved, but because they want credit for accomplishing something. Perhaps they're trying to justify their high salaries, or perhaps they're trying to build their résumés. But if you split a program in two, you can claim that you've "created new programs," even if the original structure was working just fine. If you consolidate three departments into one, you can say that you've increased efficiency, even if no cost savings result and no genuine advantages can be identified.

Much of this suspicion may result from the lack of trust that often exists between faculty and administration. But regardless of whether we agree with the argument, let's recall some of the reasons people use to justify their belief that all administrative-initiated change is bad.

As we just saw, perhaps the most common factor behind this point of view is that presidents, provosts, and deans want to promote change so that they'll be viewed as having made a difference at the institution. Many faculty members suspect that the reason that so many presidents arrive at institutions ready to become change agents is that they want to impress their boards. At lower levels of the hierarchy, deans and provosts are sometimes accused of promoting a change as a way of earning their next promotion. The real needs of an institution, such as repairing infrastructure and advocating for higher faculty salaries, go unaddressed, it is argued, because these problems don't sound exciting when a president makes an annual report to the board or a dean is applying to become a provost. The suspicion is that academic leaders fall into the trap known as action bias—the fallacy that it's always better to be doing something rather than nothing. (On action bias, see Dobelli, 2013.)

The second common suspicion is that administrators initiate change because they favor mission creep—the desire of all community colleges to become state colleges, state colleges to become state universities, state universities to become research universities, research universities to achieve the RU/VH Carnegie classification (i.e., very high research activity, similar to the old Research 1 category), and RU/VH universities to be among the top ten such institutions worldwide. Mission creep is the academic equivalent of keeping up with the Joneses—or, more accurately, getting ahead of the Joneses. It's the belief that wherever we are now, we'll be far better off if only we can reach "the next level of excellence." As a result, faculty members who were hired by an institution with a long-standing commitment to teaching sometimes worry that they'll never be promoted to the rank of full professor because the criteria for such a promotion are a constantly moving target.

A third claim made by those who are skeptical of administratively initiated change is that these changes usually occur for reasons that don't have a valid pedagogical basis. For example, many faculty members don't trust statements made by presidents and provosts that they're excited about the expansion of MOOCs because this new delivery platform will improve learning. Instead these faculty members believe that the real reason universities are jumping onto the MOOC bandwagon is that they want to control costs and reduce the number of full-time faculty positions (Kolowich, 2013). In a similar way, faculty members often mistrust claims by administrators that a larger percentage of adjuncts is needed on the faculty so that students will have increased access to "practitioners who are currently working in the field." Even when disciplinary accrediting bodies support the hiring of part-time faculty members who are still actively involved in their professions, college professors often suspect that the university is more interested in avoiding the high cost of employee benefits than in improving the experience of its students.

The fourth reason that faculty members often question the value of changes they didn't initiate themselves is that they believe groups from outside the institution are increasingly interfering in the future of higher education. To be sure, governors and legislatures, regents and trustees who have been appointed by those governors and legislatures, and even certain accrediting bodies are often regarded as interlopers who make decisions with little concern for a school's distinctive history, mission, and organizational culture. While presidents and provosts may view these constituents as valued stakeholders, faculty members usually adopt a closed-system perspective (see chapter 2) and accuse those outside the institution of pursuing an agenda different from their own. Even presidents or provosts who have recently been hired from outside the institution may be regarded with suspicion if they propose too many changes too soon or treat the school as though they have arrived to save it (see Buller, 2010). These administrators and their initiatives are treated like invasive species in a highly sensitive ecosystem. They're met with opposition because they "haven't taken time to understand us" and "want us to become something we're not." In fact, all four of these suspicions at times fuse into a single conviction that an unnecessary and highly disruptive change is being imposed on an internal us by an external them.

Finally, faculty members are sometimes suspicious of changes that administrators propose because they believe these initiatives are merely vain attempts to improve the institution's standing in national or international rankings. Legislators, trustees, presidents, and parents of students often care about national rankings; faculty members usually don't. College professors tend to be highly critical of the methodology used to generate such lists, reject many of the criteria used to develop the rankings, and resent the way these flawed instruments can affect internal budgeting priorities. Catalogues of the purportedly "best colleges," such as those prepared by *US News and World Report* and *Forbes Magazine*, frequently ignore the mission and values of individual institutions and assume that a single set of criteria can be used to evaluate any school, regardless of its focus, history, or strategic direction. So when governing boards and administrators are suddenly motivated to increase admissions standards, improve retention and graduate rates, expand diversity, or raise the test scores of incoming students, there is widespread suspicion that they're trying to game the system of national or international rankings, not pursue goals that genuinely reflect the quality of the institution. The resulting changes are, in the minds of many faculty members, likely to be unnecessary at best and highly destructive at worst.

In order for a change to be warranted, therefore, proponents of the "no change is good change" perspective believe you must first provide an utterly compelling answer to the question, "What is the problem we're trying to solve?" Then, only if a consensus among all constituencies emerges that the problem is truly significant, should you proceed to explore alternative solutions, concentrate on the initiatives that have the greatest likelihood of producing a positive difference, and then adopt the approach that requires the least amount of change while effecting the greatest amount of good. Administrators who advocate for change that doesn't meet these criteria, critics will say, are doing little more than creating work for others that will ultimately serve no useful purpose to the school's educational and research missions.

Is Some Change Good for Higher Education?

Like so many other stark contrasts confronting higher education, the choice between considering all change to be good and all change to be bad is really a false dichotomy. Of course, there are certain administrators who advocate for change largely to satisfy their own egos, justify their own existence, or make their own résumés more attractive when they apply for future positions. And of course the continuing progress of higher education requires administrators to get ahead of the curve at times, not merely wait for problems to arise and only then respond to them. Change in higher education can't be an all-or-nothing proposition. Academic leaders have to bring about desirable changes that benefit their stakeholders while holding the line on initiatives that are likely to be short-lived fads. The key is being objective enough to recognize when an initiative is attractive mostly for what it'll do to one's reputation as an administrator, not the needs and best interests of the program's stakeholders.

As I noted in the earlier discussion of organizational culture, it's poor administrative practice to make major decisions, including those that involve introducing a significant change, without considering the larger context these decisions will affect. The mistake many administrators make at the beginning of their positions is acting precipitously because they believe there will be only a limited window of opportunity for them to secure new resources or implement major new policies. Particularly when administrators are hired from outside the institution, they're tempted to take action before they understand all of the issues involved. Unless it's absolutely necessary for a decision to be implemented immediately, it's far better to spend some time learning the values and history of a program before proposing significant changes to it. In fact, all academic leaders who are new to an institution should make it a practice to recite the following paragraph repeatedly:

> The area I've come here to lead wouldn't have survived until now if it was doing everything wrong. The people who came before me must have been doing something right. I need to be sure I understand exactly what those right things were before I start making changes that could damage them. And I need to demonstrate appreciation for the contributions those people made.

In short, if you don't pause long enough to learn the reasons that a certain policy, procedure, or organizational structure was put in place to begin with, you may well make the false assumption that it was put in place for no reason at all.

Nevertheless, just as it's foolish to think that everything about your institution's current structure needs to be reorganized, it can be equally foolish simply to accept the status quo as the only possible way of doing things. Many policies and procedures that made perfectly good sense at one time are no longer useful or have grown more cumbersome than they need to be. So although effective academic leaders don't try to change everything, they have to be willing to question everything. The goal is to ask, "Why do we do it this way?" in a manner that seeks genuine understanding, not a manner that implies you think it should be done differently. One of the many advantages administrators receive from working at several different institutions or participating in opportunities like the American Council on Education (ACE) Fellows Program is being exposed to various approaches and their rationales. They learn that there can be more than one way to achieve almost any goal and that not every solution is suitable for every academic environment.

For this reason, academic leaders should neither idealize nor fear change. Just as not every change results in an improvement, so too is it true that not every change is destructive. Good academic leadership involves a willingness to consider alternative approaches, refusing to stifle debate with arguments like, "We already tried that, and it didn't work," and freely admitting when an approach has failed. Rather than digging in your heels and defending a decision that didn't pan out, it's far better to admit that although you were willing to take a calculated risk, the idea didn't succeed in the way you'd hoped. Indeed, there will be times when the best change you can implement is a change that restores things to the way they were before you "improved" them.

Case Study: Pursuing Innovation without First Establishing Need

As an illustration of the damage that can be done when a significant change is proposed without first establishing whether it's really needed, I'll tell my own story. (Admitting mistakes seems only fair since I don't want to leave the false impression that I've been flawless when it comes to leading change. I haven't. In fact, many of the lessons I'm presenting here I learned painfully over a long period of time.)

I was hired into a college from the outside to serve as its dean. One of the distinctive features of this institution was that it had an extraordinarily flat administrative structure. There was the president. There was me. And there was the faculty. There were no other line positions, like heads of schools or departments, separating us. The school itself was well established, a very traditional institution that prided itself on the quality of its teaching. But it was also champing at the bit of long-outdated curricula and policies that kept it from developing its full potential. All through my interviews, people had told me how hungry they were for change and how, as far as they were concerned, I couldn't shake things up fast enough to suit them. They wanted me to hit the ground running and serve as the type of radical change agent they had long been lacking. In addition, I wanted to do something significant that could serve as my legacy at the college and as a point of pride in what I assumed would be later interviews to serve as a president or provost.

Since both of my previous institutions had revised their general education programs while I was there—one to a system that had grown over time to become unnecessarily complex and unwieldy, the other because it was under a state mandate to convert from the quarter system to the semester system—I decided that the area in which I was most experienced in leading change was general education reform. The school's general education program at the time had already been in place for eighteen years. As I saw the situation, it had been adopted in the same year that most of that fall's freshman class was born, and the world had changed mightily since then. For many years, people had been reluctant to propose any major reforms because the process that developed the current general education program had been so painful. The school had very little faculty turnover, with the result that many people still working there could remember the bitter arguments, tense meetings, and ruined friendships that resulted from the earlier process. "There's still blood on the floor," people frequently told me, and almost no one had the stomach to go through such a divisive process again. At the same time, everyone knew that the existing program lacked a clear rationale. Like many general education programs at other institutions, people regarded the current system not so much as a carefully designed and scaffolded curriculum but as a nonaggression pact where one faction of the faculty agreed to let certain courses count for core credit as long as their own pet courses were treated as favorably.

When I proposed that we begin a process of reform at the end of my first year, I based my recommendation on three arguments that I genuinely regarded as compelling:

1. *It was time.* The college had undergone many changes during the past eighteen years. It had developed several new graduate programs, established a leadership training program that was widely studied as a model, added hundreds of new courses to the catalogue, and implemented an innovative program that allowed gifted students to enter college early without finishing (or, in many cases, even attending) high school. The existing general education program, as I pointed out in speech after speech, had been designed before the advent of the Internet; in fact, personal computers

hadn't been particularly common when the program was first designed. Our current students had different needs and different ways of learning, and we needed to reflect these changes. Our existing requirements struck me as stemming from a dated, rather generic distribution requirement program that had long outlived its usefulness. We needed a tighter, more clearly focused curriculum to start the new century.

2. *It was beneficial.* As a private college without a large endowment, the school was heavily tuition dependent. An increase or decrease of as few as ten students in the entering class had a major effect on the budget, and so it was useful for us to distinguish ourselves in the marketplace. At the time I was serving as dean, a lot of truly innovative work had been done at the upper division and in graduate programs. It seemed desirable at that time to be just as innovative in the college's general education program in order to appeal to prospective students and boost enrollment. Moreover, a truly distinctive general education program might attract external funding and so assist the college's budget in other ways.

3. *It was essential.* In addition to challenges in the area of student recruitment, the college had an attrition rate that was unacceptably high. Some students left before they had a chance to sample the school's innovative majors because they decided that their initial course work wasn't challenging enough or "just wasn't for them." Others flunked out because they weren't developing the skills and knowledge base in their lower-division courses that they would need in order to succeed in their majors. A more carefully designed general education program could solve this problem by being exciting to students and preparing them for more advanced course work. In short, a revision of the general education program wasn't just desirable; it was critically necessary for the school's survival.

It all sounds pretty convincing, doesn't it? In fact, as I was writing those paragraphs, I found myself getting talked into the idea all over again. But I have the advantage now of knowing how that particular process played out, and from my use of it as a case study, you probably do too. The reform that I imposed on the school proved to be a rancorous, highly disruptive process that forced people's workload to increase significantly for more than three years and cost the institution money it could ill afford for consultants, travel to conferences, and released time for the faculty members I had cajoled into working on the revision.

After many arguments and mutual recriminations, the faculty and I limped along to the process's highly unsatisfactory conclusion. In the phrase often (although inaccurately) attributed to Senator George Aiken of Vermont, we simply "declared victory and went home." When a new president arrived with new institutional priorities, all of us—myself included—decided we couldn't endure any genuine curricular reform because of the hostility the process had generated, and we simply stopped trying. We made one single small tweak in the existing program in order to save face, left the bulk of it intact, and declared our reform initiative a resounding success. The effort, expense, and time were completely out of proportion with any benefit that may have been gained.

What went wrong?

The Ten Analytical Lenses and the Need for Change

If you read that case study carefully, it's probably already apparent to you that I began that change process for all the wrong reasons. The rationale I shared with the public (and even managed to talk myself into) was never my primary cause for initiating the reform. My real reasons (to build a résumé; to leave a legacy; to be perceived as more than a mere caretaker) became the drivers of a change that ultimately no one wanted and, even worse, no one needed. That inherent problem with the proposed change would have been clear to me if I had used our ten analytical lenses before embarking on my ill-fated general education reform. If I had done so, here's what I may have learned.

Lens	Perspective Provided
20/20 lens	The college's general education program has already been in place for a long time and looks dated to an outside observer. But there has not been a groundswell of sentiment inside the institution to change the system. In fact, not a single person within the institution is requesting a change. Most general education reviews end up taking longer than anticipated, and there is no guarantee of success.
Concave lens	A more distinctive and visionary approach to general education could, if marketed properly, give the institution a competitive advantage in recruiting students, securing grants, and attracting the interest of donors.

Convex lens

Since the desire for change did not arise internally, it will be necessary to persuade the college's major stakeholders of the need to change, then work with opinion leaders among the faculty to develop a suitable new direction, secure approval for course changes from the curriculum committee, and have the reform approved by the full faculty. Because this process will be long and intense, the proposed benefits would have to outweigh this cost in time, labor, and other institutional resources.

Telephoto lens

While general education reform has been a major concern of higher education for the past few decades, there are other issues—such as service-learning, social entrepreneurship, and civic engagement—that are becoming the hot new topics at conferences. (These topics may not seem so revolutionary now, but they were when this school's general education reform was under way.) By the time the institution adopts the type of curricular reform I am proposing, it is likely to be yesterday's news unless a concerted effort is made to incorporate these emerging new educational issues.

Bifocal lens

The one true problem I can identify in the college's general education program is its complexity and the exceptionally large number of courses that have been approved over the years to meet various requirements. These problems might be more effectively addressed through a pruning and tightening of the current system than a wholesale revision of the entire system. Moreover, deferred maintenance at the institution has resulted in expense problems for its aging facilities, suggesting that there may be more significant problems than those found in the curriculum.

Rose-colored glasses

A truly innovative system could bring the institution some positive publicity, increase enrollments, improve retention, and open the door to some new funding opportunities.

The best-case scenario for this change process would be a swift, smooth transition that achieves a high degree of consensus.

Sunglasses

A prolonged, divisive general education review would divert the institution's attention and resources from more pressing concerns and further damage the strained relationship that already exists between the upper administration and the faculty. The worst-case scenario for this change process would be a lengthy, bitter, and expensive review that ends up changing little if anything.

Rearview mirror

The vast majority of the faculty members who developed the current general education program still work at the institution, many of them in leadership roles on key committees. As a result, pushback against change is likely to be even stronger than usual. The current members of the governing board are particularly interested in issues related to student recruitment and retention; as a result, if the general education review moves too far afield from that goal, additional resistance may develop from the trustees.

Contact lenses

The impetus for this change is not arising from any major stakeholder group: students, faculty, alumni, employers of graduates, parents of current students, accrediting bodies, state higher education bodies, or donors. It is an issue that seems to matter to me as dean but no one else.

Wide-angle lens

If all these perspectives are taken together, I have to conclude that embarking on a major revision of the general education program seems unwise at this time. Other priorities seem more pressing. The support of key constituencies is missing and can be acquired only with a large investment of political capital. The chance of success seems small, with potential benefits far outweighed by the cost involved. It is preferable to direct energy and resources elsewhere.

In short, what the ten analytical lenses would have told me is that I had failed to answer the most basic question that has to be addressed in all change processes: *What problem is it that I'm trying to solve?* If I had raised that question, I would have realized that the issues that were causing us difficulties—the cumbersome nature of the current system, its lack of a distinctive theme, and the school's need to recruit and retain more students—were better and more easily addressed in other ways. It was my own desire to do something significant at the school that became the primary driver for the change. I could have satisfied that personal need in far less destructive ways. For example, rather than trying to embark on a major new reform, I could have partnered with the faculty in clarifying and strengthening our existing core requirements, channeled our energies to matters more closely related to student recruitment and retention, and devoted more time to the truly severe infrastructure needs the college had. But as we saw earlier, many faculty members suspect that restoring infrastructure doesn't sound as attractive to administrators and governing boards as does creating something new. I had fallen into that trap and wasn't seeing everything my bifocal lenses should have revealed to me.

The Drivers of Change

Another way of describing what went wrong in this case is to say that, without using the ten analytical lenses to provide a corrective view, I simply focused on the wrong drivers of change. A driver of change is a factor you can't control that has a significant impact on the factors you can control. One example in higher education might be a demographic shift that results in a severe decline in the traditional college-aged population of a school's primary service area. If the school had been concentrating its recruitment efforts in that primary service area, this demographic shift would serve a driver of change for that school. The college or university can't control the driver itself, but it can control its own response to that driver by creating more educational opportunities for nontraditional-aged students, making a greater effort to recruit internationally, increasing its market share in its primary service area by developing additional innovative and highly attractive programs, reducing tuition costs as an enrollment incentive, and so on. If you understand the drivers of change that have created the specific situation you're facing, you often discover what you need to do to respond to them. But without a clear understanding of what the current drivers of change are, it's almost impossible to be effective in developing a change process that makes a meaningful difference.

Moreover, as the Krüger change model suggested, the actual drivers of change in higher education often lie well below the surface of where most college administrators make policy. As we'll see in chapter 5, the tool most commonly used to plan strategic change—SWOT (strengths, weaknesses, opportunities, and threats) analysis—rarely probes the environment deeply enough to reveal the real underlying dangers a school is facing. SWOT analysis might suggest that a current weakness is declining enrollment and that a current threat is an aggressive new for-profit competitor that has entered the local market, but it doesn't often cause institutions to explore the root causes of those weakness and threats. As a result, colleges and universities either end up making cosmetic changes (such as developing new websites and advertising campaigns) or solving the wrong problem (as I tried to do with my general education initiative), thereby missing their opportunities to deal with the issues that really matter.

A good way to move beyond the symptoms of a problem and to uncover the actual causes of the "disease" is to adopt the approach known as STEEPLED analysis (Cadle, Paul, and Turner, 2010). This approach encourages leaders to make a systematic scan of eight different areas in order to determine which drivers of change may be relevant in each of them. Together the first letters of these eight important areas produce the acronym STEEPLED. Here's how the approach might be used at a college or university:

Social drivers	The impact of the media on public attitudes and priorities
	Increases or decreases in parental education levels
	Preferences for or against specific educational environments (e.g., single-sex education and religion-based education)
	Preferences for leisure-time activities
Technological drivers	New pedagogical platforms
	New research tools or laboratory methods
	Student familiarity with and expectations for technology
	New forms of communication
	Improvements in health care technology
	New industrial techniques
Economic drivers	Rises or declines in the income of stakeholders
	The impact of the market on endowment funds

	Price undercutting by competitor institutions
	The cost of local housing
	Utility costs
	Outsourcing or insourcing of services
	Value of foreign currency (for institutions with international students or programs)
	Interest rates (for student loans and capital projects)
Ecological drivers	Ecological issues involving the campus, including wetlands and protected species issues
	Student interest in issues of sustainability, energy policy, and the like
	Governmental policies affecting zoning, regulation, reporting requirements, and the like
	Weather-related threats, such as hurricanes and tornadoes
	Deferred maintenance issues
Political drivers	Relations with local, state, and federal political officials
	Shifts in emphasis due to changes in political leadership
	Levels of support for the administration in decision-making bodies at the institution
	The composition and priorities of the governing board
	Relationships with faculty and staff unions
	The priorities of the internal political leadership, such as the composition and priorities of the faculty senate
	Personalities and priorities of the administrative leadership
	The politicization (or lack thereof) of the student body and student government
Legislative drivers	Local, state, and federal educational policies
	Collective bargaining agreements
	Tax policy
	Proposed or pending legislation

	Standards of accrediting bodies
	Decisions made by internal political bodies, such as the faculty senate and curriculum committee
	Employment law
	Unfunded mandates
	Legislation affecting benefits packages
Ethical drivers	Conflicts of interest
	Shifts in public values
	Responses to public scandals or crises
	Challenges involving traditional values of higher education, such as academic freedom
Demographic drivers	Population shifts and trends
	Enrollment and retention rates
	The rise of new stakeholder groups (such as returning adult students at an institution that historically served only traditional-aged college students)
	Social mobility
	Life expectancy
	Population movements to or from the institution's service area

In the case of my doomed general education reform, what I regarded as the most essential drivers of change wouldn't have struck me as significant factors if I had done a STEEPLED analysis. And the institution's most pressing needs, such as upgrading its physical plant and addressing its enrollment challenges, would have leaped off the page. Moreover, if I had paid closer attention to the political drivers of change at the college—in particular, the lack of support the administration had from key faculty committees and the priorities of opinion leaders among the faculty and staff—the amount of resistance my proposal received wouldn't have come as such a surprise. The mistake I made isn't uncommon for administrators in higher education. As academic leaders, we too often seek changes that aren't driven by the actual needs of the institution. Even when a leader is enticed by a compelling vision for the future, he or she could end up being the sole advocate for that vision unless it aligns well with the other drivers of change affecting that college, university, or program.

In *Beyond Change Management* (2010), Dean Anderson and Linda Ackerman Anderson note that in addition to the external and impersonal drivers of change involved in transforming an organization, there are also simultaneous internal and personal drivers. Examples of the latter include *cultural imperatives* (the established ways of interacting in that organization that can necessitate, facilitate, and block a change), *leader and employee behavior* (the way in which specific work teams interact, such as fear-based interaction, reward-seeking interaction, and trust-based interaction), and *leader and employee mind-set* (the way in which the members of an organization look at the world). For example, at an institution where the cultural imperative is that the president, provost, or dean articulates a "change of the year" at the beginning of the fall term, a certain degree of change becomes driven merely as the result of expectation and habit. At an institution where the tradition has been that overloads are paid every time someone does anything not specifically listed in his or her job description, effective drivers of change are likely to be those that are either based on financial rewards (which may produce faster results but become a consistent drain on resources) or an intentional effort to transform the local culture (which may be easier to sustain in times of limited resources while requiring a prolonged period of cultural adjustment before the change can begin).

The Central Role of the Needs Case in Change Leadership

The authors of the American Council on Education's report *On Change* observed that successful change "leaders make a clear and compelling case to key stakeholders about why things must change" Eckel, Hill, Green, and Mallon, 1999, 2). While in one sense this conclusion seems to echo the first step in the Kotter change model—establish a sense of urgency—on a deeper level it reflects a lesson commonly taught in the study of policy debate: your argument for change is far more effective when you can demonstrate that change is needed rather than merely desired. That approach is what is known in the field of policy debate as making a *needs case*. In order to understand how this type of case works and why it's relevant to leading change in higher education, we first have to review what policy debate is.

Policy debate is a formal, academic approach to arguing whether a specific change from the status quo should be adopted. The side in the discussion that proposes and supports this change is known as the affirmative team; the opposing side, which argues against the proposed change, is called the negative team. The goal of the negative team is to persuade a panel of judges that the change proposed by the affirmative team is unnecessary, unlikely to solve the problem in question, capable of producing even greater problems than those resulting from the status quo, or simply not the best possible solution to the problem that has been identified. Change processes in higher education frequently mimic the general features of a policy debate. An affirmative team (the proponents of the change) argues that its plan will solve a significant problem, while a negative team (the opponents of the change) declare that it won't.

In fact, the parallels between policy debate and academic change processes are quite interesting and tell us a great deal about how we can be more effective in our role as change leaders. The first speech of a policy debate, known as the first affirmative constructive speech (1AC), begins with the affirmative team building a prima facie case: an argument based on sufficient evidence and logic to persuade a reasonable individual that a problem exists. If the 1AC fails to achieve this goal, the affirmative team automatically loses the debate. For this reason, most policy debates begin with the affirmative team adopting what is known as a stock issues format—an appeal to four key reasons that change is necessary:

1. *Harm:* The status quo is causing a significant problem that is unlikely to be solved unless action is taken.

2. *Inherency:* The cause of the problem can be identified.

3. *Solvency:* A plan can be developed that will eliminate or alleviate the cause of the problem.

4. *Disadvantages:* The proposed plan does not lead to problems that are equal to or greater than those of the status quo.

That speech is then followed by the first negative constructive speech (1NC), which seeks to refute the four stock issues of the 1AC (or however else the prima facie case is presented), frequently by introducing one or more of its own four stock issues:

1. *Topicality:* The plan proposed by the affirmative team does not technically fulfill the topic of the debate. In formal debates, the topic takes the form of a resolution, such as, "Resolved: The US federal government should substantially increase its exploration and/or development of space beyond the Earth's mesosphere," or, "Resolved: The US federal government should substantially increase its transportation infrastructure investment in the United States" (the policy debate topics selected by the National Forensics League for 2011–2012 and 2012–2013, respectively; see www.nflonline.org/StudentResources/PastPolicyDebateTopics). Challenges to topicality are frequently made by arguing that various terms used by the affirmative team should be defined differently from

how that team has tried to define them or that its claims aren't really relevant to the issue being discussed.

2. *Disadvantages:* Despite the claims of the affirmative team, its plan would indeed create problems that would be equal to or greater than those of the status quo.

3. *Counterplans:* There is a better way of solving the problem under discussion than the plan proposed by the affirmative team.

4. *Kritiks:* The philosophical basis of the 1AC is an assumption that's flawed, immoral, or dishonest. For instance, if the plan proposed during the 1AC would require implementation by the department of education, a kritik might attack the very legitimacy of the department of education, not the logic of the plan itself.

If you've ever been at a faculty meeting for a discussion of a curricular or structural change you proposed, those types of arguments will all sound familiar. Some people will claim that you've misunderstood the real nature of the problem (topicality), others will claim that your proposal will actually make things worse (disadvantages), still others will claim that they have better ideas for fixing the problem (counterplans), and some will even question why you, rather than the faculty, are making this proposal in the first place (kritiks).

Those similarities are not coincidental. The procedures of policy debate arose in academic settings, and they reflect how academics make and counter arguments, use evidence to advance their perspectives, and are persuaded when a suitable case has been made. That's important, because it helps us understand why faculty members sometimes seem to resist any change that's proposed to them and how we can make the case for a truly beneficial change more compelling. First, the similarity of policy debate to the academic change process illustrates how we have to go about making a prima facie case that the status quo isn't working. We need to speak in terms of harm, inherency, solvency, and disadvantages in order to illustrate the genuine need for change. If we can't make a compelling case even to ourselves that these stock issues exist, then, like the affirmative team in a policy debate, we've lost automatically and there's no reason to drag our institutions through a pointless process.

Second, the 1NC stock issues alert us to the arguments we're likely to hear from the defenders of the status quo and others who are simply opposed to change of any kind. By understanding the underlying basis on which an objection is made, we can better craft a response (and objectively determine whether a response is warranted). Here are some examples.

TOPICALITY

Argument: "But we are and always have been a liberal arts college. The assumptions you're making about placement rates for our graduates might be germane to a vocational school. They don't really have anything to do with who we are and what we say we're trying to accomplish." *Response:* "It's precisely because of our liberal arts tradition that the proposal needs to be considered. We've always said that our goal is to educate the whole person. And although the employability of our graduates isn't identical to educating the whole person, it is a part of it. If we fail to make our graduates employable, we fail our graduates."

DISADVANTAGES

Argument: "Increasing the number of people in marketing and development is going to make an already strained faculty workload even worse. If we've got resources to spend on additional hires, we need to expand the faculty, not the administrative staff. You'll only increase our budgetary problems." *Response:* "Remember that funding directed to marketing and development isn't money spent; it's money invested. The people we hire will provide outreach to additional students, who will bring us much-needed tuition; potential donors, who can increase the endowment and annual fund; and the legislature, which can provide additional state support. The payoff from these positions will be far greater than if we ate our seed corn by converting these lines to faculty positions now."

COUNTERPLANS

Argument: "Why, during times of budgetary constraint, do we always talk about collapsing departments and eliminating programs? Why don't we increase the number of programs we offer, which might attract more students and further investment, while collapsing administrative units and eliminating some of the vice dean and associate provost positions?" *Response:* "As a matter of fact, we've already cut back on staffing in the dean's office and reduced the number of associate provosts from four to two. There simply isn't any other administrative area to cut that wouldn't adversely affect teaching load by pushing a number of administrative duties onto the faculty. Besides, the programs that we're cutting wouldn't be productive even if they tripled in size. None of them graduate more than a major every year or two, and they don't contribute significantly to the course requirements of other programs."

KRITIKS

Argument: "You're approaching the issue completely backward. We don't make curricular decisions in order to drive enrollment. The admissions office doesn't tell us what to teach. We, as academic professionals, decide what to teach. Then it's the job of the admissions office to find prospective students who want that curriculum, not the other way around." *Response:* "Actually, it's in the best interest of faculty members to play a more active role in recruiting prospective students. These are the students who will be in your courses and completing your degrees. You're in a better position than anyone else to explain to a really capable student why we have the best program for what he or she wants. Far more than the admissions office, *you* have a vested interest in attracting the best and brightest students to enroll here."

Third, and most important, a study of policy debate is useful because it reminds us that the needs case is not the only type of justification an affirmative team can make for changing the status quo. There are a number of alternative strategies for making this argument, but for our purpose, let's focus on the four most common types. I'll choose examples of each argument from higher education because each approach has significant problems compared to the needs case when it comes to supporting an academic change process:

○ *Comparative advantages case.* This is an argument that although there's not an absolute need for change, a proposed plan will produce better results than the status quo—for example: "Even though our current undergraduate program seems to be working fine, we'll probably place more of our graduates into high-paying jobs if we replace our thesis requirement with an internship requirement." The case has these problems:

- Since you're not arguing that you positively must change, you'll need to provide overwhelming evidence that the advantages you foresee are likely to occur and that they outweigh the cost and inconvenience of the change.
- This case is extremely vulnerable to attacks based on a counterplan (that could result in even greater advantages) or kritiks (that sidetrack the argument by refocusing attention on the assumptions made about what is or is not truly advantageous)

○ *Alternative justification case.* This argument presents several different alternatives to the current policy or situation. The assumption is that if the decision-making body adopts any of the alternatives, it must be admitting de facto that the current situation should be changed—for example: "As an alternative to having our students write and defend a thesis, we could institute an internship requirement, convert our degree into a co-op program, offer a comprehensive examination, or waive the thesis for those who already have five or more years of relevant work experience." These are the problems:

- To many observers, an alternative justification case appears to be a desperate attempt to secure any change at all rather than a reasoned, well-articulated vision of the future. Opponents can attack this type of argumentation with a variety of images like, "You're just running random ideas up the flagpole to see if anyone salutes them," "It's merely a shotgun approach," or "All you're doing is throwing mud at the wall to see if any of it sticks."

- Administrators who wish to pursue a particular vision of the future rather than any method at all that solves the problem will find the alternative justification case unsuitable. It surrenders a significant amount of control over the change process to others since they, not the person making the argument, will decide which alternative to pursue.

○ *Criteria case.* This argument is similar to a needs case or a comparative advantage case that claims the discussion must begin with an agreement that specific criteria should be used to measure success—for example: "The whole purpose of our program is to get students jobs, increase their incomes, and make it more likely that they will remain employable throughout their working lives. Eighteen percent of our current graduates do not find suitable employment for two or more years after completing our program. Twenty-one percent of those who do find employment report on our alumni surveys that they are 'stuck in dead-end jobs.' And 11 percent of our alumni who find work immediately after graduation experience periods of unemployment lasting six months or more at some point during their careers. Since our program is not meeting the very criteria we have for its success, we have to decide how to change it." A criteria case has these problems:

- It easily becomes sidetracked by a prolonged discussion of the criteria themselves rather than an analysis of the problem and its possible solutions.

- It offers critics numerous points of attack. They can object to the criteria, the need, the plan, or the proposed manner of implementing the plan. If they find a significant flaw in any one of these elements, the case is likely to fail.

o *Net benefits case.* This is an argument that even if the proposed change turns out to be more difficult or costly than the current policy, its resulting benefits will at least make it more desirable than the status quo—for example: "It's true that if we pursue this initiative, the placement rate of our graduates into jobs will probably decline a bit in the short term. Enrollment may also suffer temporarily. But I'm convinced that the publicity our program will receive from this bold and innovative new curriculum, coupled with the new corporate networks with industry we create due to the plan to require all students to complete an internship, will be of even greater benefit to us in the long run." The net benefit case has these problems:

- People are more troubled by imminent disadvantages than they are excited by the possibility of delayed gratification. As a result, a net benefits case is often a hard sell.

- Any argument based on long-term benefits is subject to the challenge that current assumptions of what is best may be invalid several years in the future. For example, there may be unanticipated changes in any of the STEEPLED analysis drivers that could negate the net benefits even before they materialize.

And here we find one of the reasons that so many change processes fail in higher education: administrators frequently feel that a change is justified because of comparative advantages, net benefits, alternative justifications, or specific criteria. But these arguments are never as compelling as a needs case. As a result, these alternative justifications inevitably leave the administrator open to the charge that he or she has failed to establish the true need for the change.

To put it another way, effective change management in higher education rarely occurs when people aren't convinced that they need to change. Presidents, provosts, deans, and chairs can talk all they want about how much better things will be if only a different vision of the future is pursued. But unless they can persuade themselves and others that there is no reasonable alternative to the proposed change, they're unlikely to receive more than superficial buy-in from key stakeholder groups. The changes, if they end up implementing them at all, will probably be short-lived. As every policy debater soon learns, these alternative justifications are much easier to discredit than a needs case. All an obstructionist needs to do is argue that since the plan hasn't yet been tried, there's no real proof that any of those advantages or net benefits will be as great as promised. (And think of how often critics of change in higher education take precisely that approach.) Yet once a strong needs case is established, the argument is no longer about whether a change should occur; it's about what kind of change it should be.

Of course, no one would suggest that leading academic change is precisely the same as engaging in a formal policy debate. The latter has specific rules, time limits, structured arguments, and traditions. The former can feel more like a free-for-all. Nevertheless, there are clear similarities. A great deal of social change occurs for emotional rather than rational reasons. Politicians appeal to people's sentiments and gut reactions at least as much as they trust in their intelligence and logical judgment. Marketing counts on consumers who make visceral responses to products, many of which the customers may not even be aware of. (See, e.g., Pradeep, 2010, Lindström, 2008, and Renvoisé and Morin, 2007, as well as the attempt to refute many of their claims in Satel and Lilienfeld, 2013.) Cults and certain religions attract converts by trying to fill an emotional need and appealing to faith, not by making a systematic and well-reasoned argument. But while no one will deny that primal and subconscious factors are present in discussions about policies in higher education (witness the role played by Bolman and Deal's political and symbolic frames), faculty members and administrators systematically debate these issues in department meetings, sessions of the faculty assembly, and curriculum committees. Using critical reasoning and systematic argumentation still matters in higher education. Moreover, college professors are trained and experienced debaters. They may not always see themselves as such, but their entire career in higher education has taught them how to identify problems, propose potential solutions, critique the merits of these solutions, and detect weaknesses in the arguments of others. If that's the environment in which we wish to lead a change, we have to pay attention to how our needs case is prepared and justified. We know that counterarguments, kritiks, and rebuttals are inevitable. If we seek to base a change on alternative justifications, we'll initiate a change process that's highly unlikely to achieve any of its goals.

Conclusion

Change processes in higher education succeed or fail largely due to how well the need for the change has been established. Administrators who argue that every change is beneficial because it shakes things up are just as misguided as are those who argue that no change is ever desirable because any departure from the status quo represents a betrayal of the institution's core mission and values. Our ten analytical lenses can be valuable tools in determining whether a need for change exists and, if so, how that need is best addressed. The drivers of change that we can identify through a STEEPLED analysis can help identify the relevant forces in the environment that have produced an identifiable need for change. Finally, the techniques of formal policy debate are useful in alerting us when we're trying to make a case based not on genuine need but on a claim that there will be comparative advantages, net benefits, and the like. Becoming familiar with the techniques of policy debate also provides useful insights into how best to make a case for a needed change and prepare for the objections that are likely to arise.

With this in mind, we can proceed to perhaps the most pressing question now facing us about change processes in higher education: since colleges and universities have such a unique organizational culture, how can we use that culture to progress from simply managing change to leading change? That's the question explored in the next chapter.

REFERENCES

American Academy for the Arts and Sciences. (2013). *The heart of the matter.* www.amacad.org.
Anderson, D., & Ackerman Anderson, L. S. (2010). *Beyond change management: How to achieve breakthrough results through conscious change leadership* (2nd ed.). San Francisco, CA: Jossey-Bass/Pfeiffer.
Buller, J. L. (2010). Rearranging the academic furniture. *Academic Leader, 26*(8), 3, 8.
Cadle, J., Paul, D., & Turner, P. (2010). *Business analysis techniques: 72 essential tools for success.* London: British Computer Society.
Dobelli, R. (2013). *The art of thinking clearly.* New York, NY: Harper.
Eckel, P., Hill, B., Green, M., & Mallon, B. (1999). *On change.* Washington, DC: American Council on Education.
Kolowich, S. (2013, May 10). Faculty backlash against online partnerships. *Chronicle of Higher Education,* A1–A4.
Lindström, M. (2008). *Buy ology: Truth and lies about why we buy.* New York, NY: Doubleday.
Pradeep, A. K. (2010). *The buying brain: Secrets of selling to the subconscious mind.* Hoboken, NJ: Wiley.
Renvoisé, P., & Morin, C. (2007). *Neuromarketing: Understanding the "buy button" in your customer's brain.* Nashville, TN: T. Nelson.

Satel, S. L., & Lilienfeld, S. O. (2013). *Brainwashed: The seductive appeal of mindless neuroscience*. New York, NY: Basic Books.

RESOURCES

Edwards, R. E. (2008). *Competitive debate: The official guide*. New York, NY: Alpha Books.

Ericson, J. M., Murphy, J. J., & Zeuschner, R. F. (2003). *The debater's guide* (3rd ed.). Carbondale: Southern Illinois University Press.

Morrow, D. R., & Weston, A. (2011). *A workbook for arguments: A complete course in critical thinking*. Indianapolis, IN: Hackett.

4

FROM CHANGE MANAGEMENT
TO CHANGE LEADERSHIP

WE HAVE ALREADY LEARNED three important lessons about change in higher education that are critically important to anyone who wants to lead rather than be led by the drivers of change affecting colleges and universities today:

1. The models of change management commonly used in the business world aren't really very effective in helping us understand what happens in higher education because its distributed organizational culture is so different from that found in hierarchical or decentralized organizations.

2. Since the distributed organizational culture of colleges and universities operates as an open system, those who are involved in change processes need to be able to see each policy, procedure, and proposal from multiple perspectives, adopting a system like Bolman and Deal's four-frame model, de Bono's six thinking hats, or our ten analytical lenses that combine features drawn from both these approaches.

3. Due to higher education's open system and distributed organizational culture, change processes are embraced by stakeholders more readily (and thus tend to proceed more smoothly) when they're based on a clearly established needs case rather than the anticipation of comparative advantages, net benefits, or any justification other than genuine need.

Those conclusions lead us to ask: If change management approaches like the Kübler-Ross model, the Krüger model, and the Kotter model aren't very effective in describing or planning for a successful change process in higher education, then which approaches work better? How, in short, can we as administrators stop trying merely to manage change and start to lead it?

Let's begin to answer these questions by reviewing certain similarities and differences among the three change management approaches examined in chapter 1. Each of them took a slightly different focus when it came to the most important aspects of change. For Kübler-Ross, it was how people respond to change; for Krüger, it was how various issues relating to change affect the progress of the change process in an organization; and for Kotter, it was how the manager should guide the change process. Yet despite these different emphases, each came to a similar conclusion: there's a right way and a wrong way to manage change. In other words, they concluded that change processes are largely the same in all types of organization. In the case of the Kübler-Ross and Kotter models, there are even specific steps we can expect to go through in a set order. That concept may bring an illusion of clarity to the often messy change processes that occur at colleges and universities, but it doesn't relate well to the actual experience most of us have when we try to propose needed changes at our institutions. Once the process is over, we can force our description of what occurred to fit those models, but they don't capture the sometimes chaotic, sometimes contentious, and sometimes painfully slow unfolding of change that we experience in higher education. In order to find a better way of describing how change occurs in the real world of colleges and universities, let's look at a few additional theoretical approaches to change. This time we'll focus not on traditional change models but on a different approach that we might call *change descriptions* or *change maps*.

The Learning Culture Theory

In *Organizational Culture and Leadership* (2010), Edgar Schein, whose insights into organizational culture we explored in chapter 1, identifies ten characteristics of organizations that accept change more readily because they develop what he calls a learning culture:

1. *These organizations are proactive.* Rather than being passive observers of their environments, they draw conclusions from experience and use the lessons they learn to avoid problems in the future.

2. *They are genuinely committed to learning.* Some organizations give lip-service to learning, believing that they're doing well since they pay attention to new developments in their external environments. But the organizations that Schein calls learning cultures also study themselves. They recognize when their administrative strategies aren't as effective as they should be and when key stakeholders are becoming disengaged. Then they take corrective action based on what they observe.

3. *They make positive assumptions about their stakeholders.* Schein finds great value in Douglas McGregor's (1960) distinction between theory X organizations (where it is taken for granted that people are basically lazy and motivated only by hope of reward or fear of punishment) and theory Y organizations (where the basic operating principle is that people usually do to the best of their abilities whatever they believe to be right, even if managers may sometimes disagree with the employees' methods). Learning cultures derive great benefits from taking a theory Y approach: they're able to make use of the talents and ideas of those who aren't technically in charge because managers don't assume their employees' ideas arise only out of narrow self-interest.

4. *They believe that change is possible, not just in themselves but also in the larger environment.* If organizations act as though every restriction on them is set by forces outside themselves, they don't even consider certain types of changes as possible. In essence, they adopt a victim mentality. For example, if a college assumes that it would never be accredited if it began accepting students who have not earned high school diplomas, it never even considers investigating the possibility of developing an admissions program that selects students based on their knowledge and skill rather than on their credentials.

5. *They understand that learning methods need to change over time.* In a true learning culture, Schein says that the organization isn't locked into any one way of gaining and evaluating information. If you assume, for instance, that hard data and empirical analysis are the only way of learning, you'll never trust an intuition that could have led you toward a truly innovative way of doing things. Steve Jobs's famous aversion to focus groups was based on his belief that customers can tell you what they want only in terms of what they already know; they can't envision a truly revolutionary product. In short, they don't know what they want because they haven't experienced it yet. Learning cultures work in a similar way: they respect facts and figures but don't become locked in by them. They do what's right even if it hasn't yet been proven.

6. *They are optimistic about the future.* When difficult economic or social problems occur, some organizations revert to past practices and comfortable habits. They try to return the world (and themselves) to an idyllic, and usually imaginary, concept of former glory. Learning cultures know that even if the near future is likely to contain a good deal of hardship, a better future is possible. And by definition, their long-term future will be dramatically different from the past.

7. *They are committed to transparent and open communication.* Many organizations hoard information, believing either that power is derived from the scarcity of knowledge or that certain stakeholders, in Jack Nicholson's famous words in the 1992 movie *A Few Good Men,* "can't handle the truth." Learning cultures aren't afraid to share information even if their plans aren't yet completely clear. They take responsibility for past and pending decisions, and they believe that their processes are strengthened, not weakened, by responding to criticism.

8. *They are committed to diversity.* A dedication to diversity occurs in different ways for different types of organizations. Schein himself was largely thinking of the need for cultural diversity in the corporate world, which long preserved a narrow view of who its stakeholders were and whether employees were capable of becoming managers. But in higher education, where gender and cultural diversity has already been a goal for many years, other types of diversity need to be considered. For example, a college may benefit from a higher degree of organizational diversity in which major decisions are not made by the governing board and upper administration alone but with a wider participation of stakeholders. Institutions that find themselves drifting into political homogeneity, such as the widespread belief that all faculty members are, in Roger Kimball's famous phrase, "tenured radicals" (Kimball, 1990), can benefit from making a consistent effort to ensure that students are exposed to a broader spectrum of philosophies, pedagogies, and political approaches.

9. *They adopt systems approaches wherever possible.* Learning cultures understand that organizations rarely operate in vacuums. They embrace the interconnectedness of people within their organization, as well as the interconnectedness of their organization with other groups. They're less likely to be blindsided by the unforeseen consequences of a decision because they're so used to considering every choice they make in terms of its potential effect on others.

10. *They believe that the study of their own organizational culture is important to their growth and development.* Learning cultures don't assume that all organizations are alike. They don't even assume that all organizations in similar fields are alike. Amazon has a distinctly different corporate culture from Google, and Harvard has a distinctly different institutional culture from UCLA. It's possible to be successful—even to reach the pinnacle of your profession—with a local culture that's different from that of even your best competitors. But it's very difficult to attain or maintain this level of success if you don't know what your organizational culture is, which elements of it are integral to your success, and which elements of it are merely customary practices that can be altered when necessary.

Schein's concept of the learning culture can provide a framework within which we can talk about change in a different way from the rather prescribed approach of the change models set out in chapter 1. Moreover, the idea of a learning culture resonates better at a university than do corporate models of change because of how a university sees its mission: it wants to be a learning culture, not a profit-generating culture or a culture that's victimized by forces beyond its control. It prefers to see itself as approaching change not in terms of becoming reconciled to death or attempting to steer clear of icebergs on a dangerous journey, but as an organic type of growth that reflects the fundamental mission of higher education: growth in knowledge and understanding.

The Change Leader's Road Map and the Change Journey

This same metaphor of change as growth, progress, discovery, and learning can be seen in the second major theory of change we'll consider in this chapter: Linda Ackerman Anderson and Dean Anderson's change leader's road map. Like Elisabeth Kübler-Ross and John Kotter, Ackerman Anderson and Anderson view change as a series of steps that usually occur in a specific order. For these authors, most change processes can be thought of as having nine distinct phases (Ackerman Anderson and Anderson, 2010):

1. Prepare to lead the change.
2. Create organizational vision, commitment, and capability.
3. Assess the situation to determine design requirements.
4. Design the required state.
5. Analyze the impact.
6. Plan and organize for implementation.
7. Implement the change.
8. Celebrate and integrate the new state.
9. Learn and course-correct.

Several of the assumptions the Andersons make about the change leader's road map are things we've come to question with regard to change in higher education. For example, the road map assumes that substantive change usually flows from the top down: the leader is the person who develops the vision and builds commitment; the members of the organization are the ones who merely embrace, accept, implement, or adapt to that vision.

But the Andersons' approach does include a major conceptual shift from the three change models we discussed earlier. The change leader's road map acknowledges that each change process will be different and that there'll be unexpected detours along the way. If the Kübler-Ross, Krüger, and Kotter models of change can be thought of as recipes for change (if you omit an ingredient or perform the steps out of order, you're unlikely to have a satisfying result), the Andersons' theory is presented as a road map for change (it outlines a commonly taken route, but allows side trips, alternative itineraries, and various diversions along the way):

> The ... Change Leader's Roadmap ... has an appealing logic and flow. Some leaders and consultants may inadvertently assume that this logic implies that transformation is controllable and predictable, and that the model is meant to be adhered to rigidly and followed sequentially. They also assume that they must do all of the tasks in it. These assumptions would be neither wise nor beneficial.... The Change Leader's Roadmap is not a cookbook for how to orchestrate transformational change. The model is designed as a *thinking discipline*, a guidance system for navigating the complexity and chaos of transformation in a conscious and thoughtful way. The structure and depth it provides are meant to support your thinking, not ... to order or dictate your actions. (Ackerman Anderson and Anderson, 2010, 278–289)

Building on this concept, Vesa Purokuru, a coach and consultant at humap.com, and Holger Nauheimer, the CEO of Change Facilitation (www.change-facilitation.com), describe what they call the change journey. In chapter 2, I used this same expression to describe that view of the world that believes change is constant and that encourages people to pay more attention to their experiences along the way than on the ultimate destination. But Purokuru and Nauheimer use this expression differently. For them, the change journey is indeed about getting somewhere, but they suggest that it's difficult, at times even impossible, to predict exactly what path a process will take in order to reach that destination. Since no two organizations or institutional cultures are alike, each change process must be unique. Moreover, since each organization or institutional culture evolves over time, no two change processes even at the same institution will ever be alike. According to Purokuru and Nauheimer, the fallacy many leaders make is to believe that any change model can predict what will occur with 100 percent accuracy or even with 50 percent accuracy. After all, organizations are highly complex systems, often with many hundreds of employees, all making unsupervised decisions on a daily basis. When we compound this situation with all the external factors promoting change (the drivers of change that we considered in the previous chapter), it becomes clear that no one can possibly predict how any particular change process will unfold. Any approach that seeks to describe specific steps that each "good" change process must go through simply distracts leaders from the way things actually work. When their organizations fail to follow the prescribed model, change managers assume that either they or their organizations have done something wrong. But all they've actually done is discovered the limitations of change models in general. (See www.changejourney.org.)

What's needed, Purokuru and Nauheimer argue, is not just another model but a far more flexible approach, something they call a change journey map. The change journey map can be envisioned as a cityscape. In it, there are numerous places that a traveler could go during a journey, although none of these places are destinations where he or she is required to go. Each change journey is different because it involves different visits of different durations to different destinations in a different order. Moreover, Purokuru and Nauheimer see their change journey map as an evolving concept. New places may be added to it as new discoveries are made about organizational culture and as individual institutions encounter their own as-yet-unmapped destinations along the way. As an illustration of how this concept works, here are a few examples of the "destinations" an organization might visit throughout its change process:

○ *The laboratory:* The point an organization reaches when it begins experimenting with pilot programs for new processes, procedures, and structures

○ *The garden of trust:* Where there's an attempt to build mutual trust as a prerequisite for positive change

○ *The labyrinth:* Where the organization temporarily gets lost during its change journey and needs to find its way back to common ground

○ *The exhibition center:* Where successes that occur along the journey are celebrated and publicized

○ *The graveyard of old habits:* Where people stagnate for a time by fixating on past practices that prevent future growth before developing new strategies to change those habits

○ *The gate to goals:* Where the group sets clear goals and decides what success will ultimately look like

○ *The opera house of emotions:* Where there is recognition that some of the drama arising in response to the change has not been based in reason

○ *The court of conflicts:* Where strained interpersonal relations that arise as a result of the change process must be mediated and resolved

○ *The studio for ideas and creativity:* Where the challenge facing the organization is addressed in innovative ways that aren't bound by past or current practice

○ *The agora:* Where constructive dialogue occurs (see www.change journey.org/page/the-map)

The change journey map makes several important contributions to our understanding of how change processes occur in higher education. First, it recognizes that each path of change is different. Despite what traditional change models argue, no institution goes through exactly the same steps in the same order as any other institution. Some colleges and universities may get hung up for a long time at destinations like the graveyard of old habits, while others may move past this site after a very brief "visit" or avoid it entirely. Second, the change journey map offers useful metaphors leaders can adopt to help themselves and others understand why their processes get hung up from time to time. It also offers ideas about how they might get their processes back on track. "I think we've become caught in the prison of inability and resistance," a change leader might conclude. "Perhaps we need to draw on the bank of diverse resources in order to take better advantage of the skills and talents we already have and thus develop a clearer idea of how we can break free." In this way, the change journey map doesn't try to offer a predictive tool in the way that traditional change models have; instead it serves as a tool for interpretation and problem solving.

C. Otto Scharmer's Theory U and Mindfulness-Based Leadership

When most people think of a leader, they tend to picture someone who has the courage to act quickly, decisively, and boldly; who moves forward despite the naysayers; and who doesn't waste time second-guessing choices that have already been made. But there are several reasons for regarding this common image as severely flawed, particularly for higher education. In a distributed organizational culture, quick, decisive, and bold actions, decisions made without adequate consultation, and a refusal to revisit issues are all fatal for morale because they cause members of the faculty and staff to feel unappreciated and out of the loop. In addition, failure to take advantage of the insights that could have been provided by a highly educated workforce is an inefficient use of resources. So rather than emphasizing speed and decisiveness, it's often more effective for academic leaders to slow down their decision-making processes, pay closer attention to the specific context in which they're operating, and place a priority on awareness of the complexities involved in an issue. In fact, two major approaches to leadership deal specifically with the role that being deliberate and reflective can play in successful change processes: theory U and mindfulness-based leadership.

The name *theory U*, which was coined by C. Otto Scharmer, senior lecturer at MIT and founding chair of the Presencing Institute, was chosen both because it served as a response to Douglas McGregor's theory X and theory Y and because Scharmer believed that effective change processes should follow a U-shaped path. In *Theory U* (Scharmer and Senge, 2009) and *Leading from the Emerging Future* (Scharmer and Kaufer, 2013), he describes how bringing about meaningful change requires us first to venture inward and downward into our own values and core beliefs and then to venture upward and outward in a way that applies the insight we gain to the challenges that surround us. This is how Scharmer describes the U-shaped change journey (figure 4.1):

INWARD AND DOWNWARD

1. *Suspending:* Being willing to set aside preconceived notions and observe the situation with eyes that are truly open

2. *Redirecting:* Developing a new understanding of the system or network in which you are operating that includes seeing yourself as part

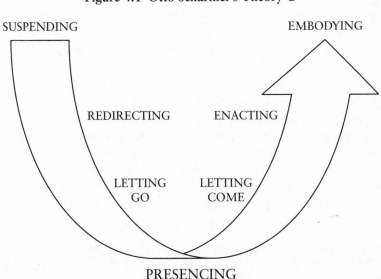

Figure 4.1 Otto Scharmer's Theory U

SUSPENDING   EMBODYING

REDIRECTING   ENACTING

LETTING   LETTING
GO   COME

PRESENCING

of the system ("How might I be contributing to the problem? How could I potentially become part of the solution?")

3. *Letting go:* Giving up your old models for understanding how things "should" or "have to" work and surrendering to uncertainty, complexity, and risk

TURNING THE CORNER

1. *Presencing:* Relating these new insights to your core values as a person or your institution's values ("Who am I in terms of the principles I'm most committed to? What is my work in terms of my mission in life and ultimate goals?" or, "What is our institution in terms of the principles it's most committed to? What is its work in terms of its mission and long-term goals?")

UPWARD AND OUTWARD

1. *Letting come:* Accepting that, on the basis of these core values and the new insights you've achieved, change must occur in you as well as in the world

2. *Enacting:* Allowing a new, compelling vision for the future to crystalize based on the insights you've received about your present circumstances, your own core values, and your institution's long-term goals

3. *Embodying:* Embedding the new ideas and changes into the institution's standard practices, resulting in "the new normal" simply becoming normal

Throughout his work, Scharmer elaborates on this process so that, by the end of *Theory U*, for example, this seven-step journey also includes a full twenty-four principles and practices and five additional movements (co-initiating, co-sensing, co-presencing, and so on). But for our purposes, the simplified structure I have outlined summarizes the essential concept. While initially theory U seems little more than a variation of traditional models—with a specific number of identifiable steps that must be completed in a specific order—it differs from those approaches in a key way: it studies organizational change not as a process that we observe externally ("I am one thing. The institution I'm observing is something else.") but as an environment we're inseparable from. To put it another way, the change leader is not a catalyst that remains unaffected by the change, but a key ingredient in the change itself.

You can't change an organization without being changed yourself.

Scharmer's emphasis on self-awareness and understanding how change leaders are inseparable from the changes they initiate also characterizes the leadership strategy known as mindfulness-based leadership. (See Buller, 2014.) A great deal of research has been done on the benefits that can result from exercises in mindfulness—the practice of paying nonjudgmental attention to each experience as it occurs. For example, mindfulness practices have been demonstrated to reduce depression following a traumatic brain injury (Bédard et al., 2012), alleviate chronic pain (Wong et al., 2011), decrease the urge to smoke (Brewer et al., 2011), help people cope with stress (Schreiner and Malcolm, 2008), and raise self-esteem (Rasmussen and Pidgeon, 2011). Most important for our purposes, training in mindfulness-based leadership strategies, as provided by such organizations as the Authentic Leadership in Action Institute (www.aliainstitute.org), the Institute for Mindful Leadership (www.instituteformindfulleadership.org), and the Bradford Clark Group (www.art-of-growth.com) is increasingly being taken seriously by executives and human resource departments throughout the corporate world (Karakas, 2011; Veil, 2011).

What mindfulness-based leadership shares with theory U is its strong emphasis on nonjudgmental awareness. Usually when we have an experience at work, our response is either a complete lack of awareness (we're too busy multitasking to pay attention to what Sarah said) or judgment ("Why is Sarah in such a bad mood today?" or, "What must I have done to annoy Sarah?"). Traditional leadership approaches exacerbate this tendency because they tend to emphasize speed and decisiveness. They encourage us to take a quick read of the situation, make a judgment, and then move on. But leadership approaches based on mindfulness run counter to that tendency. Scharmer's theory U encourages us to become more aware of our perspectives by looking inward before moving onward. Mindfulness-based leadership encourages us to become more aware of our environments by taking each experience as it comes, without attaching a story or meaning to it. If Sarah said something that seemed abrupt or curt, what we should conclude is simply that Sarah said something that seemed abrupt or curt, not necessarily that she's a bad person, in a foul mood, angry with us (justifiably or not), in need of customer service training, or anything else we may be tempted to conclude. Withholding judgment helps us keep our options open. We're less likely to box ourselves into a small number of possible responses (such as our habitual ways of dealing with an angry person) because we train ourselves to approach each experience with an open mind. We exchange quick decisiveness or rashness for a generous and compassionate range of possibilities.

Creative Leadership

Of course, just as we might fault a decisive person who turns out to be wrong, so might someone fault us for indecisiveness if we fail to act on first instincts that turn out to be right. In fact, Malcolm Gladwell in *Blink* (2005) argues that gut reactions prove to be right far more often than they're wrong. Is there any way to reconcile mindfulness with a willingness to trust our instincts? One possibility might be found in the leadership philosophy known as creative leadership. As described by Gerard Puccio, Marie Mance, and Mary Murdock (2011), creative leadership "can be defined as the ability to deliberately engage one's imagination to define and guide a group toward a novel goal—a direction that is new for the group. As a consequence of bringing about this creative change, creative leaders have a profoundly positive influence on their context (i.e., workplace, community, school, family) and the individuals in that situation" (28).

What Puccio, Mance, and Murdock are suggesting is that rather than viewing change as a process that's separate from organizational culture—as something that happens to an institution, willingly or unwillingly—our goal should be to understand that change is an integral part of that culture. But rather than simply reverting to the continual view of change as outlined in chapter 2, creative leadership views ongoing, open-ended change not as an inevitable occurrence that must be managed and endured, but as a daily opportunity to do something desirable in an organization. Think of it this way: we all know people who are highly creative, just as we're all familiar with those who seem utterly uncreative in everything they do. What distinguishes one from the other is that the former group possesses an openness to new ideas; a conviction that innovation is exciting, not threatening; and an opportunity to see the world in new ways. In the same way that we're familiar with people who fall into each of these two categories, so can we imagine both creative and uncreative organizations. A creative organization is one that regards change as stimulating and exciting; an uncreative organization prefers the tried and true even when it no longer works as well as it once did.

What creative leadership does is turn our entire discussion of change on its head. Rather than trying to manage change in an organization just as you might manage cash flow or inventory, you focus on developing a new organizational culture. Change management is goal oriented; it keeps its eyes on the prize and continually measures its progress toward its predetermined destination. Creative leadership is systems oriented; it devotes its energy toward building a more creative organizational culture. Rather than defining a goal and establishing a plan to get there, creative leaders build a culture of innovation and expect change and innovation to flow naturally from it. With creative leadership, supervisors don't waste their time trying to impose change on a recalcitrant group of stakeholders; they invest their time in learning how to be more creative themselves and how to instill an outlook that celebrates innovation in those who work with them. This approach has a natural affinity with distributed organizations like colleges and universities since it doesn't involve driving a new idea downward through a hierarchy; instead, it works to foster the type of organic environment in which new ideas are born, nurtured, grow, and reproduce.

In addition, creative leadership involves processes at which academics are highly skilled—problem solving, cultivating and refining new ideas, developing ideas that initially go against the mainstream—with the result that it uses the faculty's talent and training to its best advantage. While organizations like the Center for Creative Leadership (www.ccl.org) and the Institute for Creative Leadership (www.instituteforcreative leadership.org) apply this approach to all kinds of organizations, it hasn't yet been fully embraced throughout higher education, the very field in which it holds so much promise.

The Pattern That Emerges

Although the change theories we've explored in this chapter seem very different, they share certain features that distinguish them from traditional change models.

The first pattern we observe as we consider these theories side by side is their insistence that, contrary to what we might conclude from traditional change models, effective change does not result from following a formula or recipe. Not every change process will be the same as any other, and there's no reason we should expect it to be. Particularly in a field as dynamic as higher education, we do our institutions a disservice by trying to force their change processes to adhere to a prescribed series of steps. Change in higher education is not like a guided tour; it's more like a voyage of discovery.

The second pattern we notice is that people unnecessarily complicate the change process by trying to divide it into silos: the leader as change agent is one type of entity, the stakeholders as change participants are another, the goal itself as a change objective is still another, those external factors that serve as change drivers are a fourth, and so on. The real world, particularly in distributed organizations like colleges and universities, can't be divided that neatly. There are change drivers both within and outside our institutions. We as change leaders are ourselves affected by the change, no less than are our organizations and stakeholders. Sometimes even the external environment can be changed by something that happens within our institutions, as occurs when technology transfer leads to the creation of a new industry or our programs have an impact on the culture and economy of our local communities. Change in higher education should not be imposed from the outside; it should grow more organically from within.

The third pattern we learn from these change theories is that the key to effective change is not, for the most part, engaging in quick and resolute decision making. It derives more gradually from awareness—awareness of our own values, of what's going on all around us, of the needs of others, and of the effect our choices have on the larger world. Being aware as academic leaders means that we often withhold judgment as a situation unfolds. We wait to see where it's going and how it fits into the bigger picture. We don't assume that opposition occurs because people are evil, stupid, lazy, or uninterested in the good of the institution. We remain open to learning more. We refrain from jumping to conclusions. In fact, we seek out diverse views, contrarians, and devil's advocates because we want to base our decisions on the fullest information possible, and we often gain new perspectives from those who don't agree with us. In short, effective change leaders apply the same academic rigor to their administrative work as they do in their teaching and research. They let the facts take them wherever they may. Change in higher education is not a matter of connecting the dots; it begins with an appreciation of the dots themselves and a willingness to understand how they got there.

The change theories summarized in this chapter demonstrate that guiding change effectively is a lot more flexible than applying a one-size-fits-all change management model. Effective change leaders are those who adopt an approach that fits their organizational culture on both the macrolevel (the culture of higher education as a whole) and the microlevel (the culture of the specific institution or academic unit that they're leading). With that in mind, what might this more effective type of change leadership in higher education look like?

Change Leadership in Higher Education

Successful change leadership at a college or university will borrow aspects of all the change theories we just explored. It will work to develop learning cultures, emphasizing the importance of adapting to new circumstances, making positive assumptions about the motives of stakeholders, encouraging transparency from all parties, and thinking in terms of inclusive systems rather than conflict between an in-group and an out-group. It will borrow from the change leader's road map and the change journey, recognizing that each change process is unique and resisting the tendency to apply artificial formulas, patterns, and precedents. It will draw inspiration from theory U and mindfulness-based leadership, encouraging leaders to reflect on their own values and the values of the programs they serve and refraining from premature judgments and false assumptions. And it will engage in creative leadership, taking time to build a culture that admires innovation and sees change as an asset, not a threat.

To see how this combination of ideas can come together to promote lasting change, let's imagine an institution that has several options about how to plan for its future. Our hypothetical university started out as a two-year college and has already gone through a number of significant transformations. Its first programs were all applied areas, particularly the practical skills needed by secretaries to work in large offices during the 1950s and 1960s. Early catalogues for the college list such courses as typing, shorthand, bookkeeping, and business writing.

Over time, as secretaries became administrative assistants and needed a different type of education, the college's academic program grew, and the school eventually offered all four years of an undergraduate degree. New academic areas were added—the arts and humanities, health professions, education, engineering, and public administration—and this expansion ultimately led to the college's first master's degrees. Enrollment rose, and the college sought university status. It began awarding doctoral degrees, first in applied areas (the EdD and PsyD) and then in research fields (the PhD).

Now the school appears to be at another crossroads. An economic downturn in its primary service area has resulted in plummeting enrollment, significant losses of philanthropic funding, and pressure from the community for the school to "stick to the knitting" (in other words, to eliminate programs that aren't vocational). Some type of change seems inevitable. The school will either have to close its doors in the near future or find a way to deal with these severe challenges. But the immediate question is: How should the university change?

Scenario One

In one possible scenario, the university hires a new president who established her reputation by saving another school on the brink of financial ruin. She's widely regarded as a visionary change agent, "just the sort of person we need," the university's governing board said when they hired her. Throughout the entire interview process, everyone she met mentioned how ready the university was for substantive change and how following its current path would destroy it.

With such a strong mandate, the new president assembled a leadership team (including a number of new vice presidents she brought in because she had worked with them before and knew she could trust them), scheduled a planning retreat with her administrative team and the governing board, and gave her first State of the University address less than a month after being hired. In it, she announced a sweeping new strategic plan that she called *10,000 in 10*, with a goal of raising the university's enrollment to ten thousand full-time students within the next ten years. To accomplish this goal, the school would radically alter its academic programs. It would refocus on professional programs, deemphasize the liberal arts and PhD programs (which were "irrelevant in the twenty-first century anyway," according to a very vocal member of the governing board), offer all its programs online, accept credit for massive open online courses and professional experience, condense each baccalaureate program to only three years, and cut the price of tuition to less than half its current rate. At the same time, the institution would aggressively recruit students into its applied doctoral programs and set an ambitious target for federal grant support, which would give it access to sizable amounts of external funding.

Since the president had been through a similar change process before, she believed she knew what to expect. The Kübler-Ross model of change told her that there would be strong resistance to her ideas initially, but the Krüger and Kotter models of change told her what she'd need to do. She'd pay close attention to the power dynamics lying just below the surface of the organization, spend her time communicating her vision to the faculty and staff, empower others to implement the initiatives developed by her leadership team, and celebrate small victories. After all, two steps in the Kotter model were already behind them: there was a strong sense of urgency at the university, and she had created her guiding coalition. As a result, she was quite surprised when the new strategic plan was met with widespread enthusiasm rather than anger and denial. Faculty and staff embraced the ideas with a sense of relief that there was finally a plan in place, and they could understand their role within in. *I must've lucked out,* the new president thought. *Things were so bad that people are just glad they finally have visionary leadership.*

As the fall semester got under way, however, that initial honeymoon period ended abruptly. A rumor emerged that in order to reduce costs, there would be layoffs of faculty members in the liberal arts and PhD programs. Even in fields like business and public administration, the rumors said, full-time faculty members would be replaced by adjuncts who would cost less since they didn't qualify for benefits. The new adjuncts could be located anywhere in the world since their courses were taught online. The faculty senate, which had once welcomed the new plan, increasingly resisted it as its members saw the impact it would have on their own workload. Once the students and alumni learned that major changes were in store, they mounted a campaign against the new plan on Facebook, wrote op-ed pieces for the local newspaper, and began showing up en masse in the president's office. "I didn't pay to get a degree from Online U," one protestor was quoted as saying, and "Stop Online U" became a new rallying cry.

By the end of the president's first year, the office of research and sponsored programs issued a report concluding that rather than increasing the amount of indirect funding received by the university, the plan to replace research doctorates with more applied degrees could reduce it by up to 90 percent. The president then fired the vice president for research for going public with this report. Opposition grew even stronger since this termination seemed to confirm everyone's fear that many people would soon lose their jobs.

The president reviewed her notes about the Kotter change model and decided that the university must be in the "never let up" stage. She redoubled her efforts to force through the new strategic plan, called additional meetings with various constituencies, and tried to counter the anger of the faculty, students, and alumni with a positive and forward-looking message. Her efforts backfired. The president's calm demeanor was misinterpreted as indifference, and she found herself increasingly isolated.

Within a year and a half of the president's arrival, the university had reached gridlock. Faculty meetings were devoted to little more than arguing about which elements of the president's new strategic plan were the worse. A vote of no confidence concluded each meeting. Over winter break of her second year, the new president released a memo stating how much she missed the classroom and intended to return to the faculty at the end of the academic year. The university limped on, but its financial problems continued, and within three years, massive layoffs proved to be unavoidable.

Scenario Two

Our second scenario also begins with a university that hires a new president. But this time the president who's been hired has worked with learning cultures, change journeys, and creative leadership at her previous institution. So rather than relying on a change model approach and prescribing her new vision for the university, she invests her first hundred days in getting to know the school's primary stakeholders, asking about the issues that matter most to them, and letting them learn a bit about her and her core values. At a public forum, she addresses this broad group of constituencies:

> It's not going to shock anyone if I tell you that our university is facing serious challenges, and that there are going to be lots of struggles ahead. But one of the things I learned in the last several months is how resilient you all are and how committed you are to the success of our university. After all, it's not as though you haven't dealt successfully with problems before. It was that innovative, entrepreneurial spirit you all have that most attracted me to this job. Just think of how creatively you've responded to every opportunity you've had in the past. You reinvented yourselves many times, first from a two-year to a four-year college, then as a university, and finally as a research university. Compared to what you've already done, the issues we're all facing together now don't seem all that threatening. It's just an opportunity for us to build on the solid foundations you've all laid. I've got confidence in you, and I want you to have confidence in me. Most of all, we're going to have fun planning our future together.

Over the next few weeks, the president worked with the governing board and various faculty committees to establish a series of task forces that would examine possible approaches to the school's challenges. Each group would have representation from multiple constituencies in order to provide a broad range of perspectives. Guidelines were established stating that no member of a working group's vote or opinion would count more than anyone else's. As a result, whenever a member of the governing board started referring to classes and degrees as "products" and to students as "customers," the alumni, students, and parents on the task force would immediately counter this language by steering the discussion toward the importance of education and research. Conversely, whenever students or faculty members began to focus too exclusively on their own programs or interests, members of the upper administration or governing board would redirect the conversation toward the big picture.

The process wasn't smooth by any means. As occurs in any discussion of substantive change, early adopters ran into conflict with those who opposed any type of change whatsoever. Arguments broke out and, not infrequently, feelings were hurt. But rather than concluding, "We must now be at the depression stage of the change process. That means the acceptance stage is just around the corner," the president would good-naturedly tease that the university was just making a short side trip to the graveyard of old habits or the opera house of emotion and respond accordingly. By being aware of the competing needs of all groups within her open system, the president was able to keep their attention on the goals they shared, not on the fears and vested interests that could divide them.

After a semester, the working groups proposed four alternative pathways that could take the university back to a state of financial health. In order to keep people from becoming attached to their pet pathway, the members of working groups were shuffled so that a new set of working groups would study the feasibility of all four approaches. These new groups used our ten analytical lenses to identify the strengths and weaknesses of each proposal, with the result that certain elements of one proposal eventually came to be combined with the best features of other proposals, resulting in a single hybrid or consensus pathway.

When this consensus pathway was brought before the governing board, faculty senate, student government association, and alumni board for their endorsement, no one was surprised by anything they heard. The details of each proposal had been shared with all constituents at various points throughout the process. Only the governing board endorsed the final proposal unanimously, although it received a majority vote (and at times an overwhelmingly majority vote) from other bodies. The resulting plan—to rebrand the institution as a national professional university, hire new recruiters who would aggressively seek out-of-state applicants (and who were each given a challenging quota so that the extra tuition that resulted would more than pay for their salaries), refocus the university's PhD programs on a few pillars of excellence that would become the focus for large federal grants, and offer thirty select programs completely online to students located anywhere in the world—received sufficient support. Although there were challenges in its implementation, momentum kept the plan moving forward. When the president stepped down after ten years in office, full-time equivalent enrollment had reached more than twelve thousand, and the school's financial status was rated "excellent" by its regional accrediting body.

A Comparison of These Strategies

Notice that the plans put in place in these two scenarios were not really all that different. But the ways in which the school developed these plans were completely dissimilar. Change models almost inevitably cause institutions to adopt hierarchical approaches, with serious problems arising for a distributed organization like a college or university. The strategy adopted in the second scenario retained enough flexibility to be workable in an open system like higher education. As counterintuitive as it may seem, the first president who seemed to be following a traditional leadership role by promoting *her* vision and *her* change process ended up trying to manage change; she never reached the point of leading it. Although the second president stayed more in the background and empowered various working groups to develop the actual strategy, she was demonstrating effective change leadership. She created an environment in which successful change became possible.

The first president focused on the intended outcome and expected the culture to adapt in such a way that it could bring it about. The second president focused on the culture and put enough trust in the process that it produced a desirable outcome. Her leadership was demonstrated through building relationships, encouraging people's confidence in themselves, and reminding the institution that it already had a creative learning culture.

The first president saw the world in dichotomies: success or failure, adoption or rejection of her vision, adherence to or violation of a specific change model, us and them, and so on. As a result, she became afflicted with what Rolf Dobelli (2013) calls alternative blindness—the failure to recognize that there may well be more options than those on the table at any given moment. The second president, by directing her energy toward the culture rather than investing in any one particular outcome, allowed a wider range of alternatives to be considered. At the same time, she developed maximum buy-in for the consensus proposal because people had already had plenty of opportunities to have their voices heard.

To be sure, these scenarios are largely hypothetical, even though I've based them on situations I witnessed firsthand. I altered only enough details to protect the innocent (as they used to say on *Dragnet*) or, perhaps, the not-so-innocent. And I'll plead guilty to the charge of constructing them in such a way as to obtain the result I want. But if you've been around higher education long enough, you probably know people who bear more than a passing similarity to the two presidents, even if the people you know happen to be provosts, deans, or board chairs. If you recall the last major change process that failed at your own college or university, it's almost certain that you'll find the missing ingredient wasn't strong, decisive leadership from the top down or sufficient adherence to one of the traditional models of change management. What's much more likely to have occurred is that someone tried to promote his or her vision for the future among stakeholders who had contributed little or nothing to its development, fell victim to alternative blindness in believing that the choice had to be all or nothing, gathered a leadership team that said only what that person wanted to hear, and to this day still hasn't taken responsibility for the way things turned out. At colleges and universities all over the world, that process is unfolding right now.

Conclusion

Although they were initially designed to describe change processes, traditional change models are all too often used to prescribe and guide change processes. In hierarchical organizations, that's not a major problem. The person at the top of the hierarchy has the ability to impose this plan throughout the chain of command. But in a distributed organization, that approach rarely works. Change leaders have to see themselves as part of the system being changed, not in control of it from on high. They need to allow each change process to find its own path. They must remain informed of what's occurring throughout the organization so that they can respond effectively. They should devote their time to building a creative learning culture rather than trying to engineer a specific outcome. Although a vision of where the institution needs to go can be a powerful motivator, assuming that there's only one right way to reach that destination will usually lead to frustration, divisiveness, and failure. The mistake many academic leaders make in attempting to guide change processes at their institutions is that they continue to pursue an approach that's consistently shown itself to be largely ineffective in bringing about meaningful change: strategic planning. Why strategic planning doesn't work—and what alternatives to this largely futile exercise exist in higher education—is the topic of the next chapter.

REFERENCES

Ackerman Anderson, L. S., & Anderson, D. (2010). *The change leader's roadmap: How to navigate your organization's transformation* (2nd ed.). San Francisco, CA: Jossey-Bass/Pfeiffer.

Bédard, M., Felteau, M., Marshall, S., Dubois, S., Gibbons, C., Klein, R., & Weaver, B. (2012). Mindfulness-based cognitive therapy: Benefits in reducing depression following a traumatic brain injury. *Advances in Mind-Body Medicine, 26*(1), 14–20.

Brewer, J. A., Mallik, S., Babuscio, T. A., Nich, C., Johnson, H. E., Deleone, C. M., ... & Rounsaville, B. J. (2011). Mindfulness training for smoking cessation: Results from a randomized controlled trial. *Drug and Alcohol Dependence, 119*(1–2), 72–80.

Buller, J. L. (May 2014). Mindful academic leadership. *Academic Leader 30*(5), 1, 6.

Dobelli, R. (2013). *The art of thinking clearly.* New York, NY: Harper.

Gladwell, M. (2005). *Blink: The power of thinking without thinking.* New York: Little, Brown.

Karakas, F. (2011). Positive management education: Creating creative minds, passionate hearts, and kindred spirits. *Journal of Management Education, 35*(2), 198–226.

Kimball, R. (1990). *Tenured radicals: How politics has corrupted our higher education.* New York, NY: Harper & Row.

McGregor, D. (1960). *The human side of enterprise.* New York, NY: McGraw Hill.

Puccio, G. J., Mance, M., & Murdock, M. (2011). *Creative leadership: Skills that drive change* (2nd ed.). Thousand Oaks, CA: Sage.

Rasmussen, M. K., & Pidgeon, A. M. (2011). The direct and indirect benefits of dispositional mindfulness on self-esteem and social anxiety. *Anxiety, Stress, and Coping, 24*(2), 227–233.

Scharmer, C. O., & Senge, P. M. (2009). *Theory U: Leading from the future as it emerges: The social technology of presencing.* San Francisco, CA: Berrett-Koehler.

Scharmer, O., & Kaufer, K. (2013). *Leading from the emerging future: From ego-system to eco-system economies.* San Francisco, CA: Berrett-Koehler.

Schein, E. H. (2010). *Organizational culture and leadership* (4th ed.). San Francisco, CA: Jossey-Bass.

Schreiner, I., & Malcolm, J. P. (2008). The benefits of mindfulness meditation: Changes in emotional states of depression, anxiety, and stress. *Behaviour Change, 25*(3), 156–168.

Veil, S. (2011). Mindful learning in crisis management. *Journal of Business Communication, 48*(2), 116–147.

Wong, S. Y., Chan, F. W., Wong, R. L., Chu, M. C., Kitty, L.Y.Y., Mercer, S. W., & Ma, S. H. (2011). Comparing the effectiveness of mindfulness-based stress reduction and multidisciplinary intervention programs for chronic pain: A randomized comparative trial. *Clinical Journal of Pain, 27*, 724–734.

5

WHY STRATEGIC PLANNING
DOESN'T WORK

IF AMERICAN HIGHER EDUCATION has had an article of faith for the past thirty to forty years, it's been this: the most effective way to implement substantive change at a college or university is to engage in strategic planning. As a result, questioning the effectiveness of strategic planning often seems a bit like administrative heresy. But the fact remains that strategic planning doesn't work. At least, it doesn't work well enough to be worth all the time and money universities spend on it. We'll examine the evidence for why that's so later in this chapter. But for now, let me explain it by means of a story.

Shortly after the collapse of the Iron Curtain in the early 1990s, a university hired me to review its administrative processes and help its leaders determine why they were achieving so few of their long-term goals. They made it clear that they didn't really need help with change processes. They were happy with what they were doing in that regard since they considered the methods they were using as state of the art. What they wanted from me was some advice on how they could better implement their ideas, since there seemed to be a disconnect between the great ideas they developed and what they could eventually get to work. When I asked them to tell me about the planning process they were using and valued so highly, they proudly showed me an incredibly elaborate flowchart of committees and approval processes that regularly resulted in a highly detailed and visionary five-year plan. "A five-year plan?" I asked. "You do know that's partly what brought down the Soviet economy, don't you?" From the look of shock on their faces, I had a feeling that this consultancy was about to be short-lived. And that's precisely what occurred. Word seemed to get around quickly, and for the rest of the day, I was asked at every single meeting why I didn't understand strategic planning and then subjected to a lecture on its incredible value to colleges and universities. I left the school the next day and was never invited back. But I still have a copy of that 1993 five-year plan, a masterpiece of detail for what an American university should do and how it should allocate its budget for the entire period from 1994 through 1999. Except there's just one thing missing—the word *Internet* never appears in all those hundreds of pages.

I'm not saying that it's never useful for colleges and universities to plan (quite the contrary), and I'm not even saying that strategic planning can't be helpful. But what I am saying is that strategic planning as a systematic process is of relatively limited use in helping colleges and universities produce the sort of transformative change they all say they're interested in and that it's rarely worth the millions of dollars they spend on it.

In this chapter, I explore why confidence in strategic planning is so misplaced and how the approaches to change leadership discussed in the previous chapter point the way toward a more effective solution. But we begin with a more fundamental question: When and why did higher education get involved in strategic planning in the first place?

A Brief Primer on Strategic Planning

Ironically, in 1994, the very year that the school that hired me for my ill-fated consultancy was scheduled to begin its next five-year plan, Henry Mintzberg, the Cleghorn Professor of Management Studies at McGill University, published *The Rise and Fall of Strategic Planning*. Mintzberg argued that strategic planning almost never achieves its objectives in any type of organization, including the corporations that had embraced it so enthusiastically, and it can actually be counterproductive in terms of helping an organization deal with drivers of change. Many of Mintzberg's reasons for opposing strategic planning are a bit different from those I discuss in this chapter, but his thesis is still relevant two decades after he wrote his book. It also includes a fascinating history of strategic planning, to which I'm indebted in preparing the summary that follows. (Other sources for the following include intranet.onec.go.th/world_ed/history.html, www.ssireview.org/blog/entry/the_strategic_plan_is_dead._long_live_strategy, and Zuckerman, 2012.)

Strategic planning, originally termed *strategic management*, developed after World War II when businesses sought to transfer the approaches that had proved successful in winning the war from the military to the corporate world. The goal was to enable a business to "capture" a segment of the economy by carefully designing a long-term plan rather than simply relying on advertising or unpredictable market forces. From the very first, therefore, the concept of strategic planning arose from the most hierarchical types of organization imaginable: the military and corporate worlds. As John Jordan, clinical professor of supply and chain information systems at Penn State, notes,

> To understand the contours of classic business strategy, it is helpful to discern its western military heritage: competitors are seen as enemies and the marketplace is typically a battleground. The similarities are more than rhetorical. Modern business strategy's kinship with military theory dates primarily to the mid-nineteenth century, when a cadre of graduates of the U.S. Military Academy at West Point came into positions of authority.... What are the key tenets of classic business strategy that emerged from these military origins? In its simplest form, an organization or military operation should resemble a pyramid: Power and intelligence are concentrated at the top and trickle down to the wide bottom of the hierarchy, where both power and intelligence are presumed to be minimal. The ultimate goal is the familiar "command and control," which necessitates getting subordinates to do what you want while preventing them from doing what you don't. (Jordan, 2012, 376)

That fundamentally hierarchical mind-set was carried over into higher education, which got its first taste of strategic planning in 1959 when the topic was discussed at a meeting of about two dozen academic leaders at MIT. (See www.psu.edu/president/pia/planning_research/reports/two decades.pdf.) Representatives from that group continued to meet periodically for the next few years, eventually organizing formally as the Society for College and University Planning in 1965. (See www.scup.org/page/about.)

The critical moment in academic strategic planning didn't come until 1983 with the publication of *Academic Strategy* by George Keller, a professor of higher education studies at the University of Pennsylvania. (We'll hear more from George Keller in chapter 7.) In the years that followed, strategic planning was embedded more and more into standard administrative practice, eventually becoming a requirement of several regional accrediting bodies. For example, Standard 2 (Planning, Resource Allocation, and Institutional Renewal) of the Middle States Commission on Higher Education reads:

> An institution conducts ongoing planning and resource allocation based on its mission and goals, develops objectives to achieve them, and utilizes the results of its assessment activities for institutional renewal. Implementation and subsequent evaluation of the success of

the strategic plan and resource allocation support the development
and change necessary to improve and to maintain institutional quality.
(http://www.msche.org/?Nav1=About&Nav2=FAQ&Nav3=Question07)

Other groups, like the Southern Association of Colleges and Schools,
while they didn't specifically require institutions to draft a strategic plan,
developed standards that were far easier to meet if the college or university
had such a document prepared:

> The institution engages in ongoing, integrated, and institution-wide
> research-based planning and evaluation processes that (1) incorpo-
> rate a systematic review of institutional mission, goals, and outcomes;
> (2) result in continuing improvement in institutional quality; and (3)
> demonstrate the institution is effectively accomplishing its mission.
> (SACS Commission on Colleges Core Requirement 2.5, http://www
> .sacscoc.org/pdf/2012PrinciplesOfAcreditation.pdf)

Notice that although the words *strategic plan* appear nowhere in
this requirement, the very phrasing practically serves as a definition
of what a strategic plan is in higher education. For this reason, by
the early twenty-first century, very few academic institutions lacked a
formal strategic plan (usually displayed prominently on the institution's
website), and many schools had entire offices devoted to the frequent
updating of the strategic plan and to documenting its progress.

The reason that so much staffing seemed necessary is that strategic
planning, as it had developed in American industry, was a good deal more
complex than the mere setting of long-term goals. It frequently began with
a SWOT (strengths, weaknesses, opportunities, and threats) analysis, a
systematic examination of internal strengths and weaknesses and external
opportunities and threats. (See figure 5.1.) SWOT analysis might be done
as informally as a series of brainstorming sessions or as elaborately as an
exhaustive market study, consideration of demographic trends, financial
scrutiny of competitors, and forecasts of emerging trends in the field and
in global society that might affect the business. This process provided the
basis for an organization's vision statement, a concise synopsis of where
the company wanted to be in a reasonable period—usually five, ten, or
twenty years. The company would then proceed to conduct gap analysis,
the comparison between actual performance and potential performance.
What, in other words, could the company possibly do in order to fulfill
the vision that was outlined? How far away from the desired level of performance was it now, and what would it take to get where the company
needed to go?

Figure 5.1 SWOT Analysis

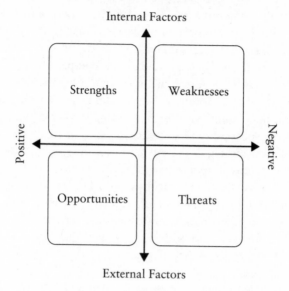

Internal Factors

Positive

Strengths   Weaknesses

Negative

Opportunities   Threats

External Factors

The strategic plan itself was then often drafted on a series of levels. The level 1 strategic plan, or strategic visioning, was usually conducted at the level of the CEO and board of directors: Where would the company be positioned relative to its competitors in the industry? What new direction would it be taking overall? The level 2 strategic plan, or strategic implementation, was usually prepared at the vice presidential level. How would the strategic vision become a reality over time? How would each area contribute to that overall effort, and what resources would be needed to do so? The level 3 strategic plan, or tactical planning, was developed at the individual unit level. It tended to focus on a shorter period of time and to address the practical steps that would need to be taken immediately in order to meet the goals set at the level above it. What, in other words, should the annual targets be for each unit as the plan becomes a reality? What options are available in case any unit misses its target? True to its roots in linear thinking and hierarchical organizations, strategic planning was a process that flowed from the top of the organizational chart downward, becoming more specific and detailed the lower one went through each successive level.

In order to measure the company's progress against the rest of the industry, most businesses adopted benchmarks (goals to aim for, usually derived from best practices elsewhere in the industry) or key performance indicators (KPIs, specific targets signifying a quality standard has been reached, such as a 95 percent approval rate or a 99.9 percent reliability rate for electronic components). The advantage of using benchmarks and KPIs was twofold. First, it gave upper levels of management what was (or at least appeared to be) hard data on whether the desired level of progress was being made. Second, it prevented the company from focusing its attention too exclusively inside the organization by requiring systematic examination of what its competitors were doing and whether there might be additional opportunities or threats lurking further down the road.

That entire process should sound quite familiar to anyone who's ever participated in a strategic planning process at a college or university. Much of the same terminology—*SWOT analysis, tactical planning, benchmarks*—was taken verbatim from the hierarchical corporate environment and imposed on a distributed academic culture. Other aspects were sometimes slightly modified—benchmarks were often recast as assessment metrics, and KPIs usually were described as targets set by offices of institutional effectiveness—but the heart of the practice remained the same. For a college or university, just as for a military unit or Fortune 500 company, strategic planning became an elaborate multilevel exercise in goal setting, data collection, and systemic progress toward a highly desirable goal.

What could possibly go wrong?

The Limitations of Strategic Planning in Higher Education

The answer is: everything. For one thing, we already know from our discussion of organizational culture that a system developed within distinctly hierarchical organizations (the military and corporate environments) will basically be an invasive species in higher education's distributed ecosystem. It runs counter to the way universities really work and the way faculty members like to think, with almost inevitable resistance arising at every stage in the process. For another thing, it ignores the fact that strategic planning has been far from a universal success even in business. The complex machinery of strategic planning simply isn't nimble enough to keep pace with a rapidly changing marketplace, and that rate of change continually accelerates:

> This kind of top-down, once-a-year process of codifying strategies may have worked well (though it often didn't) when the environment was calmer, when you sold the same people every year, when life was more predictable. It was assumed, not always wrongly, that important changes in the marketplace would become apparent to top

management in time to be incorporated into the next plan; customer loyalty and a generally moderate level of competition ensured that there would be time to adapt before any damage was done to the organization's competitiveness. If the ongoing process of correcting for mistakes was slow, so were the shifts in the marketplace itself. (Wall and Wall, 1995, 21–22)

But even beyond these considerations, we can point to eight ways in which strategic planning can't possibly live up to its hype, at least when it comes to bringing about effective, transformative change in higher education.

Little Advice on How to Plan

As Mintzberg himself noted in *The Rise and Fall of Strategic Planning* (1994), the entire cumbersome process of strategic planning can tell us quite a lot about how to structure and monitor the planning process, but it's not designed to tell us anything at all about how we're actually supposed to come up with the ideas for our plan. If the CEO and governing board aren't creative enough to get the strategic visioning right, if the vice presidents aren't imaginative enough to get the strategic implementation right, or if those in the trenches aren't insightful enough to get the tactical planning right, then having the most elegant process in the world isn't going to result in a workable plan. In fact, the more closely you examine it, the more the entire concept of strategic planning comes to resemble that Sidney Harris cartoon in which two scientists are examining a complex equation on a chalkboard with the phrase "then a miracle occurs" scrawled across the middle (www.sciencecartoonsplus.com/pages/gallery.php). The caption of that cartoon applies in the case of strategic planning as well: "I think you should be more explicit here in step 2." The problem is that when it comes to strategic planning, step 2 (the actual creation of the plan) is never really spelled out.

Overly Generic Mission Statements

If the mission and vision statements of an institution are so generic that they provide relatively little guidance for the planning process, the whole exercise starts to look like a quest in which you have no idea at all what you're questing for. I'll come back to the problem of vague mission statements later in this chapter, but for now, suffice it to say that certain mission statements are almost necessarily generic. If a university truly has a comprehensive mission, then by definition, its mission must be to do a lot of (sometimes unrelated) things on a lot of different levels in a lot of different ways. Finding the least common denominator in all that often results in a mission statement that contains merely empty verbiage, and that certainly doesn't provide a great deal of guidance when it comes to planning.

Limited Options

Planning necessarily limits options. For example, if you plan to get married and raise a family, then implementing that plan means that you can't also remain single and childless. Planning is about making choices, and those choices depend on the best estimate you can make now about what your future needs and interests are likely to be. But not all drivers of change are predictable. New technologies will emerge, new markets will arise, new problems will occur, and highly desirable new opportunities will develop. If you plan too generally, you run the risk of not having a plan at all. If you plan too specifically, you can end up limiting your options so that you don't have the agility to respond to a rapidly changing environment. So it's rather naive to think that strategic planning is an effective way to prepare for the future. It's more likely to be a very expensive gamble that one scenario of what will happen is more probable than any other.

Mission Creep

Strategic planning almost inevitably leads to mission creep. Since the entire goal of strategic planning is to develop a logically determined and carefully considered road map to the future, the process of developing that road map causes managers to ask, "Where do we want to go in the next five, ten, or twenty years?" And the answer to that question is almost never going to be, "Right where we are right now," even though certain leaders may claim at the beginning of the process that such an answer is possible. When the institution's attention is always focused on what's stronger, bigger, larger, and better, strategic plans become expansion plans. They encourage institutions to expand into new territories or programs, seek out new markets, and do something they're not already doing. In short, they promote mission creep.

Mission creep is particularly severe in higher education because although the organizational culture within an institution is distributed, the organizational culture of the higher education system is as hierar-chical as it comes. For example, if a two-year college wants to become stronger, bigger, larger, and better, almost certainly it will plan on one day becoming a four-year college. And if a four-year college wants to become stronger, bigger, larger, and better, in all likelihood, the plan will move the institution toward university status. And so on. Strategic planning encourages each institution to become something it's not, even when its strengths and successes lie in what it already is. Although almost all academic strategic plans claim to proceed from the mission statement, they end up to causing that institution to creep beyond its stated mission.

The Planning Fallacy

Strategic planning encourages institutions to succumb to the planning fallacy—the tendency to underestimate the time and resources needed to complete a task and to overestimate their likelihood of success. We encounter the planning fallacy in students all the time. They often bud-get the amount of time they need to complete a paper by assuming that everything is going to work out exactly as they hope: resources will be available when they need them, and unexpected obstacles won't emerge. Then, when their computer crashes, their car has a flat tire, or the library can't provide a resource through interlibrary loan, they want the dead-line for the assignment extended because, they say, these problems were "unforeseeable." We sometimes mock their lack of foresight and expe-rience, but then go on to engage in the same type of wishful thinking ourselves when it comes to strategic planning. The management of time and resources is an area in which it actually pays to be pessimistic: it will almost always cost more and take longer to achieve an ambitious goal than we initially believe. But no one wants to write a strategic plan that makes it look as though the university will take an extremely long time to accomplish relatively little. And so no matter how careful the strategic planners are, they continue to succumb to the planning fallacy (Kruger and Evans, 2004; Buehler, Griffin, and Ross, 1994; Sanna, Parks, Chang, and Carter, 2005).

The Need to Measure the Measurable

Benchmarks and KPIs cause us to value only what we can measure. A met-ric is, by definition, something that we can quantify, weigh, categorize, or at least determine whether it has occurred. People tend to overvalue met-rics throughout the strategic planning process because of the fallacy of mathematical precision—the belief that simply because a phenomenon is quantified (especially if it is quantified down to two or more decimal places), it is much more reliable than phenomena we can't quantify. But colleges and universities also have to respond to intangibles. Some hot new programs maintain strong enrollments year after year; others prove to be a fad. Sometimes the mood of donors seems to be optimistic and generous; at other times, everyone we meet appears pessimistic and convinced that we're heading in the wrong direction. Moreover, even if something is measurable, it may not be measurable with the precision needed to allow effective decision making. Many social trends are quite subtle in their development. Unless you're asking the right questions on your prospective student surveys or in your focus groups, you're not going to get useful information. As but one example, the rapid shift in attitudes about gay marriage and marriage equality remained all but undetectable until public opinion had already begun to change. Many polls couldn't predict the trend because they hadn't foreseen it well enough to ask people about it. Something similar can occur in the data collected for strategic plans: we're unlikely to know which academic programs the next generation of students will want and that industry will need twenty years from now because we can't predict every trend well enough to ask about it. The result is that the metrics we use to judge the effectiveness of a strategic plan don't necessarily measure the most important things; they simply measure the most measurable things.

"What gets measured gets done" (Osborne and Gaebler, 1992, 146). But many strategic planning processes track far too many metrics. Collecting data on them all occupies time and resources that institutions could devote to more important activities—such as actually meeting the goals of the plan. A good rule of thumb is that it's better to have fewer metrics that are actually meaningful than more metrics simply because you know the data are readily available.

Since many of the things we'd really like to know about higher education—such as the impact programs will have on the quality of students' lives twenty or thirty years after they graduate, the way in which society benefits because a university decides to expand one program while phasing out another, or even how someone who never graduates from a school is happier and more fulfilled by having gone there—are so hard to quantify that schools ignore them entirely. Worse, we often cherry-pick the data to make whatever case we wish. If raw numbers prove the point we want to make, we use raw numbers. If the raw numbers look bad but percentages took better, we use percentages. If percentages look bad but rates of change look better, we report the delta. If the delta looks bad, we rely on anecdotal evidence. As a result, although we often claim to be engaging in data-driven decision making, the dirty secret of higher education is that much of strategic planning involves decision-driven data making.

Perhaps the strangest aspect of most strategic planning metrics is that they don't even document everything they claim to be documenting. The goal of using metrics in strategic planning is, after all, to illustrate the effect the school has on the people who work and study there. For this reason, although input metrics, such as a student's high school GPA and standardized test scores, are frequently important for things like national rankings (which reflect how selective a school is), most strategic planning processes claim to be tracking output metrics, that is, the "value added" to the student's life because of the educational experience at that institution. Common output metrics include such factors as retention rates, graduation rates, and job placement rates. But the problem with this approach is that in higher education, the output metrics correlate heavily with input metrics. For example, if you want to be able to predict a school's freshman-to-sophomore retention rate, six-year graduation rate, and one-year-after-graduation job placement rate, where would you look? The most sensible thing to look at is the median high school GPA and standardized test scores of the school's incoming class. Those data are better predictors of the institution's output metrics than any initiative it takes as the result of a strategic planning process. Schools with certain entrance requirements tend to have certain graduation rates (Wiesenfeld, 2014). Whatever you do to change that result is likely to have a modest effect at best. Of course, if you want to have a dramatic effect on the output metrics tracked by most strategic plans, there's an easy way to do it: refuse admission to anyone who doesn't have stellar grades and test scores in high school. But that approach runs counter to most institutions' desire to provide students with expanded access to higher education and, quite frankly, their need for tuition income. And so they go on chasing their tails, tracing metrics that are predetermined, overinterpreted, and used simply because they happen to be available (Pollard, Williams, Williams, Bertram, and Buzzeo, 2013).

Shallow SWOT Analysis

SWOT analysis really doesn't tell much about the environment in which you're operating. It's like doing a surface scan of a territory that tends to miss the sinkholes, veins of gold, and untapped springs that lie just beneath that surface. Like benchmarks and KPIs, SWOT analysis prefers to deal with factors that can be quantified or pigeonholed. It assesses the assessable; it doesn't unearth the buried. Moreover, obtaining reliable information about external threats is extremely difficult. Other institutions aren't going to share their plans or proprietary information with a school it regards as a competitor, so much of what's included in the typical SWOT analysis is little better than a guess. Finally, SWOT analysis doesn't really help prioritize the issues that you're facing. Every weakness and threat is usually given equal space on the list, with the result that ten or twelve trivial problems might end up distracting attention from the one real challenge that ought to be addressed immediately. To paraphrase David Osborne and Ted Gaebler from earlier in this chapter, always make sure you really want what you measure because what you measure is what you'll get.

Platonicity, Reification, and the Lorenz Butterfly Effect

Perhaps most destructive, strategic planning leaves institutions vulnerable to the triple threat of Platonicity, reification, and the Lorenz butterfly effect (see Buller, 2013, for a discussion of these concepts). Nassim Taleb coined the term *Platonicity* in *The Black Swan* (2010) to describe our tendency to confuse models and ideal scenarios for reality when there can never be a model with enough detail to account for every contingency.

Reification is a similar idea: it relates to the fallacy of assuming that our mental constructs or descriptions of reality are the same as reality itself. They're not; it's perfectly possible for us to develop ideas that can't be found in the physical world (such as a perfect cell phone or the square root of negative pi). And the Lorenz butterfly effect refers to the notion, first suggested by the mathematician Edward Lorenz, that it's impossible to identify every causal factor in a complex chain of events. It could always be the case, to use Lorenz's own example, that the way a butterfly flaps its wings on a March day in Beijing could ultimately have an effect on hurricane patterns in the Atlantic later that summer. Collectively these three ideas tell us that we can plan all we want, but those plans may ultimately have very little resemblance to what's actually going to happen.

Fitting the Culture

If strategic planning is to have any chance of working at all, it needs to operate within the sort of hierarchical organization that developed this approach. But although colleges and universities regularly create organization charts that make it look as though they're designed in clear chain-of-command structures, the reality is far messier. Do faculty members, we might ask, actually "report" to chairs and deans? Well, yes and no. In matters that are clearly administrative, such as the allocation of institutional budgets and the assignment of space, they certainly do. But in curricular matters regarding course content and standards, faculty maintain that independent contractor status we talked about in chapter 1. And other areas of faculty work are even more difficult to describe in terms of who is reporting to whom. There are probably very few universities that don't have a policy specifying that the dean and chair have the responsibility of deciding who teaches what and when. But there are probably equally few universities that don't also acknowledge that in actual practice, most faculty members decide what they're going to teach and when their courses are going to be scheduled. Universities simply don't work the way in which the chain of command is depicted on paper.

As a result, shadow hierarchies are common at many institutions in an effort to make the strategic planning process work. These shadow hierarchies are pyramid-shaped reporting structures that mimic the chain-of-command structures in the military and corporate worlds. For instance, an office of strategic planning or institutional research may be created, often at the vice presidential level or reporting directly to the president. Within that office, units dedicated to institutional effectiveness, outcomes assessment, data management, internal auditing, and report generation are developed. This shadow hierarchy overlays the more distributed academic side of the institution, with the latter dedicated to teaching and research and the former dedicated to documenting the quality of that teaching and research and planning how the institution should conduct its teaching and research in the future. Inevitably this shadow hierarchy begins to seep into the academic side of the institution. Faculty members are instructed to design their syllabi so that they contain assessable outcomes. They're told to rewrite their final exams so that these tests embed questions designed for assessment. And faculty time is shifted from teaching, research, and service to data collection and reporting in order to provide all the information the shadow hierarchy requires. In the end, rather than spending resources to achieve a worthwhile goal, the institution devotes more and more of its resources to documenting how it's achieving a goal, regardless of whether that goal is worthwhile.

If that were not bad enough, all the other problems that strategic planning has in corporate environments get magnified many times in higher education. After all, if the marketplace for business is changing rapidly, the marketplace for education is changing at warp speed. Students, the primary stakeholders at educational institutions, stay for a relatively short time—usually between two and six years—and then are replaced with other students with their own distinct interests, challenges, and needs. Chairs, deans, and provosts also have rapid turnover. At some schools, department chairs rotate every two years; at most colleges and universities, an administrative tenure of five years is considered typical for deans and vice presidents. Ten- to twenty-year plans thus become meaningless in an environment when both the leadership and consumer base is so fluid. As a result, many new presidents arrive at an institution, spend one to three years developing a new strategic plan, devote a year or so to pursuing it, and then are replaced by the next president, who starts the strategic planning process all over again. There's nothing particularly strategic in that.

The Lack of Mission in Mission Statements

The mission statements of colleges and universities tend to be extremely vague. Sometimes generality is unavoidable, as in the cases of the comprehensive institutions I mentioned earlier. But sometimes that generality exists for no apparent reason. Many mission statements are so long that no one can possibly remember them, confuse mission (who we are right now) with vision (who we aspire to be), or use language that is superficially impressive but does not really say very much. Compare, for example, the mission statements of Duke University (three paragraphs, 304 words, www.trustees.duke.edu/governing/mission.php), the University of Notre Dame (seven paragraphs, 523 words, www.nd .edu/about/mission-statement/), and Williams College (nine paragraphs, 597 words, archives.williams.edu/mission-and-purposes-2007.php). The length of these documents detracts from their clarity.

   As another way of illustrating how overly generic mission statements provide little guidance or no guidance about what makes that school distinctive from its peers, let's conduct a brief thought experiment. Here are five actual mission statements drawn from the websites of different colleges or universities. (I'll reveal later in this chapter which schools are represented in this exercise. For now, the name of each school has been suppressed.) Read the mission statements and then answer the questions that follow.

   o "The mission of [institution A] is to serve the community, the
      nation, and the world by discovering, communicating, and preserv-
      ing knowledge and understanding in a spirit of free inquiry, and
      by educating and preparing students to discharge the offices of life

with usefulness and reputation. We do this through a partnership of students and teachers in a unified community known as a university-college."

o "[Institution B] provides access to higher education opportunities that enable students to develop knowledge and skills necessary to achieve their professional goals, improve the productivity of their organizations and provide leadership and service to their communities."

o "The distinctive mission of [institution C] is to serve society as a center of higher learning, providing long-term societal benefits through transmitting advanced knowledge, discovering new knowledge, and functioning as an active working repository of organized knowledge. That obligation, more specifically, includes undergraduate education, graduate and professional education, research, and other kinds of public service, which are shaped and bounded by the central pervasive mission of discovering and advancing knowledge."

o "[Institution D's] mission is to educate and nurture students, to create knowledge, and to provide service to our community and beyond. Committed to excellence and proud of the diversity of our University family, we strive to develop future leaders of our nation and the world."

o "[Institution E] is a dynamic and responsive institution of higher education committed to improving and enriching individual lives and society through comprehensive, high quality and accessible learning opportunities that allow students to contribute and compete in a diverse and global community."

As you answer the following questions, try not to look ahead but rather decide how you'd respond to each question before proceeding to the next.

1. What do you learn from each mission statement that would distinguish that institution from any other college or university? How does it present its role in higher education as better than or different from that of any other postsecondary school?

2. Which of these mission statements belongs to a(n):

   a. Community college?

   b. Major multicampus university system?

   c. For-profit university with a significant commitment to online education?

    d. Ivy League institution?

    e. Research university that regularly appears in *US News & World Report*'s "top 50 best colleges" list?

3. Which of these mission statements belongs to:

    a. Brown University?

    b. Miami University?

    c. Craven Community College?

    d. University of California?

    e. University of Phoenix?

When I conduct this exercise at administrative workshops, virtually no one can identify anything at all distinctive about the mission statements in response to question 1. Indeed, about the only thing there is to notice in this regard is the reference made about access to higher education opportunities in institution B's mission statement. People's answers to questions 2 and 3 are usually no better than, and often worse than, random chance. In fact, it is not uncommon for everyone in the room to get every section of the last three questions wrong. (To avoid prolonging the suspense, here are the answers. Institution A is Brown University, an Ivy League institution: www.brown.edu/about/mission. Institution B is the University of Phoenix, a for-profit university with a significant commitment to online education: www.phoenix.edu / about_us / about_university_of_phoenix /mission_and_purpose.html. Institution C is the University of California, a major multicampus university system: www.universityofcalifornia.edu /aboutuc/missionstatement.html. Institution D is the University of Miami, a research university that regularly appears in *US News & World Report*'s "Top 50 Best Colleges" list: www.miami.edu/index.php/about_us/leader ship/mission_statement/. And University E is Craven Community College: www.cravencc.edu/about/missionstatement.cfm.)

I mention these five colleges and universities not to pick on them—all five are excellent schools that are widely regarded as leaders among their peers—but rather to indicate the extent of the problem. From mission statements like these, you get absolutely no sense that the schools are leaders among their peers, much less why they've achieved that status. Since one of the commonplaces of strategic planning processes is that the plan must flow logically from the mission statement, documents like these make that progression all but impossible. One good exercise at a strategic planning retreat would be to include your own school's mission statement in that mix. Can anyone recognize your institution's own mission among these other generic statements? Then, as a follow-up exercise, go through the mission statement and cross out anything that would apply to most, if not all, other colleges and universities. In particular, be sure to eliminate any phrasing that mentions:

- The importance of teaching, research (including making discoveries or discovering new ideas or knowledge), and service
- The quality of the faculty
- A dedication to students ("We care about the students," "Students come first," and so on)
- The excellence of the curriculum
- The idea that you're a community, family, or partnership
- Your school's strong commitment to helping students reach their goals or dreams
- The diversity of your community
- Preparation of students for life in a global economy or environment

The fact is that every institution of higher education believes those things about itself (even if you might disagree). None of those factors make a school unique or even distinctive. What the phrases above really describe is not the mission of a particular college or university but the mission of any college or university. It's no wonder that so many strategic planning processes simply promote mission drift.

If you haven't taken the time to figure out who you are and why that's important, the only future identity you're likely to aspire to is to be exactly like someone else.

Better Approaches to Strategic Change

Undoubtedly some readers will reject the central theme of this chapter: that strategic planning in higher education does not and cannot live up to its promises. They will cite genuine achievements and changes that have occurred because of strategic planning initiatives they've participated in. I won't deny that those achievements exist. My point isn't that strategic planning can't create any benefits at all but that it doesn't do so consistently or efficiently and thus is far less strategic than its title would have us believe. To put it most succinctly, strategic planning in higher education produces results, but those results are rarely worth the time and expense involved.

If governing boards and legislatures are truly interested in decreasing the cost of attending college and improving efficiencies throughout higher education, here's a good place to begin: rather than creating additional reporting requirements that force colleges and universities to document the degree to which they're achieving their goals, require instead that the same amount of money and effort be invested in pedagogy and research. Those are the real "products" of higher education, and we can't improve their quality simply by increasing the number of ways we document that quality. And if you're still not convinced that strategic planning is not the most effective way to bring about constructive change in higher education, conduct the following thought experiment. If you've been involved in higher education for more than a decade, ask yourself whether you've ever heard a board chair, president, or chancellor say, "The one thing I'm sure of is that *this* strategic plan isn't going to be one of those that just sits on a shelf somewhere." And didn't that very same plan (or at least most of it) end up sitting on the shelf somewhere anyway? When strategic plans are implemented in higher education at all, they help shape a year or two at most. After that, situations change, stakeholders change, administrators change, and the long-term strategic value of the plan diminishes to nothing.

So if we want to lead change more strategically, we need better alternatives—processes that really work with the type of organizational culture in higher education. Fortunately those alternatives exist. Let's consider two excellent alternatives that flow logically from the type of change leadership I discussed in chapter 4: scenario planning and the strategic compass.

Scenario Planning

Scenario planning is an approach to thinking about the future that's much more flexible than strategic planning. For one thing, it seeks to produce not a single strategic plan, but an entire set of possible contingencies that can continue to provide guidance as the situation evolves. Scenario planning begins with the same sort of STEEPLED analysis considered in chapter 3. Take each of the drivers of change that are part of a STEEPLED analysis, choose a reasonable point in the future (no longer than ten years out, with a window of three to five years yielding the most fruitful results), and ask the following questions.

- What is the worst-case scenario of what our world will look like at that time? How might this driver change our environment in a way that is most destructive to our interests?

- What is the most-likely-case scenario? Given the direction in which higher education appears to be moving, what effect will this driver probably have on our environment?

○ What is the best-case scenario? How might this driver change our environment in a way that is most beneficial for our interests?

For instance, a university might decide that its worst-case scenario in terms of enrollment trends (one of the demographic drivers) in five years would be either a loss of 35 percent of its current enrollment or an increase of more than 50 percent. Losing more than a third of the student body would make the current budget unsustainable; layoffs would be likely, and programs would need to close. Increasing enrollment more than 50 percent would create unbearable strains on infrastructure. Even an increase of 25 to 30 percent would stretch certain resources thin, at least in the short term. The most-likely-case scenario is growth that averages about 3 percent a year over the next five years, and the best-case scenario is growth that averages between 8 percent and 10 percent per year over that period. With roughly 8 percent growth, the school could expand in a systematic and carefully managed manner.

With these scenarios in mind, the school can make reasonable plans for each contingency. The result is much more productive than a brainstorming session in which people share whatever thoughts they happened to have at the moment. With specific scenarios, mathematical models can be developed, and the leadership team can examine case studies of other schools that have undergone similar changes. Then, when all the different scenarios are identified with as much precision as possible, they're assembled in various combinations and permutations in order to determine which even more complex scenarios might occur.

For example, suppose we were to face our best-case scenario in terms of enrollment, but our worst-case scenario in terms of governmental support (one of the legislative drivers) and our most-likely-case scenario in terms of the region's economy (one of the economic drivers)? What steps could we take if enrollment dropped, but the economy was even better than expected and support from the legislature remained strong? The advantage of this approach is that although we can never account for every possible contingency, it frees us from ignoring the possibility (in fact, the near certainty) that the environment in which our institution will be operating in five to ten years will be dramatically different from its environment today. We can then begin to act on the basis of the scenario that best reflects the different drivers of change as they occur. The other scenarios provide contingency plans to adopt if matters become better or worse than expected.

Scenario planning allows schools to plan in a way that doesn't paint them into a corner. There might be a decision, for example, to begin converting more temporary faculty lines to tenure track because it seems likely that the economy is improving, the school is growing, and the need for tenured faculty members to boost the institution's research portfolio appears to be trending upward. But because the institution has also studied worst-case scenarios and the problems that could arise if retrenchment is needed at a school with a high percentage of tenured faculty, it may choose to move more cautiously in this direction than it might have done if it had given in to the unbridled enthusiasm that often accompanies the initial phases of strategic planning (an extreme form of the planning fallacy).

The Strategic Compass

The second major alternative to strategic planning, the strategic compass, is particularly useful in highly dynamic environments like higher education. The value of a strategic compass is that although it points the institution in a general direction, it doesn't do so in the overly detailed and costly manner of most strategic plans. It asks, "Since what our environment will be like in the future is inherently ambiguous, how can we best position ourselves so that we'll be prepared to take advantage of unexpected opportunities when they arise, to remain resilient in the face of unanticipated challenges, and to adapt in a way that will keep us relevant in the years to come?" One way of answering this question is to break it into four steps.

STEP 1: WHAT DO WE DO BEST? Setting a strategic compass begins with appreciative inquiry, the systematic exploration of where your institution's strengths lie. Although the process of appreciative inquiry is far more involved than I depict it here (see, e.g., Cockell and McArthur-Blair, 2012, and Kelly, 2013), its central premise may be stated as follows: find out what you do best and then do more of it. That bit of common sense is a good antidote against mission drift. It directs attention to our strengths and keeps us from overlooking the fact that we wouldn't have come this far if we weren't doing something right.

STEP 2: WHAT DO OUR STRENGTHS TELL US ABOUT WHO WE REALLY ARE? If we examine what a school does well and what it does poorly, we get a pretty good indication of what the mission of that school really is as opposed to what its public statements may claim it is. In other words, a college may see itself as well on its way toward becoming a major research university but discover, when it takes an objective look at its strengths and weaknesses, that it's not as close to that goal as it had thought. Perhaps what it does best is provide educational opportunities to students who wouldn't otherwise have had them and what it does worst is retain graduate students. Rather than chase after research grants that it may not get anyway, its best option may be to develop more programs for first-generation college students with only modest academic records, provide flexible scheduling for working adults who are able to take only a course or two at a time, and expand its evening program for place-bound residents with few educational options. While its four- and six-year graduation rates may still pale in comparison to those of many other schools, its success in helping students eventually graduate (even if they end up transferring after a few years and graduating elsewhere) is a valid and important mission. So instead of becoming a second-rate research university, it may decide instead to become a first-rate source of educational opportunities to the very people who need them the most.

> It's always better to be excellent at something you know you can do well than to try to be only adequate at something that someone else will always do better.

The result of setting the institution's strategic compass might be the development not of a mission statement but of an identity statement: a concise description of the institution's core values, strengths, and distinction—for example:

- ○ "We provide educational opportunities to motivated undergraduates who might not otherwise have them and offer graduate programs in select applied areas that are critical to our region."

- ○ "We are a multicampus comprehensive university that is committed to providing a broad range of educational opportunities so that no resident in our service area need travel more than twenty-five miles to receive a college degree."

- ○ "We are an international research university that recruits only world-class students who have their choice of numerous educational options. We then develop the skills of these highly select students through demanding academic programs, while expanding global knowledge by means of research programs in the arts and sciences."

o "We are devoted to developing the whole person—mind, body, and spirit—of undergraduate students through course work, residence life, leadership opportunities, and community service."

o "We prepare the educators and leaders of tomorrow."

STEP 3: WHAT DOES THIS IDENTITY TELL US ABOUT WHERE WE SHOULD DIRECT OUR RESOURCES?   By focusing our attention on who we are, how we have achieved our success, and which strengths distinguish us from others, we gain a clearer sense of what our priorities must be. A clear sense of our identity frees us to devote our time, energy, and other resources toward positive change (improvement) rather than change for the sake of change (plans we pursue simply because we would feel stagnant if we weren't trying to change something). For example, if we discover that we've made a difference in the world by accepting students who couldn't get into highly selective schools and providing them with the skills they need to achieve their goals, we don't automatically assume that our next step should be to become more selective in our admissions "since that's what the prestigious schools do." Rather, we should direct even more resources to fulfilling that core mission, marketing our success in such a way that our message reaches those who may not otherwise hear it, and further distinguishing ourselves from our peers by embracing our identity and achievements. Using our resources in this way helps us follow our strategic compass. It makes the whole institution stronger so that we're in a position to take full advantage of opportunities when they arise and be resilient when setbacks occur.

STEP 4. HOW DO WE DEVELOP A CULTURE OF INNOVATION THAT EXTENDS BUT DOESN'T ALTER THIS IDENTITY?   At this point, I can easily imagine someone asking, "But if all we ever do is shore up strengths and wait for the next opportunity or problem, are we really leading change at all? Aren't we just preserving the status quo, reacting to whatever happens, and allowing others to determine our destiny?" What makes a strategic compass truly valuable is the final step in the process: using everything learned so far to create a culture of innovation. In the previous chapter, we saw how Edgar Schein's learning culture theory, coupled with the creative leadership approach developed by Gerard Puccio, Marie Mance, Mary Murdock, and others, placed an emphasis on developing a certain type of environment rather than pursuing a certain type of goal. That's what change leaders do in higher education: they build a culture; they don't just articulate a vision. As Peter Eckel, Barbara Hill, Madeleine Green, and Bill Mallon stated in their 1999 report, *On Change,* "Institutional change leaders work within a culture while challenging its comfort zone to change the culture" (p. 7).

As an example, consider the case of a hypothetical institution that concludes step 2 with the first identity statement we considered: "We provide educational opportunities to motivated undergraduates who might not otherwise have them and offer graduate programs in select applied areas that are critical to our region." Such a statement provides not only a description of where the school is right now but also a sense of where it can go in the future if it's willing to be creative enough. It can partner with local government officials, donors, and industries to build programs to meet the greatest needs of local residents. It can redirect scholarship funding from being primarily merit based to being primarily need based, with priority given to students who have overcome adversity or demonstrated their determination to succeed against the odds. It can use this awareness of its identity to redesign its entire marketing campaign ("A Great Place for Second Acts" and "We're Looking for B Students Who Have the Drive to Become A Students") and promote this message aggressively throughout its service area. It can begin honoring famous people who, after struggling in high school, finally came into their own during college. It can rename its athletic teams the Diamonds in the Rough and use the resulting publicity to underscore the school's academic mission. In short, by being creative about who they are rather than envious about who they wish they were, the stakeholders of the institution can help the school become truly distinctive.

Stephen Wall and Shannon Wall (1995) describe the benefits that result from this approach of what they refer to as strategic foresight:

> When strategic leaders capitalize on the wealth of information and knowledge that is accumulated by front-line strategists, they develop *strategic foresight*—the ability to discover unanticipated market trends and as yet unarticulated customer needs. Businesses with strategic foresight avoid the trap of developing strategies that are merely reactive, and are able to discover possibilities that may ultimately transform their companies and their industries. (19)

At a college or university, strategic foresight allows an institution to identify trends in how to best serve students' needs and engage in the type of research that best suits their mission. Academic leaders with strategic foresight don't assume they have all the answers; they know they won't be able to spot each emerging trend from their vantage point. These leaders have a healthy respect for what Wall and Wall call "the wealth of information and knowledge that is accumulated" throughout the institution. As they strive to be catalysts for positive change, they remain skeptical of any plan that might carry their schools too far away from the identity that has made them successful in the past.

Conclusion

A logical conclusion at this point would be, "If the corporate style of top-down strategic planning doesn't work in higher education, then what we must need is a bottom-up process. Strategic planning should begin with the faculty. They're the ones who know their fields the best and understand where academic disciplines are heading." Unfortunately bottom-up strategic plans don't have a particularly good track record either. Since every constituency wants its own ideas incorporated into the plan, any proposal that results is likely to try to contain something for everyone. As a result, bottom-up strategic plans tend to be watered down and bland, more of a mutual nonaggression pact than a compelling vision of the future. Academic consultant and former dean John Wiesenfeld calls bottom-up strategic plans "letters to Santa": "They basically say, 'We've been good, and so here are all the things we want'" (conversation with John Wiesenfeld, January 21, 2014). If you keep adding different colors to a pinwheel, all you see is a white blur once it starts to move.

The proper alternative to top-down strategic planning isn't bottom-up strategic planning; it's no strategic planning at all. Alternative approaches like scenario planning and the strategic compass are more flexible, cost-effective, and likely to produce lasting results. Many presidents, chancellors, and governing boards of universities will reject this conclusion and say, "But look at us! We engaged in a wonderful, broad-based strategic planning process, and it transformed our institution to a degree that wouldn't have been possible any other way." As we know, every rule has its exceptions, and any given college or university may decide that all the energy and resources it devoted to strategic planning was completely worthwhile. But if you're an objective reviewer and you take a close look at the vast majority of "transformations" produced by traditional strategic planning, it becomes apparent that the rhetoric rarely matches the reality. In many cases, administrators do exactly what I did at the end of my ill-fated general education review in chapter 3: they simply declare victory and go home. They'll use new language to describe programs that are basically unchanged from what they were before the strategic plan was ever developed. A new name might appear on a building. Modest reorganization of colleges or departments may occur. But despite all the sound and fury, what real impact has been made on the quality of the education students receive or the nature of the research that faculty perform?

In his harsh but not entirely unjustified critique of the expanding administrative structure at American universities, Benjamin Ginsberg argues that strategic planning isn't genuine leadership at all; it's a facade designed to convey the impression that one is leading when actually very little meaningful work is being accomplished:

> When they organize a planning process and later trumpet their new strategic plan, senior administrators are signaling to the faculty, to the trustees, and to the general community that they are in charge. The plan is an assertion of leadership and a claim to control university resources and priorities. This function of planning helps to explain why new presidents and sometimes new deans usually develop new strategic plans. We would not expect newly elected presidents of the United States simply to affirm their predecessors' inaugural addresses. In order to demonstrate leadership to the nation, they must present their own bold initiatives and vision for the future. For college leaders, the strategic plan serves this purpose. (Ginsberg, 2011, 48–49)

Rather than "shrinking the change" to make a major transition feel more comfortable to constituents (Heath and Heath, 2010; see chapter 2, this volume), many administrators exaggerate the significance of small changes in order to make themselves seem more effective as administrators. But an illusion of leadership won't be enough to address the genuine challenges that higher education faces in the twenty-first century. With increasing competition for students and the most renowned faculty, colleges and universities can't afford to engage in change processes that merely make their leaders feel as though they're accomplishing something. If approaches like scenario planning and the strategic compass replaced strategic planning and the resulting savings were redirected from administration into pedagogy, does anyone seriously doubt that the result would be an overall improvement in the quality of American higher education?

It's ironic that at the same time many leaders in the business world are becoming increasingly dubious about the value of strategic planning, many leaders in higher education continue to embrace it. It's now part of the standard operating procedures at most institutions, touted as a way of making each institution more distinctive. But as we've seen, any approach that merely encourages institutions to become stronger, bigger, larger, and better leads inevitably to mission drift, producing institutions that are more, not less, like all of the others.

REFERENCES

Buehler, R., Griffin, D., & Ross, M. (1994). Exploring the "planning fallacy": Why people underestimate their task completion times. *Journal of Personality and Social Psychology, 67*(3), 366–381.

Buller, J. L. (2013). *Positive academic leadership: How to stop putting out fires and start making a difference.* San Francisco, CA: Jossey-Bass, 2013.

Cockell, J., & McArthur-Blair, J. (2012). *Appreciative inquiry in higher education: A transformative force.* San Francisco, CA: Jossey-Bass.

Eckel, P., Hill, B., Green, M., & Mallon, B. (1999). *On change.* Washington, DC: American Council on Education.

Ginsberg, B. (2011). *The fall of the faculty: The rise of the all-administrative university and why it matters.* New York, NY: Oxford University Press.

Heath, C., & Heath, D. (2010). *Switch: How to change things when change is hard.* New York, NY: Broadway Books.

Jordan, J. M. (2012). *Information, technology, and innovation: Resources for growth in a connected world.* Hoboken, NJ: Wiley.

Keller, G. (1983). *Academic strategy: The management revolution in American higher education.* Baltimore, MD: Johns Hopkins University Press.

Kelly, R. (2013). Appreciative inquiry: A way to a more positive future. *Academic Leader, 29*(12), 2, 8.

Kruger, J., & Evans, M. (2004). If you don't want to be late, enumerate: Unpacking reduces the planning fallacy. *Journal of Experimental Social Psychology, 40*(5), 586–598.

Mintzberg, H. (1994). *The rise and fall of strategic planning: Reconceiving roles for planning, plans, planners.* New York, NY: Free Press.

Osborne, D., & Gaebler, T. (1992). *Reinventing government: How the entrepreneurial spirit is transforming the public sector.* Reading, MA: Addison-Wesley.

Pollard, E., Williams, M., Williams, J., Bertram, C., & Buzzeo, J. (2013). *How should we measure higher education? A fundamental review of the performance indicators.* Brighton, UK: Institute for Employment Studies. Retrieved from http://dera.ioe.ac.uk/18967/2/2013_ukpireview2.pdf

Sanna, L. J., Parks, C. D., Chang, E. C., & Carter, S. E. (2005). The hourglass is half full or half empty: Temporal framing and the group planning fallacy. *Group Dynamics: Theory, Research, and Practice, 9*(3), 173–188.

Taleb, N. (2010). *The black swan: The impact of the highly improbable.* New York: Random House.

Wall, S. J., & Wall, S. R. (1995). *The new strategists: Creating leaders at all levels.* New York, NY: Free Press.

Wiesenfeld, J. (2014, February 18). *A peer cohort analysis of graduation rates.* Presentation to the Florida Atlantic University Board of Trustees. Retrieved from www.fau.edu/bot/meetings/02182014_committee_meetings/sp/SPI1 .pdf

Zuckerman, A. M. (2012). *Healthcare strategic planning* (3rd ed.). Chicago, IL: Health Administration Press.

RESOURCES

Chermack, T. J. (2011). *Scenario planning in organizations: How to create, use, and assess scenarios.* San Francisco, CA: Berrett-Koehler.

Lindgren, M., & Bandhold, H. (2009). *Scenario planning: The link between future and strategy* (2nd ed.). London/Basingstoke: Palgrave Macmillan.

Ronis, S. R. (2007). *Timelines into the future: Strategic visioning methods for government, business, and other organizations.* Lanham, MD: Hamilton Books.

Senge, P. M. (2006). *The fifth discipline.* New York, NY: Random House Business.

Wade, W., & Wagner, N. (2012). *Scenario planning: A field guide to the future.* Hoboken, NJ: Wiley.

6

CREATING A CULTURE OF INNOVATION

WE'VE SEEN THAT THE standard approach colleges and universities take to promote change, strategic planning, is not worth the resources it takes to bring about what are often very minor changes. We've also seen that alternatives like scenario planning and setting a strategic compass fit the organizational culture of higher education far better than strategic planning does. Finally, we've seen that the most important task for change leaders in higher education is not to announce a specific goal but rather to spend their time creating a culture of innovation and continuous learning. That last observation leads to several important questions: How do you do that? Can you do that? In other words, is it possible to make the people who report to us more innovative, receptive to change, and imaginative in their approach to problem solving? Or is creativity just something you have to be born with?

Fortunately a great deal of research into creativity has been done over the past several decades, and many of these discoveries can guide us in how we can effectively develop a culture of innovation at colleges and universities. For example, Mark Runco, the E. Paul Torrance Professor of Creativity Studies at the University of Georgia, discusses the extensive academic research that has been conducted on creativity—from psychological, biological, cultural, educational, and social perspectives—in *Creativity: Theories and Themes; Research, Development, and Practice* (2007). He concludes that this skill or ability

> is not the same thing as intelligence, originality, innovation, nor invention. It may, however, play a role in each. Distinguishing creativity from these things ... is not just an academic exercise. It is often practical. We can best fulfill potentials if we are specific about what is involved .... The fact that creativity is largely intentional supports the notions that "we can do something about creativity." It is not fixed at

birth, nor necessarily lost in midlife or late adulthood. Many adults may lose the spontaneity that allows children to be creative, but those same adults can compensate by employing an intentional tactic and by choosing to renew their spontaneity. (410–411)

In other words, it's not the case that creativity is something you have to be born with. With the right practice, we can become more creative than we are right now—perhaps not as creative as a great virtuoso or a Nobel Prize winner but more creative than we've ever been before. And if it's possible for individuals to become more creative, it's also possible for departments, divisions, and even entire institutions. So, what approaches seem to work?

Creativity as Lateral Thinking

Since the 1960s one of the most familiar ways of developing creativity has been associated with the term *lateral thinking*. This expression was coined by Edward de Bono, whose six thinking hats I discussed in chapter 2. It refers to a suspension of linear, step-by-step logic and a willingness to set aside our initial assumptions about how things "should" work. Often associated with such expressions as "think outside the box" and Apple Computer's "Think Different" ads of the late 1990s, lateral thinking involves acting deliberately so as to free ourselves from orthodox approaches, ask speculative "What if?" questions, and change our frame of reference. Perhaps the most famous lateral thinking puzzle is the so-called nine dots problem (figure 6.1): connecting nine dots laid out in a three-by-three square while not

- ○ Using more than four lines
- ○ Removing the pen or pencil from the paper
- ○ Tracing the same line more than once
- ○ Or touching the same dot more than once

Figure 6.1 Nine
Dots Problem

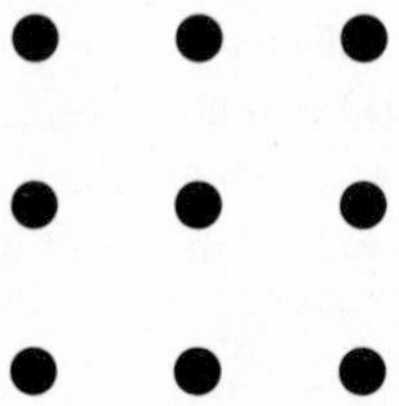

Most people approach this challenge with the assumption that the lines they draw can't extend beyond the outermost dots. When they try to do so, however, they find that it takes at least five lines to connect every dot in the pattern. Only when they realize (or someone shows them) that the instructions never said the lines can't extend outside the dots does a four-line solution become possible (figure 6.2). The exercise becomes quite literally about learning to "think outside the box."

Nevertheless, Dani Raviv, a professor of computer and electrical engineering and computer science at Florida Atlantic University, has argued that even the common four-line solution doesn't begin to challenge the assumptions most people bring to the puzzle. In his book *Everyone Loves Speed Bumps, Don't You?* (2011), Raviv points out the following:

○ While the instructions say that the lines have to be straight, they don't require them to go through the center of the dot. By tilting the lines and touching some of the dots only obliquely, it's possible to connect them with only three lines (figure 6.3).

○ In addition, the instructions don't say how big the pen is relative to the dots. With a broad enough nib, it's possible to connect all nine dots with a single line that covers the entire puzzle.

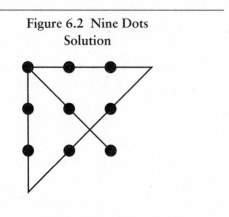

**Figure 6.2 Nine Dots
Solution**

Figure 6.3 Alternative Nine Dots Solution

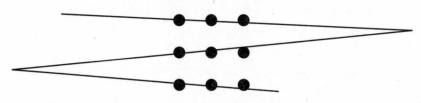

○ Nor do the instructions say that the puzzle has to be solved in only two dimensions. If you wrap the puzzle around a cylinder like the label on a soup can, you're able to connect all nine dots with a single "straight" line that spirals all the way around the now three-dimensional object.

○ Finally, the instructions don't say that the paper can't be folded. If it's folded tightly enough that the nine dots lie one on top of another, it's possible to connect them all with a single line that traverses the paper perpendicularly.

Encouraging people to engage in lateral thinking offers an initial way of promoting innovation in programs. Here's how this approach might look in an actual administrative situation:

1. A challenge is identified, and you define it by means of a needs case as described in chapter 3. Let's assume that the problem is a program that has declining enrollment and thus has been operating at an unsustainable deficit.

2. By working with the faculty and staff, you use a combination of SWOT analysis, STEEPLED analysis, and appreciative inquiry to identify the program's current strengths and opportunities, how various drivers of change might affect the overall environment in which the program operates, and what the program is doing right that it can do more of.

3. With this information as a context, you work with the faculty and staff to brainstorm possible ways of dealing with the challenge. Let's suppose that the brainstorming session yields these possibilities:

   • Launch an aggressive marketing campaign that highlights the strengths of the program.

   • Reduce staff and increase the caps on course sections so as to improve efficiency.

   • Begin a development campaign that can provide an endowment to supplement other sources of funding.

   • Target grant opportunities that are likely to yield the largest amount of indirect costs.

   • Reduce requirements and increase electives in the program so as to make it more flexible and easier to complete.

   • Create new scholarships that are available only to students majoring in the program.

- Offer a free computer to students who complete a major in the program.
- Subsidize tuition for students who major in the program.
- Provide free housing and a meal plan to students who take at least two courses per semester in the program.

4. A week or so later, you ask the same group to meet again. You needed to allow some time to go by so that the people in the exercise can distance themselves from the assumptions they brought to that initial meeting. You then have the group go through the list of ideas they developed and try to identify the underlying assumptions that led to each idea. Let's imagine that our hypothetical group concludes that they made the following assumptions in proposing their ideas:

- Students aren't enrolling in the program because they don't know about it at all or don't have enough information about it.
- Students aren't enrolling in the program because it's expensive.
- Students aren't completing the program because of complex requirements.
- Students aren't completing the program because of course availability.
- Personnel costs are largely responsible for the program's deficit.
- The program has been relying too heavily on the institutionally provided funds that form its operating budget.
- Untapped sources of grant funding are available.
- Financial incentives will attract additional students.
- A significant number of students who would be interested in the program would also be interested in on-campus housing.

5. You work with the faculty and staff systematically to challenge each of their underlying assumptions:

- What makes us assume that students don't have information about the program? What if they are getting plenty of information but don't like what they see? How would we go about learning whether this is true?
- What makes us assume that students find our program too expensive and that financial incentives will attract more students? Maybe the current disincentives aren't financial but are more a matter of scheduling, the job placement rate of our graduates, or

some other factor? How would we go about learning whether this is true?

- What makes us assume that the only students who will be interested in our program will be traditional-aged college students? Maybe if we market the program to working adults and offer courses online, during the evening, on weekends, and in short modules, we can develop an entirely new market for the program.

6. As each assumption is questioned, you open the way to new possibilities. For example, our hypothetical group may decide that a sensible next step is to invest in a marketing study to find out exactly what prospective students are looking for in programs of this kind, what prevents them from enrolling or completing these programs, and what type of incentive matters to them. Rather than becoming locked into an assumption like, "Students aren't enrolling in the program because it's expensive," the group may discover that other factors are causing enrollment to decline. Armed with this new information, they can now address the actual cause of the problem rather than their false assumptions.

This strategy, *formalized lateral thinking*, is useful in helping people uncover solutions and possibilities that they may not otherwise have considered. By combining a needs case with SWOT analysis, STEEPLED analysis, and appreciative inquiry, we can help those we work with become much more methodical in identifying relevant issues, particularly those that our common assumptions prevent us from recognizing. Then by combining brainstorming with the systematic challenging of underlying assumptions, we can begin to see new possibilities and think in more creative ways about which strategies to pursue.

Preparing a Program for Formalized Lateral Thinking

Certain departments may find it harder to engage in this approach than others. If you can't imagine the people you work with conducting an exercise like the one just outlined, there are a number of warm-up exercises you can do to get people thinking about familiar issues in unfamiliar ways. Edward de Bono (2008) published an entire book of such exercises, and other useful collections have been developed by Michalko (2006), Mumaw and Oldfield (2006), Miller (2012), and Sawyer (2013).

A sample exercise works as follows. Choose a common object that has a distinctive shape, like a funnel, frying pan, screwdriver, umbrella, or

Frisbee. Then challenge the group to come up with at least three answers to each of the following questions:

1. What could we use this object for besides its intended function?
2. What else could we use to perform this object's intended function?
3. How could we improve this object?
4. What benefits could occur if we made this object larger, thicker, heavier, or stronger?
5. What disadvantages could occur if we made this object larger, thicker, heavier, or stronger?
6. What benefits could occur if we made this object smaller, thinner, lighter, or shorter?
7. What disadvantages could occur if we made this object smaller, thinner, lighter, or shorter?
8. How could we use this object if we turned it upside down from its current position?

The value of this exercise is that it quickly underscores the idea that there are plenty of alternatives to straight-line thinking. If you do it in successive rounds—starting first, for example, with a colander, then using a coffee mug, and finally trying the exercise with a shoehorn—you're likely to find that ideas become more and more inventive each round. You can then say something like, "Okay, now let's apply that same level of creativity to solving our problem with our graduation rate. What are our immediate assumptions, and what happens when we set those aside?"

Refinements to Formalized Lateral Thinking

Although formalized lateral thinking is very useful, it doesn't work with every group and for every problem. One limitation is that the third step in the process requires people to engage in a session of intense brainstorming, and some groups are better at brainstorming than others. To begin with, groupthink can arise. The whole premise of brainstorming is that we'll come up with better ideas if we don't have to worry about our suggestions being dismissed as foolish, impractical, or just plain weird. But what actually happens in most brainstorming sessions is that the first few ideas that people propose tend to guide the rest of the discussion. As a thought experiment, imagine a situation in which you're leading a brainstorming session about how to improve a lightweight vacuum cleaner. These are the first few ideas people propose:

o Give it a brighter color so that it's easier to find in the closet.

o Make the handle longer so that it's easier to use on stairs. ·

o Widen the base so that it takes fewer passes to cover the same area.

o Put a light on the front so that dirt will be easier to see.

o Round off the sharp edges to make it safer and more attractive.

Now add five ideas of your own. If you're like most other people, the ideas you come up with will be mostly about the appliance's appearance rather than such matters as its cost, efficiency, suction, motor design, or durability. Why? All the ideas I listed had to do with the vacuum cleaner's appearance and external shape. Once we start thinking along a certain line, it becomes very difficult to break out of that mind-set. We begin making even more assumptions that we don't stop to challenge. In fact, in actual situations, groupthink is an even more pronounced factor than in this experiment. Actual brainstorming groups often include people with different positions and ranks. If one of the participants has a status differential from the others—either because this person happens to be their boss or because he or she speaks more loudly or with greater confidence—it can be a natural reaction for other people to self-edit their responses, promoting them less forcefully than they would in other circumstances, or for the group as a whole to favor one particular idea because of the person proposing it, not its inherent quality.

Traditional brainstorming also has one of the drawbacks we associated with SWOT analysis: it results in an undifferentiated list of ideas, with foolish and impractical suggestions given an equal place with the truly revolutionary. In fact, that's part of the ground rules of brainstorming: no idea is rejected outright. The result is that many brainstorming sessions produce entire lists of foolish and impractical ideas without generating a single workable possibility. People may come away from them feeling that they've participated in a wonderfully creative exercise, but you may end up no closer to a solution than you were before. As the old cynic's motto says, none of us individually can waste as much time as all of us collectively, and many brainstorming sessions prove that point splendidly. They leave you with attractive-sounding ideas that are impossible to implement, and many of them don't even seem all that attractive when examined again days or weeks later.

Fortunately, there are several refinements to make brainstorming sessions more productive. The first refinement is *segmented brainstorming*. Rather than beginning in the typical way, with everyone sharing ideas and thoughts as a group, a certain amount of time is set aside for people to think of as many possibilities as they can on their own. For example, the process might begin with each person taking approximately twenty minutes to write down as many ideas as he or she can think of independently. Then the organizer of the activity breaks the participants into subgroups of five to eight people. These subgroups go over each member's list, combining ideas where appropriate and generating new ideas from the discussion that follows. Finally, the full set of participants reassembles to consider the ideas each group produced; examine each of them in terms of its feasibility, likely impact, and originality; and propose an action plan for moving forward.

A second refinement is *anonymous brainstorming*: rather than having each person present his or her own ideas to the group, people write ideas on individual slips of paper. The slips are then gathered up and distributed randomly to subgroups that discuss, refine, and improve the ideas. The advantage of anonymous brainstorming is that it reduces the likelihood that a single dominant voice will overpower the discussion before every possibility is considered. Moreover, people are less likely to champion ideas simply because they are their own (or were proposed by a friend or supervisor) if no names are attached to the suggestions.

Structured brainstorming imposes artificial limits on the ideas that people are asked to generate. While we might expect added rules to reduce the creativity of the suggestions people come up with, in actual practice the results tend to be even better than those produced by traditional brainstorming.

Here's an example of the type of restriction that might be imposed during structured brainstorming. A group needs to come up with ideas that can reverse the declining enrollment occurring in a particular program. The group is told that they can propose only ideas that could be implemented

o Within six months
o At a cost of no more than $250,000
o Without increasing the number of credits students must complete for graduation
o By adding no more than three new courses to the current curriculum
o Falling completely within the requirements of the program's accrediting body

Limitations of this sort often help a group focus much more quickly on ideas that are innovative but not overly impractical. Moreover, many people find that having a few restrictions placed on them primes the pump for their own thoughts and helps them generate creative suggestions far more quickly.

Reverse brainstorming turns the traditional brainstorming session on its head. Instead of asking, "What are some possible solutions to this problem?" the group is asked, "What are some possible causes of the problem?" After it has determined all the possible challenges it is facing, the group explores ways of preventing each cause from occurring or mitigating the effects of that cause if it turns out to be unavoidable. Reverse brainstorming can be particularly effective in encouraging people to identify the elephant in the room by challenging the common assumption that every problem must have one and only one cause.

Systematic inventive thinking similarly reverses the brainstorming process and attempts to address the issue in a different way. For example, rather than using formalized lateral thinking to challenge current assumptions, it encourages participants to identify creative ideas that were right in front of them all along. It does so through a five-step process:

1. *Subtraction:* What would happen if we were to remove an element from the situation? Could a process be streamlined? Could savings result without a sacrifice in quality? Could other types of efficiencies be obtained? Could a sleeker, simpler, more elegant approach be found? *Examples:* What if we don't charge an application fee for our program? What if we eliminate the "last day to withdraw from a class without failing" from the academic calendar? What if we don't pursue specialized accreditation for professional programs? What if we don't offer any scholarships or financial aid but instead lower the cost of tuition for everyone?

2. *Unification:* What would happen if separate entities were combined in some way? Could administrative costs be reduced? Could greater efficiencies be found? Could improved synergy result? Could an economy of scale be achieved? *Examples:* What if we combine the departments of geology, geography, anthropology, history, and cultural studies into a single unit? What if, instead of charging students a complex array of fees based on the number of credit hours they take, we charged a single all-inclusive fee? What if, rather than assigning an administrative assistant to each department regardless of its size, we created an administrative services center that served all departments with five or fewer faculty members?

3. *Multiplication:* Are there any ways in which duplicating efforts or multiplying offices actually saves money or brings additional advantages? Where are economies of scale offset by greater access, reduced wait times, or higher levels of service? *Examples:* If we doubled the number of recruiters in the admissions office and the number of development officers in the advancement office, would the resulting added income more

than compensate for the expenditure? If, instead of centralizing the budget office and student affairs operations on our main campus, we were to open a separate office for students on each campus, would the improvement in services improve retention?

4. *Division:* Is there a feature or activity that can be divided from another unit and made independent? Could greater prestige or opportunities for funding occur if strong programs were split off and made their own schools? Could we be more innovative if we divided units in nontraditional ways? *Examples:* What if we divided the College of Arts and Sciences into a College of Fine Arts, a College of Humanities, and a College of Science? Would each unit attract larger donations and grant support independently than they do as part of a single large unit? What if we split off faculty members in psychology, biology, nursing, the medical school, and philosophy who are all working in neuroscience and created a new College of Neuroscience?

5. *Attribute dependency:* Are there unnecessary connections between attributes that can be dissolved? Alternatively, are there unconnected attributes that are better joined? *Examples:* Currently no food or drink is allowed in the library. The idea is that books and foods don't mix because of the danger that the books can be damaged. But chain bookstores regularly have coffee shops inside them. What if we eliminate the "no food or drink" rule, open a coffee shop in the library, and see what happens? Could we create a new revenue stream at the same time that we encourage greater student use of the library? Currently each faculty member proctors his or her own exams. But we also have a testing center that administers the standardized tests for graduate school. What if we were to link all testing activities in the same center? Would faculty time be better used? Could the freed-up time in class be better used for other activities? Would we be making more efficient use of our underused testing center?

One final refinement to formalized lateral thinking and brainstorming is the alternative strategy known as *brainwriting,* which works as follows. Give each person in the group a blank sheet of paper. At the top of the paper, have each person write what he or she sees as the biggest challenge or opportunity facing the program. Resist the urge to define the problem for the group. Insist that each person is free to define the matter however he or she sees it. When you review the results of this exercise later, don't be surprised if one person describes the situation in broad and general terms, such as, "We need to increase enrollment," while others focus in on a very specific aspect of the issue, such as, "How can we attract more junior-level transfers into our program from Middle Southwestern State Community College?" Understanding how different people view the opportunity or challenge you're dealing with is a valuable product of this activity. Once everyone has defined the issue, have each person number a series of spaces on the paper starting from the bottom. Create the same number of spaces as there are people participating in the exercise. In other words, if there are eight people in your brainwriting group, there should now be eight pieces of paper, each with an individual description of the issue at the top, with a numeral 8 below it, a numeral 7 below that, and so on, all the way down to the numeral 1 at the bottom of the page.

Arrange the group in a circle and then have each person pass his or her sheet of paper to the left. Each person should read the issue as it's described at the top and then write his or her best recommendation beside the numeral at the bottom of the page. When all the participants are done, they should fold their pieces of paper so that suggestion 1 is no longer visible and pass the sheet to the left. Everyone now reads the description of the issue he or she just received from the person to the right, writes a suggestion next to the number 2, folds the paper again, and passes it to the left. Encourage the participants to avoid writing similar suggestions on each paper they receive. Suggest that they try to develop a new idea each time, even if the problem or opportunity is one they've already seen. Eventually each person will receive his or her own paper back again and provide one final suggestion beside the number 8. When this entire exercise is completed, each participant should unfold the paper, review the suggestions recorded on it, and then begin a discussion of how best to begin solving the problem or taking advantage of the opportunity.

Brainwriting has several advantages to traditional brainstorming. First, by having each person define the issue in his or her own words, you discover how much consensus there is on the actual problem or opportunity. Some people may view a challenge only in terms of resources ("How can we increase our budget?"), while others view it only in terms of expenditures ("How can we reduce our costs?"), and still others perceive it in entirely different terms (such as, "How can we get the upper administration to understand that our program, while extremely valuable and central to our institution's mission, will never be able to pay for itself?"). Those different characterizations can produce a far more fruitful discussion than you would have had if you simply asked people to brainstorm ways to improve retention or recruit more students. Second, brainwriting compels everyone to participate equally and avoids the problem of someone hanging back, even though he or she has a valuable perspective to share. In traditional brainstorming sessions, certain people begin by contributing a lot of ideas but then fall silent because they don't feel their ideas have been good enough or they're afraid of what one of their colleagues might say. Brainwriting provides at least a small amount of anonymity, equalizes participation among all participants, and usually results in far more suggestions (including far more good suggestions) than does traditional brainstorming. Third, the structure of the process encourages people to think more creatively.

When you review the suggestions, you'll probably find that the first few recorded on each sheet are relatively uninspired. People tend to respond initially by relying on familiar ways of approaching opportunities and challenges. But as the process continues and they see different people describing the central issue in different ways, they're more likely to begin challenging their own assumptions. In fact, by encouraging or requiring the participants to make a new suggestion each time, you're forcing them to move beyond their first impressions and come up with more innovative ideas.

The Role of Mind-Set, Outliers, and Learned Optimism

When I do workshops on change leadership and have people practice the exercises we've just explored, at least one person will always conclude, "That was fun, but that sort of thing just doesn't seem to work here." The person will go on to explain that there have been creativity workshops in the past that didn't change anyone's behavior. People may feel more creative while they're doing the exercises, but they find it almost impossible to transfer those skills to what they actually do in their jobs. That's because most creativity training is done with what I call *magic trick creativity*: the trainer presents participants with questions or story problems that seem impossible to solve and then, after people struggle with them for several minutes, reveals an answer or trick that shows the participants how they've made a number of false assumptions. "Oh, I get it now," the participants think. "I had automatically assumed that the wrestler, firefighter, welder, and engineer were all men. But if three of the four were actually women, the solution becomes easy," or "I had been thinking that the two people you were talking about were unrelated. But if they're a mother and child, then I see how it all works out." Just as when you watch a YouTube video and discover how a baffling magic trick was performed, learning the secret behind this type of creativity exercise makes an apparently impossible situation easy to understand. The conclusion we're supposed to make in this type of training is that we're uncreative when we let our assumptions get in our way and far more creative when we think outside the box.

That's certainly a valuable lesson to learn, and challenging assumptions is one of the prerequisites to greater innovation. But here's the problem with magic trick creativity: it's not transferable. In other words, learning the solution to one problem doesn't help people the next time they encounter an actual challenge on the job. When we learn how a magician does one trick, we don't necessarily learn how all magic tricks are performed. It's the same with most creativity training. When we do the exercises we're given, we figure out how to solve that particular problem but learn next to nothing about how to solve any other kind of problem. In order for creativity training to be effective, it has to move beyond teaching us to challenge our assumptions and teach us how to change our mind-set and perspective.

In her critically acclaimed book *Mindset: The New Psychology of Success* (2006), Carol Dweck distinguishes two ways in which people look at themselves, their opportunities for success, and their role in the world: with a growth mind-set and with a fixed mind-set. People with a growth mind-set view the world largely through the lens of nurture, not nature. They believe that although they may have been born into a particular social stratum and with a certain set of attributes, they can still progress, improve, and develop. In the minds of these people, all it takes to grow and improve is hard work. Obstacles are not failures but opportunities to learn something new. However, for people with a fixed mind-set, this entire picture is reversed. They believe that intelligence, athleticism, physical attractiveness, and other attributes are a matter of luck and genetics. Some people are just "born smart," while others "just aren't good at math" or learning a foreign language or playing a musical instrument or whatever else they assume is beyond their reach. As a result, they stop trying when they face challenges they don't believe they can solve. They develop an understanding of themselves that locks them into one particular role with specific strengths and weaknesses they don't believe they can change. Their inability to improve in certain areas becomes a self-fulfilling prophecy. As Henry Ford said, "Whether you think you can or think you can't, you're usually right."

Ironically, although higher education is a profession that values new ideas and challenges students to master subjects they don't believe they can master, we tend to favor a fixed mind-set over a growth mind-set in the people we hire and promote. Consider the way in which most faculty members and administrators receive their credentials. They study a broad range of subjects and engage in a wide array of academic activities throughout their schooling until about the second year of their undergraduate work. By that time, we expect people to "discover who they are" and choose a major. Once in their major, they tend to study that subject to the exclusion of everything else. As their work becomes more and more demanding, their extracurricular activities typically become more focused and are eventually reduced to those activities that complement and advance their chosen major. Then, if students are successful at this level, they may continue to graduate school where they become even more focused on a specialty, eventually becoming faculty members by demonstrating they can make a significant, original contribution to a highly specialized field.

The entire system seems designed to create graduates who think of themselves as, say, "seventeenth-century Belgian economic historians" rather than as broadly educated and capable human beings. If you've served on promotion and tenure committees, you've probably heard such comments as, "I can't possibly recognize excellence in the teaching and research of a faculty member who deals with the phylogenetic analysis and taxonomy of asiloid flies. After all, I work with the biodiversity and social evolution of cynipoidea, proctotrupoidea, and platygastroidea. These are two completely different fields." So if your fixed mind-set means that you view yourself as someone who is competent within only a very narrow set of parameters, you're going to feel uncomfortable when the dean asks you to propose new ideas about institutional structure, pedagogical platforms, funding formulas, evaluation strategies, and all the other phenomena that appear to be in a constant state of flux in higher education.

Fortunately, as Dweck reveals, mind-set is not fixed. We can learn to move from a fixed to a growth mind-set, and she describes a number of programs that have been successful in helping people adopt a completely new attitude about their ability to learn and develop. Unfortunately, Dweck (2006) doesn't provide many details about how these programs work besides noting that "over a series of sessions, through activities and discussions, students are taught study skills and shown how to apply the lessons of the growth mind-set to their studying and their schoolwork" (229). That description doesn't provide much help when we want to create a culture of innovation within our own academic units. Certainly we can begin to advocate for improvements in graduate programs so that the college professors of the future have more confidence in themselves as change agents. But a solution of that sort will take many years before it yields tangible benefits and, besides, it begs a rather important question: How could we possibly implement such a sweeping change in graduate education when the very problem we're trying to solve is that academics resist sweeping changes?

A more helpful solution may be found if we combine the lessons appearing in two other books that were published at roughly the same time as Dweck's *Mindset*: Malcolm Gladwell's *Outliers* (2008) and Martin Seligman's *Learned Optimism* (2006). In *Outliers*, Gladwell popularized the research of K. Anders Ericsson, Ralph Krampe, Clemens Tesch-Römer, and others, suggesting that prolonged, consistent work at a task, not innate genius, leads to the greatest amount of success, even in such supposedly "talent-driven" fields as music, sports, and mathematics (see Ericsson, Krampe, and Tesch-Römer, 1993, Ericsson, 1996). In Gladwell's now-famous formulation, if you devote ten thousand hours of intense practice to any pursuit—the rough equivalent of putting in five years' worth of forty-hour workweeks—you can become an expert at practically anything.

That idea complements perfectly a notion that Martin Seligman presents in *Learned Optimism*. Like Dweck, Seligman documented how people's experience is affected greatly by their mind-set or perspective. Rather than dealing with the fixed or growth mind-set, however, Seligman studied the impact of optimism and pessimism. Optimistic people, Seligman concludes, view the frustrations they encounter as temporary setbacks and exceptional situations they can manage if only they try hard enough. They see their successes in the opposite way: these good things were perfectly normal and expected; they were the way the world was supposed to work, and they prove how we can accomplish great things if only we work hard enough. Pessimists had a different outlook. When bad things happened, they tended to view themselves as "born losers." It was failure and frustration that defined the way in which the world worked for pessimists, not their own achievements and happiness.

Like Dweck, Seligman suggests that these mind-sets can be changed— that pessimists can indeed become "learned optimists." But unlike Dweck, he provides a detailed strategy for making a transition in one's mind-set. First, Seligman notes that systematic and regular reflection on the good things that happen to us, rather than fixating on the bad things, gradually shifts our worldview from pessimistic to optimistic. Ending a specific period (such as a day, week, or academic term) by listing five good things that happened during that period makes even pessimistic and clinically depressed people feel better about what will happen during the next such period. Sonja Lyubomirsky carried Seligman's research even further and identified the optimal frequency for a reflective exercise: people tend to exhibit the greatest increase in optimism when they reflect once a week on the good things that happened to them; if they conduct this exercise more often than that, the activity becomes too routine to be meaningful; if they engage in it less often, the activity doesn't demonstrate an accumulating benefit over time (Lyubomirsky, 2008, 92).

Second, Seligman (2006) recommends an approach that he calls the ABC method, which provides a system for reflecting on the assumptions we make when we try to interpret any given situation. Like systematic inventive thinking and formalized lateral thinking, Seligman's ABC method is structured so as to make our unconscious assumptions apparent to us and thus enable us to decide whether these assumptions are really valid. The five steps of Seligman's method are identified with the first five letters of the alphabet:

Adversity	*What is the problem we're facing?* More generally we might ask, What are the facts that we know about the situation? If we adopt the 20/20 lens of our ten analytical lenses (or use de Bono's white hat thinking), what can we say that we know for an absolute fact?
Belief	*What belief system or assumptions are we bringing to the situation?* What strikes us as similar about this situation to something that has occurred in the past? Are those similarities valid, or do they break down at some point? What about the situation resonates with or repels us?
Consequences	*What conclusions result from the belief system or assumptions we brought to this situation?* What are the outcomes not simply in terms of what we think, but also in terms of how we feel about the problem and its possible solution?
Disputation	*If we were to approach the problem by adopting a different belief system or set of assumptions, how might the results change?* Can we reasonably challenge our initial assumptions and conclude that they are not necessary but are simply one of several possibilities?
Energization	*If we then adopt an alternate belief system or set of assumptions, how might we feel differently about the problem?* If the result is that we feel more optimistic or excited about the prospect, how can we channel that energy toward effective action?

Several important conclusions result from the lessons found in *Mindset*, *Outliers*, and *Learned Optimism*. First, groups have mind-sets just as people do. We're all familiar with institutions or units within institutions that embraced change gladly while others were resistant to the very idea of change. But mind-set can change. For this reason, we don't have to give up if we find ourselves working in an environment that seems hidebound, inflexible, and convinced that our current way of doing things is the only possible way of doing things. That's not the nature of academics or administrators; it's simply their current mind-set. Second, creativity and receptivity to change are the result of mind-set. Even people who don't view themselves as particularly innovative can become adaptable and innovative if they devote prolonged, consistent effort to developing these new habits. In higher education, we disprove the maxim that "you can't teach an old dog new tricks" on a daily basis. When a new technology comes along, we may grumble a bit, but soon we become familiar with it or perhaps even excel at it. When the curriculum has to be modified because of the demands of an accrediting agency or state legislature, we initially fume that these new requirements are impossible, but gradually we start to implement them (and sometimes discover that we prefer them). Faculty members at institutions on the quarter system or with a 4–1–4 calendar resist conversion to the semester system just as loudly as do those at schools on the semester system believe it's impossible to change to quarters or adopt a January term, and yet institutions do it all the time, and they become even stronger for the transition.

Third, although it may take a prolonged, consistent effort to effect a radical change in mind-set, some improvements can occur much more rapidly. Seligman (2006) found that clinically depressed and pessimistic patients often began to respond to his optimism exercises within only a few weeks. The same thing can occur within an institution or academic unit. But the complete transformation of a program from rigidly unimaginative to highly innovative will probably require a significant investment of time. Even so, institutions and units usually take their cue from opinion leaders. Once those major opinion leaders begin to demonstrate a new mind-set, others in the area will begin acting differently as a result.

Innovation Killers and Innovation Midwives

The single most important thing academic leaders can do to help their programs move from a fixed, pessimistic, or can't-do mind-set to a growth, optimistic, or can-do mind-set is to identify the innovation killers in their environment and replace them with innovation midwives. An innovation killer is any commonly repeated saying that reinforces the idea that change is impossible, extremely difficult, unwanted, unwarranted, destructive, or .

unreasonable. As you go through the following list of statements, you'll undoubtedly find many that you've heard at your own institution, perhaps even coming from your own mouth:

- We tried that before.
- Has anyone ever done that before?
- We haven't got that kind of time.
- We've already got too much to do.
- Our budget's too limited.
- With the reductions we've had lately, we're just trying to stay afloat.
- That'll never work.
- That's not my job.
- That's not how we do things here.
- It's impossible.
- Maybe next year.
- You may be right, but ...
- The trustees/president/provost/dean would never go for that.
- My mind is already made up.
- I don't think it's all that important.
- It's good enough already.
- If it ain't broke, don't fix it.
- That just sounds crazy.
- You don't know the people I have to deal with.
- If we've got money for that, why don't we ever seem to have enough money for raises?

These sentiments kill innovation because they reinforce the assumption that change is a bad thing. They stifle creativity before it has an opportunity to flourish.

Innovation midwives, by contrast, assist the birth of creative ideas by reinforcing the notion that change is a good thing; in fact, it's the norm. These statements convey a welcoming attitude toward lateral thinking and experimental approaches. Repeated often enough, they can shift the mind-set of an entire academic unit. Here are a few examples of innovation midwives that need to be heard more often at colleges and universities:

- Before we make a final decision, let's review all our options.
- Where can we go for additional information on that?

o You can always change your mind, you know.

o In light of the new information, I've changed my mind.

o Excuse me. I don't think I really understood that.

o I'd like to get your help with an idea I'm working on.

o How could we improve … ?

o What would happen if … ?

o Wouldn't it be fun if … ?

o What might we have missed?

o What would we do if cost were no object?

o Who else will be affected?

o Who else has a suggestion?

o Why do we always do it like that?

o I don't know much about that. What can you tell me?

o What are some of your own ideas on … ?

o How many ways could we … ?

o You know, it's so crazy that it just might work.

o Why don't we try it for a year and see what happens?

o Wow! Thank you! That's a great idea! Let's explore it together.

Innovation midwives underscore the idea that nothing can remain unchanged for very long and that not all good ideas have to come from a single source. They imply that creativity isn't just accepted; it's expected—of everyone. They reward people for coming up with new ideas and, as Linus Pauling said, "The best way to get good ideas is to have lots of ideas" (quoted in Brandt, 1986, 65).

Conclusion

Effective change leadership in higher education does not occur when legislatures, governing boards, or presidents impose a new vision for an institution from the top down. The distributed organizational structure of colleges and universities guarantees that such a process will be acrimonious at best and highly destructive at worse. It will intensify the us-versus-them dynamics that all too often exist between the faculty and administration. Because supervisor-initiated change processes require such a large investment of energy, resources, and political capital, few of them succeed beyond their initial phases. The only creativity they promote is to encourage the faculty and staff to find creative ways of scuttling the process.

A far more effective way of bringing about meaningful change in higher education is for academic leaders to create a widespread culture of innovation in which change is seen as originating from above but generated throughout the institution. In a culture of innovation:

- New ideas are encouraged, recognized, and rewarded, even when they're not practical or implemented. Academic leaders understand that people stop innovating when they believe their suggestions are going to be mocked, ignored, or disparaged.

- As many people as possible are given the freedom to do their work in their own way. Effective change leaders don't micromanage. If they need to set goals, they provide the necessary resources to achieve those goals and allow people to have as much freedom as possible to decide how to achieve them.

- Most decisions don't have to be cleared through a person's supervisor. The constant need to check with one's boss stifles creativity. Even when supervisors insist that they just need to be in the loop on everything that happens in their area, they create a chilling effect that curbs innovation and promotes a fixed mind-set.

- People feel comfortable talking with anyone in the organization (including the upper administration and the governing board) about issues of common concern. Academic leaders understand that although a chain of command may be required for certain approval and evaluation purposes, colleges and universities really have a flat administrative structure. Any member of the system should feel empowered to talk to any other member of the system without repercussions for going over someone's head or violating their sphere of authority.

- People are appreciated for what they do.

- People are appreciated for who they are.

No unit or institution is like every other. Ideas that work in one environment may be impossible somewhere else. Different traditions, values, and personalities mean that each system must be understood on its own terms. For this reason, I devote the next three chapters to examining institutions and programs that implemented successful change processes for different reasons and in different ways, thus coming to realize just how diverse change leadership in higher education actually is.

REFERENCES

Brandt, S. C. (1986). *Entrepreneuring in established companies: Managing toward the year 2000.* Homewood, IL: Dow Jones-Irwin.

De Bono, E. (2008). *Creativity workout: 62 exercises to unlock your most creative ideas.* Berkeley, CA: Ulysses Press.

Dweck, C. S. (2006). *Mindset: The new psychology of success.* New York, NY: Random House.

Ericsson, K. A. (Ed.). (1996). *The road to excellence: The acquisition of expert performance in the arts and sciences, sports, and games.* Mahwah, NJ: Erlbaum.

Ericsson, K. A., Krampe, R. T., & Tesch-Romer, C. (1993). The role of deliberate practices in the acquisition of expert performance. *Psychological Review, 100*(3), 363–406.

Gladwell, M. (2008). *Outliers: The story of success.* New York, NY: Little, Brown.

Lyubomirsky, S. (2008). *The how of happiness: A scientific approach to getting the life you want.* New York, NY: Penguin.

Michalko, M. (2006). *Thinkertoys: A handbook of creative-thinking techniques.* Berkeley, CA: Ten Speed.

Miller, B. C. (2012). *Quick brainstorming activities for busy managers: 50 exercises to spark your team's creativity and get results fast.* New York, NY: AMACOM.

Mumaw, S., & Oldfield, W. L. (2006). *Caffeine for the creative mind: 250 exercises to wake up your brain.* Cincinnati, OH: HOW Books.

Raviv, D. (2011). *Everyone loves speed bumps, don't you? A guide to innovative thinking.* Lexington, KY: Townsend Union.

Runco, M. A. (2007). *Creativity: Theories and themes; research, development, and practice.* San Diego, CA: Elsevier/Academic.

Sawyer, K. (2013). *Zig zag: The surprising path to greater creativity.* San Francisco, CA: Jossey-Bass.

Seligman, M.E.P. (2006). *Learned optimism: How to change your mind and your life.* New York, NY: Vintage Books.

RESOURCES

Brown, T. (2009). *Change by design: How design thinking transforms organizations and inspires innovation.* New York, NY: Harper Business.

Kelly, R. (2013). Encouraging a growth mind-set to help lead change. *Academic Leader, 39*(8), 1, 6.

Spitzer, R. J. (2000). *The spirit of leadership: Optimizing creativity and change in organizations.* Provo, UT: Executive Excellence Publications.

Thompson, L. L. (2013). *Creative conspiracy: The new rules of breakthrough collaboration.* Boston, MA: Harvard Business Review Press.

7

LEADING REACTIVE CHANGE

SO FAR IN OUR examination of change leadership in higher education, we've seen a number of reasons that many change processes fail—or at least aren't as successful as they were expected to be—at colleges and universities: They are based on management models that don't suit the environment of higher education, fail to develop an adequate needs case, depend on methods like strategic planning that don't work very well in an academic environment, and don't pay enough attention to creating a culture that embraces rather than resists change.

Over this and the next two chapters, we will explore one additional flaw found in many academic change processes: the assumption (often unconscious) that all change is alike. You see this assumption in the way institutions describe change in their strategic plans: "Here's where we are right now. Here's where we want to be five, ten, or twenty years from now. And the pathway between those two points is what this plan will outline." But actual change processes are rarely that simple. If we want to be effective change leaders in higher education, we have to develop a clearer understanding of the different types of change that can occur at colleges and universities and the best practices to use in dealing with each type.

Fighting Icebergs with ICE

In chapter 1, I discussed the Krüger model of change, also known as the iceberg model because it suggests that the dangers on which most change processes run aground lie hidden below the surface. Although we're usually aware of the obvious factors involved in change—like expense, time, and quality—we tend to overlook more intangible factors like power relationships, the ego investment certain stakeholders have in the status quo, and the distrust that may exist between labor and management. I return to the Krüger iceberg now that we're a bit further in this examination of change in higher education because we finally have some idea of how to deal with all those unseen factors lying just below the surface.

In creating the culture of innovation, we have three resources available to us, easily remembered by their acronym ICE: innovation, creativity, and entrepreneurship.

1. *Innovation.* In higher education, truly transformative change is rarely imposed from above by a single innovative individual. Rather, this change grows out of a broadly innovative environment. The more innovative a system becomes through the use of scenario planning, the strategic compass, and innovation midwives, the more dramatic the results will be.

2. *Creativity.* Like people, systems can learn how to become more creative over time. Their default perspective can change—the lesson of *Mindset* (Dweck, 2006)—by means of an ongoing, consistent effort—the lesson of *Outliers* (Gladwell, 2008). Although the ultimate goal is long-term transformation, some of the benefits resulting from this effort will emerge rather quickly—the lesson of *Learned Optimism* (Seligman, 2006). In short, academic change leaders can be intentional and systematic about making their systems more creative. They don't have to wait Gladwell's full ten thousand hours to start seeing a difference.

3. *Entrepreneurship.* When we replace innovation killers with innovation midwives, we signal that we're working in an environment where new ideas are embraced and welcomed rather than shot down or disparaged. We produce a culture where people are expected to be entrepreneurial and to take calculated risks, fully aware that not every risk will pay off. We know from experience that most truly radical ideas won't work, but the ones that do can produce major benefits for years to come. An entrepreneurial system is therefore not just one in which successful gambles are celebrated, but also one in which every calculated risk is celebrated. As Bob Cipriano, the author of *Facilitating a Collegial Department in Higher Education* (2011), is fond of saying, "**What gets rewarded gets repeated.**" Effective change leaders reward risk takers because they know they're committed to finding solutions that haven't already been tried and to being distinctive rather than simply being bigger.

Taking advantage of these three ICE resources helps avoid the lurking dangers that the Krüger model warns about. We encourage people not to destroy the status quo but to build on it, not to see administrators and faculty members as competitors but as colleagues in a joint enterprise, and not to fear being wrong for making a suggestion that didn't work but to keep trying out new ideas until together we get it right.

Types of Change

The way in which ICE initiatives help overcome institution icebergs depends to a great extent on the type of change that's being pursued. We saw in chapter 3 that the distributed organizational structure of colleges and universities means that most stakeholders regard a needs case for change as far more compelling than alternative justifications such as comparative advantages, net benefits, and so on. But not all needs are alike. Here are three different ways in which institutions may discover that they need to change:

1. *Changes that are forced on them.* Certain changes are utterly beyond an institution's control. Economic necessities, a disaster, a vote by the legislature or governing board, or some other driver of change may compel a response. In certain cases, the institution may have some flexibility in precisely how they decide to respond, but the decision about whether to change (and sometimes even the timetable for the change) is out of the institution's hands. I call this type of change *reactive change.*

2. *Changes that would eventually be forced on them.* Other changes are needed because the school needs to alter its course in order to avoid a crisis. In this situation, although it may appear that the institution has many more options than it would have if confronting a reactive change, there may still be many constraints. The college or university has to identify precisely what is causing the looming threat, map a course that avoids it (more iceberg imagery again), and shift direction on a new, safer course. This type of change can be called *proactive change.*

3. *Changes that are needed because of internal rather than external factors.* Still other changes are implemented not because a present or future obstacle requires the institution to make the change, but because internal factors have made it more difficult for the school to fulfill its mission in the best or most efficient way. These changes are often the most difficult to lead because there will be a tendency to justify them in terms of comparative advantages ("Oh, but we'd just be so much better off if we did this") or net benefits ("Sure we can keep doing exactly what we've been doing, but imagine how much better things could be

if we bit the bullet now and tried going in a new direction"). But we know that those are the very types of argument that are the hardest to sell to stakeholders in higher education. Changes caused by internal factors can be just as transformative as reactive or proactive change, but it's the ability to distinguish between what is needed because of internal forces as opposed to what is being compelled by outside forces. We'll call this type of change *interactive change*.

For more on the different types of change that colleges and universities can experience, see Kezar (2014).

Is Reacting Actually Leading?

How do we best demonstrate academic leadership when we're confronted with a change we have little or no control over? At first glance, we might think that simply reacting to a situation doesn't offer any leadership opportunities at all. What initially seems to be involved is a management challenge: How can we control the situation so as to result in the most acceptable and painless outcome? But as you already know if you've ever been in one of these situations, even problems that are forced on us call for leadership.

Think for a moment about a genuine crisis. If you suddenly receive word that a shooter is on campus, you have to demonstrate leadership by putting the campus on lockdown, notifying the authorities, helping people shelter in place, and adhering to the policies of your institution's emergency plan. You may be reacting to something that's beyond your control, but you're still leading because you've acted in a way that deals with the threat effectively. You've placed the good of the entire institution over your own individual interests.

Other types of reactive change are similar. You may be responding to external forces because you have to, but if you're an effective leader, you're making your response in a timely manner and in a way that's effective, creative, and appropriate. As case studies in how reactive change can truly be transformative, we examine two small institutions in North Carolina—Elon College and High Point College—that faced threats to their very existence and emerged from the challenge as universities and as models of best practices in reactive change leadership.

The Transformation from Elon College to Elon University

The remarkable story of how Elon College moved from being a struggling, largely local school to becoming a highly respected national liberal arts university has become one of the best-known cases of institutional rein-vention ever to occur in American higher education. This case is presented in great detail in George Keller's book-length analysis, *Transforming a College* (2004), and in more condensed form in Ellington (2012), Brown (2012), and Kuh (2005). It's easy to draw the wrong conclusions from Elon's transformation. It can be tempting to see this case as a valida-tion of the effectiveness of strategic planning—not surprising, since the George Keller who wrote *Transforming a College* is the same George Keller whose *Academic Strategy* (1983) had been instrumental, as we saw in chapter 5, in introducing much of higher education to the concept of strategic planning—and the visionary leadership of a single individ-ual, Elon's longstanding president, Leo Lambert. But is that an accurate assessment of what happened? Let's start at the beginning.

Elon College in North Carolina was founded in 1889 by a denomina-tion that would later become part of the United Church of Christ. For many years, it primarily served local students, many of whom required remediation before they could be successful at college-level work. Elon survived difficult financial challenges during World War II by convinc-ing the US Army to train pilots there. The GI Bill in the 1950s permitted the school to undergo a small period of growth. Nevertheless, as late as the early 1970s,

> Elon College was scarcely known outside central North Carolina. Its
> dozen buildings beside the town's railroad tracks struck visitors as
> undistinguished, with a parking lot smack in the center of the campus.
> The students mostly came from working-class families in the nearby
> mill town of Burlington, local farming families, and religious fami-
> lies from nearby small towns. The academic program was solid but
> without distinction. (Keller, 2004, 6)

Like many other tuition-driven colleges with very small endowments, Elon probably could have struggled along for a few decades longer if it weren't for a crisis that cast its very existence in doubt. To serve the increased demand for higher education, North Carolina rapidly expanded its community college system. In 1971 Alamance Community College began building an attractive new campus not far from Elon. Tuition at Alamance was a mere fraction of Elon's, and it was becoming increasingly difficult to make the case to the sort of students who had traditionally enrolled at Elon that the greater expense of attending a private college was worth it. Moreover, there was increasing competition for good stu-dents from Duke, North Carolina State, and the University of North Carolina, all located only about fifty miles away in the Research Triangle.

Students who were interested in attending a small private college tended to prefer Guilford, Catawba, or Davidson, which had stronger academic reputations than Elon. Finally, analysis of demographic data suggested that the number of traditional college-aged students—Elon's most important market—was about to enter a period of sharp decline. With all these factors coming together in a perfect storm of external pressures, change at Elon was no longer an option; it was a matter of survival.

Admittedly, what happened next in Elon's transformation followed the Kotter change model perfectly. The college's president at the time, J. Fred Young, used the enrollment threat to establish a sense of urgency and then created a guiding coalition consisting of certain trustees, the vice president for student and academic affairs, and a visionary landscape architect. But it was at this point that Elon's process began to deviate from traditional change management models and to incorporate the ICE resources of innovation, creativity, and entrepreneurship. Although the term wasn't explicitly used, what the guiding coalition engaged in can best be described as scenario planning. When it examined the economic drivers of change that were threatening the school, the worst-case scenario it identified was that a shrinking population of traditional-aged college students would increasingly shift from enrolling at relatively expensive schools like Elon to enrolling at less expensive schools like Alamance Community College or one of the state's public universities. The problem was that this worst-case scenario was also identical to what the college would be facing in its most-likely-case scenario. Short-term fixes wouldn't be enough. What was needed was an approach that was more innovative, creative, and entrepreneurial.

The process used to determine what approach might work was essentially the setting of a strategic compass. As a way of making its curriculum more distinctive, Elon switched from the standard three-credit course used by almost every other college or university to a large number of four-credit courses, with the added hour devoted to active and experiential learning.

The school discovered that its success with this approach was causing the student body to skew toward an atypical Myers-Briggs profile. While the largest groups in American society are those who fall into the ISFJ (Introverted, Sensing, Feeling, Judging) and INTJ (Introverted, iNtuitive, Thinking, Judging) profiles, Elon's student body tended to cluster around two less common profiles: ENFP (Extraverted, iNtuitive, Feeling, Perceiving) and ESTJ (Extraverted, Sensing, Thinking, Judging) profiles. These were the very sorts of students who are most likely to be attracted to a highly experiential curriculum. Recall that in chapter 5, we saw four questions guide an institution toward setting a strategic compass:

1. What do we do best?
2. What do our strengths tell us about who we really are?
3. What does this identity tell us about where we should direct our resources?
4. How do we develop a culture of innovation that extends but doesn't alter this identity?

While no one at Elon may have thought of their process in exactly this way, the next phase of Elon's transformation essentially consisted of answering these four questions. What the institution did best was to take students who had strong potential but often didn't have an academic record suitable for admission to a highly selective school and find ways of tapping into that potential through experiential learning. That strength meant that Elon was no longer well positioned as a primarily local school that served students in need of remediation. It had a new national and even international potential market that it could tap into and serve.

What that identity told Elon about how it should direct its resources was that it should make greater efforts to market the school to students with a Myers-Briggs profile of ENFP and ESTJ students (since the rates of success and satisfaction of those students were so high at Elon), to double-down on the role that hands-on, group learning played in the curriculum, and to beautify the campus so as to make it more attractive to its new national and international market. It reduced tuition discounting and made a greater investment in the school's physical plant. Study-abroad and internship opportunities were increased. And a new identity for Elon began to emerge: a school for students who were not content merely to think great thoughts but who also felt compelled to do great deeds. With that new identity, the fourth component of a strategic compass—creating a culture of innovation—also fell into place. Elon's transformation wasn't the vision of just one person, but a full range of innovations proposed by a highly creative culture. At the presidential level, Fred Young was succeeded by Leo Lambert, who introduced new ideas of his own, and the school's faculty felt empowered to add further innovations as the process continued:

> When Dr. Julianne Maher, the newly selected vice president for academic affairs, arrived at North Carolina's Elon College in the fall of 1995, she inquired about the rivalries and policy disagreements on campus to prepare herself for her first year. To her astonishment,

she was told repeatedly that there were none....."There are almost no petty feuds or intrigues here. Most faculty care for the students and teach imaginatively; they support each other and actually like the administration. And the faculty have renovated their own general education program. The administrators, too, are a talented, collaborating team." (Keller, 2004, 1)

There are several key phrases in this description. First, notice how collegial and cooperative the environment at Elon became. Although creating an academic culture of innovation cannot guarantee positive changes in interpersonal relations, this surprising level of faculty-administrative harmony is not uncommon at institutions that empower the faculty and staff and work systematically to embrace ICE resources across campus. (We'll see another example of a school where innovation and a positive institutional spirit go hand-in-hand in chapter 9.) Second, the faculty is described as teaching imaginatively and to have renovated their own general education program. The transformation of Elon College to Elon University was not the result of what one office or even one guiding coalition decided. It involved the full range of the school's stakeholders, a situation that becomes possible only when everyone feels invested in the creative process and is aware that their contributions are valued.

For all of these reasons, the transformation of Elon College into Elon University shouldn't be seen as a case study in effective strategic planning but rather as an example of how substantive change becomes possible when leaders make creating a culture of innovation a priority. A major goal at the school became first establishing and then sustaining an operating environment that expected, valued, and embraced change:

> New instructors begin with a week-long orientation to Elon and then continue to attend monthly orientation sessions. Each is assigned a senior faculty mentor to assist with his or her new life at Elon and to sharpen teaching skills. Deans, other academics, and administrators invite the novices to lunch. Monies have been set aside for summertime travel and research by new faculty members, and Lambert has raised funds for something he calls "emerging scholar professorships" for those who appear to have exceptional promise in their pretenure years. (Keller, 2004, 60)

This investment in socializing new members to the culture and encouraging them to adopt new techniques in their teaching and research pays off in a faculty that's less resistant to change and more creative, resilient, and innovative in its problem solving.

None of this is to suggest, of course, that the change process at Elon never met with resistance, even strong resistance, at times. Leading change by means of scenario planning, a strategic compass, and the development of a culture of innovation doesn't preclude debate and disagreement. But it does help channel that debate and disagreement into positive action instead of aimless grumbling. To think of it another way, most traditional strategic planning processes generate a lot of heat; the alternatives that we're considering are more likely to generate light. In fact, that was precisely what occurred at Elon. Opposing voices weren't dismissed as mere obstacles, and administrators at the institution didn't simply ignore them and forge ahead. Rather, differing views were valued as useful sources of information about how this profound change was being viewed by various groups of stakeholders. They helped the change leaders understand how the advantages of the college's transformation could better be explained to all constituents and where modifications were necessary in the overall plan.

The conclusions to be drawn from Elon's change process are not that a top-down strategic planning effort is a particularly effective way to bring about substantive change at a college or university. To the contrary, this case study reveals that broad-based participation in the activity of change, scenario planning, and the creation of a new organizational culture can yield impressive results even if the initial cause of the process is a looming threat. Some people assume that problems can be solved only through authoritarian leadership. They believe that universities are governed best when a strong hand is at the tiller, steering the institution on a set course despite any objections and cries of outrage that might occur. We might call this approach the David Farragut model of leadership, after the Civil War admiral's cry: "Damn the torpedoes! Full speed ahead!" But the fact of the matter is that the David Farragut model of leadership is far more likely to fail than to succeed. In his revealing analysis of why so many university presidents fail, Stephen Trachtenberg (2013) presents numerous case studies of leaders whose strong, top-down imposition of change collided sharply with the culture, traditions, and expectations of their colleges and universities. An example is the case of the president who

> did not foster open dialogue among various constituencies, nor did he seek input from stakeholders about changes at [the school]. He was known to call faculty members into his office and demand that they publicly support his ideas, insinuating that they would be subject to disciplinary action if they did not.... "Rather than using proven university processes to move faculty, he brought his political skills to

bear to get a desired result. That was a very huge clash." In short, he did not respect preexisting institutional processes and acted as if he had unilateral authority. (Julie Longmire in Trachtenberg, 2013, 41–42)

In fact, of the six reasons that Trachtenberg cites for failed university leadership, two are directly related to the problems caused by this style of leadership: poor interpersonal skills, including failure to listen, arrogance, and a preoccupation with one's own importance; and challenges in adapting to the culture of higher education itself or the culture of a specific institution. We'll see further evidence of how ineffective the David Farragut model of leadership is in higher education when we consider the myth of visionary leadership and the telling-is-leading fallacy in the next chapter.

The Transformation from High Point College to High Point University

Elon is far from being the only school where the right process brought about a positive result even though that change occurred in reaction to an external threat. High Point College, also located in North Carolina, faced many of the same challenges as Elon. It too was a private school that served a largely local population and lacked a reputation for distinction. But in many ways High Point's problems were even more severe than Elon's. Founded in 1924, it faced bankruptcy only a decade later. While it managed to survive that first crisis, economic and enrollment challenges persisted for much of its history. In May 1989, under president Jacob C. Martinson, a task force of 142 members was charged with developing a blueprint for the college's future. The goal of the task force was not merely to keep the school open, but to accomplish a more ambitious goal: making High Point a leader in its service area. The report that was released the following January made four major recommendations:

1. The college should participate more actively in international programs and seek additional exchanges of students with colleges abroad.

2. The college should build more attractive residence halls.

3. The college should begin laying the groundwork that would give it university status.

4. The college should take full advantage of its faith-based heritage by focusing on ethical issues across the curriculum.

It's worth noticing that Elon also adopted the first three of these four strategies. But while Elon's Christian origins and emphasis on service also meant that its curriculum placed more emphasis on values than did most public institutions, High Point's goal was more ambitious. The school began to use the theme of principled leadership extensively in its recruitment materials and increasingly to tie the curriculum to this theme. In terms of the strategic compass, High Point's answer to the question, "What do we do best?" was, "We incorporate high moral values into everything we do." That answer gave the college a compelling response to anyone who asked why tuition at High Point was higher than at a community college or state university. "We provide something you can't get there," the school was saying. "We teach students not only how to make a living but also how to lead a life worth living."

The next major step in the school's transformation came in 2005 with the arrival of its seventh president, Nido R. Qubein. Qubein had an unusual background for a college president. Rather than rising through the ranks as a college professor, dean, or provost, he was a business leader and philanthropist. That unusual preparation for the president's role gave him a different perspective. He proposed new ways of developing a culture of innovation, creativity, and entrepreneurship that extended but didn't alter this identity. For instance, the college had already discovered that it could justify its tuition in terms of providing an experience students couldn't get elsewhere. But what would happen if this principle were carried even further? Working with faculty and other administrators—most important, his creative vice president of communications, Roger D. Clodfelter—Qubein set out to build an academic environment that included (see Bartlett, 2008):

o An ice cream truck that distributes free snacks to anyone at the school

o Frequent live music in the dining hall

o Cards or personal phone calls to each student from the president on his or her birthday

o Impressive fountains at various locations on campus

o Free T-shirts and food for students at many athletic events

o Free bingo nights with prizes like Xboxes, iPads, and gift cards

In addition, High Point began a campuswide concierge that offers students:

o Complimentary Kindles, iPads, TI-89 calculators, and GPS units

○ A scheduling service for tutoring, research appointments in the library, and restaurant reservations
○ A library book drop-off point
○ Dry cleaning service
○ Tickets to cultural events

The result was an educational environment that was absolutely unlike anywhere else. Residents halls were more luxurious. Services were more comprehensive. The campus atmosphere was more exciting. With these innovations in place, High Point's enrollment began to grow. Like Elon, it changed its status from college to university and expanded its academic programs. Many of the new degrees (in such areas as entrepreneurship, interactive gaming, commerce, pharmacy, physical therapy, and physician assistantship) were in direct response to student demand. With additional tuition income now available, High Point continued to invest in improving the students' experience. Many more members of the faculty and staff were hired. The campus was beautified and expanded. And High Point rose significantly in the US News & World Report annual rankings.

Since so many of these changes followed Qubein's arrival in 2005, it's easy to interpret High Point's success as the product of strategic planning and visionary leadership. But as in Elon's case, the university's transformation actually spanned two presidencies and involved the leadership of more than just the person at the top of the org chart. As we teach students, correlation does not guarantee causality, and something that appears to be a cause may actually be an effect of something else.

> Creative leaders often do produce cultures of innovation. But it is also the case that cultures of innovation often attract creative leaders.

What happened at High Point in 2005 and 2006 didn't start in 2005 and 2006. Nor did it result from a traditional strategic planning process, superficial SWOT (strengths, weaknesses, opportunities, and threats) analysis, or adoption of a typical change model. It resulted from an institutional culture that was willing to ask what it did best, what those strengths indicated about what the institution really was, what that identity suggested about how resources should be allocated, and how the existing culture could be extended without losing its fundamental identity. The clues to what happened at High Point were visible as early as 1989 when the first task force was appointed. Its title, the National Commission on the Future of High

Point College, demonstrates that even then, the school was thinking of its stakeholders in terms of their role within an open system. The National Commission included representatives "selected from business, government, the professions, education, college alumni, students, faculty and friends, and the United Methodist Church" (library .highpoint.edu/archives/hi-po/1980_90/1989-hi-po-SpringSemester.pdf). While many schools shy away from large advisory groups because they can take so long to reach consensus, High Point's task force proved to be an exception. Receiving its charge in May, the group delivered its recommendations the following January and launched the change process that resulted in the unique environment that is High Point University today.

The Lessons to Be Learned

We learn several important lessons from the change processes that occurred at Elon University and High Point University. The first is that even when the need to change is imposed by external forces, we can still control a great deal in terms of what we change and how that change occurs. In the cases of these two universities, change was a matter of survival. The pool of prospective students was shrinking. Competition was increasing from rival institutions that could afford to charge lower tuition. And aging physical plants at both schools challenged the budget through mounting deferred maintenance and the need to replace aging facilities. If we were to follow a traditional change model, we'd probably resort to a strategy something like the following.

1. We'd almost certainly start by supplementing the population of traditional-aged students, which is decreasing, with new programs for nontraditional students. We'd invest heavily in marketing these programs and reaching out to international students, inmates of state and federal prisons, retirees, and similar untapped markets. In short, we'd change from being the type of college we were (a model that didn't seem to be working) and try to be a more general provider of postsecondary education to broad markets.

2. Since the cost of tuition is a factor that seems to be dissuading students from enrolling, we'd next either reduce tuition across the board or substantially increase the amount of certain scholarships through aggressive tuition discounting. In this way, we would compete more effectively with state-supported institutions and be able to argue that although the sticker price of our tuition is high, almost no one actually pays the full published amount.

3. To reduce expenditures further, we'd explore alternatives to maintenance and construction by minimizing our reliance on a physical campus. We'd provide as many programs as possible off-site and through distance learning. We'd offer adult students credit for life experience. We'd maximize the amount of credit students could transfer in from Advanced Placement courses and credit by examination. We'd eliminate all programs that require large labs, studios, or specialized instruction space.

Does any of that sound familiar? If you examine the websites of small private colleges throughout the United States, you'll find that these three strategies are precisely what many of them have pursued. Traditional change models and strategic planning processes often lead institutions to address threats with a full-frontal attack: if costs are too high, lower them; if students are too few, find more of them; if maintaining a campus is too expensive, go virtual. But the case studies of Elon and High Point illustrate that even in a situation so bad that it threatens a school's very existence, the use of innovation, creativity, and entrepreneurship can lead to inspired solutions. Effective change leaders don't just point to a destination and say, "Let's go there!" They work on shaping the culture so that it becomes an engine for producing better ideas.

The second lesson is that the approaches suggested by full use of ICE resources are often counterintuitive, even contrarian, in nature:

○ In order to attract more high-ability students, many schools expand their honors programs. Elon actually made its honors program smaller, thus increasing its prestige among those who were accepted and causing prospective students to compete for admission.

○ Some faith-based colleges distance themselves from their heritage so that they might be more attractive to students from diverse backgrounds. But High Point strongly recommitted to its heritage, placing renewed emphasis on the school's values-based curriculum as a way of distinguishing itself in the marketplace.

○ Rather than lowering tuition and increasing financial aid in order to make the schools more affordable, both Elon and High Point held the line on tuition and made their scholarships more competitive. What they did right was not simply to think, "If we charge more, people will believe they're getting more," but to invest their extra income from high tuition in noticeable improvements to the students' experience.

The point isn't simply to do the opposite of whatever the received wisdom happens to be. Rather it's to use techniques like those considered in the previous chapter to develop a wider range of possible solutions. When you realize, even in a crisis, that you have multiple options, you understand that you don't have to be limited by received wisdom. Instead, you can create new received wisdom for other schools to imitate.

The third lesson from these case studies is that tracking metrics and assessing the assessable aren't, despite the claims of legislatures and governing boards, the only (or even an effective) way of bringing about transformation. At the time Elon and High Point began their transformations, neither school was in a financial position to afford the type of data-driven strategic planning process outlined in books like Michael Middaugh's *Planning and Assessment in Higher Education: Demonstrating Institutional Effectiveness* (2010) or Richard Morrill's *Strategic Leadership: Integrating Strategy and Leadership in Colleges and Universities* (2007). Rather than tracking data that may or may not have helped them in deciding what course to take, the cultures of innovation at these schools recognized good ideas when they saw them and implemented them. That doesn't mean there weren't setbacks and opposition along the way. But the process was overwhelmingly supported because people could see that an investment was being made in doing something, not in documenting that they were doing something. Metrics used to note progress, when they were considered at all, were relatively simple: it didn't take an enormous staff to determine whether enrollment and graduation rates were increasing and deficits, student attrition, and deferred maintenance were decreasing. The most important data that were used were ones that any layperson could understand.

Finally, change leaders didn't allow these processes to atrophy in the way they do at so many universities. Ironically for a process that claims to be devoted to change, many university-level change processes are surprisingly change resistant. Once they are set in motion by the governing board and CEO, they often become quite rigid ("We can't do that. It may be a good idea, but it's not part of the plan."), with the result that they break rather than bend. Soon a new president or chancellor arrives, starts the strategic planning process all over again, and substitutes a new inflexible plan for the old inflexible plan. None of that happened at Elon and High Point. Leo Lambert built on what Fred Young had begun, and Nido Qubein extended what Jacob Martinson had initiated. The entire process was natural, evolutionary, and organic. By relying on the institutions' full range of stakeholders, ideas that may have withered elsewhere were given a chance to grow. It was this organic culture of innovation that kept these change processes from devolving into crisis management or a bunker mentality. Even when faced with severe threats, these schools trusted creativity enough to embrace creative solutions.

Levels of Change

These two case studies in reactive change offer a framework that we can use when we turn to proactive and interactive change in the next two chapters. Seeing how Elon and High Point brought about their transformations, we might say that in addition to changing an institution's culture, there are five levels of institutional change that are particularly common in higher education:

1. *Changes in direction.* Overall changes in direction are the most challenging levels at which to conduct effective change at a college or university. These changes typically involve a shift in overall mission, usually because the current mission is no longer needed. In order to produce a transformation this extensive, it's not enough for administrators to adopt a new management technique or try out a new leadership style. Changes in direction require widespread shifts in attitude throughout the entire organization. For this reason, academic leaders who are committed to changing the direction of an institution must become invested in the process for the long term. They're unlikely to see the fruits of their labor for at least five years. At times, changes in direction may not be completed during any one leader's tenure in his or her position. When St. Leo College moved from being a small Benedictine school in 1973 to offering degree programs on military bases around the world, it fundamentally changed direction, eventually growing to become St. Leo University, which now has multiple centers, an extensive virtual campus, and a highly developed online program.

2. *Changes in personnel.* While personnel at colleges and universities are always in flux—with some people departing or retiring each year just as others arrive—the changes in personnel that truly transform an institution go far deeper than that. They reflect Jim Collins's (2001) oft-cited maxim that the great leaders he studied began by getting "the right people on the bus, the wrong people off the bus, and the right people in the right seats—and *then* they figured out where to drive it" (13). In other words, Collins argued that changes in personnel should precede other levels of change. In higher education, we're familiar with this approach when a new president or chancellor replaces all of the vice presidents and deans shortly after his or her arrival. This approach is sometimes effective, sometimes not, but it is always traumatic for the people being replaced and those who fear they may be next.

3. *Changes in tactics.* Tactical changes occur when an institution retains its existing mission but alters the way in which it fulfills that mission. For example, Brenau University in Georgia is a single-sex institution that, like other women's colleges, found that its traditional residential program was increasingly operating at a deficit. It began subsidizing its on-campus offerings with a more profitable online program. The distance learning initiative was proving so successful, in fact, that the school considered phasing out the residential women's college. But a detailed analysis of the student body revealed that a significant proportion of those taking online courses were women who were attracted to the school specifically because it was a women's college. As a result, Brenau recommitted to its mission but altered its tactics by exploring new ways of promoting women's education through a variety of delivery systems (Carlson, 2014).

4. *Changes in structure.* Structural changes are usually tied to significant increases or decreases in enrollment, a change in direction or personnel, or the desire to serve a new constituency group. Examples of changes in structure include the reorganization of a college consisting of schools or departments into a university consisting of colleges or faculties or the conversion of a single-campus institution into a multicampus entity, serving several states or regions. St. Leo's change in direction also required a change in structure, but not all such changes are so extensive. For example, when the John H. Lounsbury School of Education at Georgia College (now Georgia College and State University) merged with the School of Liberal Arts and Sciences in 1977 to become the College of Arts and Sciences, it was engaging in a change of structure designed to provide greater efficiency. Similarly, when those two units split again in 2009—creating a College of Education and a College of Arts and Sciences—that structural change was intended to provide a more focused academic structure for the school's growing student population.

5. *Changes in procedures.* Procedural changes, while certainly important and potentially beneficial to institutions, tend to be far less dramatic than the other levels of change we considered. Changes in procedure include such actions as moving items that formerly required a specific vote by a committee or governing board to a consent agenda, adding or eliminating levels of approval to a tenure process, and requiring that an institution notify other schools in its system that it is considering creating or deleting certain academic programs. Although a change in procedure might ultimately cause an institution to consider another level of change, it rarely, if ever, results in institutional transformation on its own.

If we consider what occurred at Elon and High Point in light of these five additional levels of changes, we learn something important about the nature of transformational change leadership in higher education: you don't need to change the mission and direction of an institution entirely in order to produce transformational change. Moreover, despite the popularity of Jim Collins's observation that effective leaders start by "getting the right people on the bus and the wrong people off the bus," wholesale changes in personnel are not a prerequisite—or even particularly desirable—for substantive change in higher education.

Colleges and universities remain highly fluid environments. New classes of students come and go, faculty members and administrators seek new opportunities, and members of advisory and governing boards are frequently subject to term limits. Since the organic change that emerges from a culture of innovation requires an extended investment over time, those for whom the new direction, tactics, structure, or procedure don't resonate will choose for themselves to seek out more congenial environments. As a result, artificial changes in personnel often create more short-term damage than long-term benefits. At Elon and High Point, new presidents or provosts didn't start "rearranging the furniture" immediately after they arrived in an effort to "shake things up" or because they wanted to be seen doing *something*. Rather they invested their time and energy in developing the culture of innovation that had begun under their predecessors. They made changes in personnel not to clean house or because they felt a need to have their own teams in place but as part of an effort to complement and expand their skill sets, reinforce the new type of organizational culture that was emerging, and preserve momentum. They made changes in tactics not because they believed that strategic planning was valuable in and of itself but because a new culture needs new tactics to address its new opportunities and challenges. Put another way, these changes in structure flowed from other changes; it didn't drive them. For example, the colleges didn't become universities as a way of forcing a change in culture; they elected to change their status from college to university in order to reflect a change in culture that had already occurred.

What we learn from these cases is that traditional strategic planning often gets the cart before the horse. It not only quantifies the quantifiable and assesses the assessable, but it also changes the most easily changeable. It gets sidetracked by a desire to implement new structures and procedures, add or eliminate vice presidential divisions, modify standards for tenure and promotion, and establish new centers or institutes—and it does so for all the wrong reasons. The instigators of these changes assume that innovation, much of it painful and costly for the institution but ultimately superficial in terms of any lasting impact, will bring about the changes in culture they're hoping for. But that's a dangerous assumption. Too many change processes stall after the first few modifications to the organization chart. They fail because they start in the wrong place: by trying to change the organization without first trying to change the organizational culture. (For numerous examples of where this failure has occurred, see Trachtenberg, 2013.)

Conclusion

Received wisdom tells us that reactive change should be the least innovative change a college or university can have. After all, when everything is collapsing all around you, your temptation is simply to run for your life. But the case studies in this chapter demonstrate that it is indeed possible to apply the principles of innovation, creativity, and entrepreneurship, even in situations of reactive change, if change leaders understand that their most important goal must be to develop a culture of innovation, not to focus solely on changes in direction, personnel, tactics, structure, and procedures. Inexperienced change leaders often become fixated on these changes because they seem so much easier than changing an entire culture. Structural or procedural changes can be made with the stroke of a pen. Cultural changes require a far greater investment of time and energy, but the evidence proves they are possible even when an institution is forced to change due to circumstances beyond its control.

REFERENCES

Bartlett, T. (2008, July 4). Club ed: This university is at your service. *Chronicle of Higher Education*, A1.
Brown, A. W. (2012). *Cautionary tales: Strategy lessons from struggling colleges.* Herndon, VA: Stylus.
Carlson, S. (2014, February 7). Accounting for success. *Chronicle of Higher Education*, A1. Retrieved from chronicle.com/article/Accounting-for-Success /144351/
Cipriano, R. E. (2011). *Facilitating a collegial department in higher education: Strategies for success.* San Francisco, CA: Jossey-Bass.
Collins, J. C. (2001). *Good to great: Why some companies make the leap—and others don't.* New York, NY: HarperBusiness.
Dweck, C. S. (2006). *Mindset: The new psychology of success.* New York, NY: Random House.

Ellington, L. (2012). Select learning organizations? *International Journal of Adult Vocational Education and Technology, 3*(2), 1–9.

Gladwell, M. (2008). *Outliers: The story of success*. New York, NY: Little, Brown.

Keller, G. (1983). *Academic strategy: The management revolution in American higher education*. Baltimore, MD: Johns Hopkins University Press.

Keller, G. (2004). *Transforming a college: The story of a little-known college's strategic climb to national distinction*. Baltimore, MD: Johns Hopkins University Press.

Kezar, A. J. (2014). *How colleges change: Understanding, leading, and enacting change*. New York, NY: Routledge.

Kuh, G. D. (2005). Putting student engagement results to use: Lessons from the field. *Assessment Update, 17*(1), 12–13.

Middaugh, M. F. (2010). *Planning and assessment in higher education: Demonstrating institutional effectiveness*. San Francisco, CA: Jossey-Bass.

Morrill, R. L. (2007). *Strategic leadership: Integrating strategy and leadership in colleges and universities*. Westport, CT: Praeger.

Trachtenberg, S. J. (2013). *Presidencies derailed: Why university leaders fail and how to prevent it*. Baltimore, MA: Johns Hopkins University Press.

RESOURCES

Buller, J. L. (2009). High impact administration. *Academic Leader, 25*(1), 2–3.

Buller, J. L. (2011). The need for linking innovation, creativity, and entrepreneurship. *Academic Leader, 27*(5), 4–5.

8

LEADING PROACTIVE CHANGE

THE SECOND MAJOR VARIETY of change to consider are changes that aren't immediately forced on an institution by circumstances beyond its control but that will be imposed on them if some kind of preventive action isn't taken now. These proactive changes occur with fewer of the time constraints associated with reactive changes and so allow for even more innovative solutions. At the same time, we'll notice that institutions engaging in successful proactive change follow processes rather similar to those that Elon and High Point adopted. We'll see change leaders who devote a great deal of time and energy to building a culture of innovation, not simply imposing their own vision, shifting the school's entire direction, or merely tinkering around the edges of change with superficial experiments in new personnel, tactics, structure, or procedure. Since proactive changes often require even more time to implement than reactive changes, they provide abundant opportunities to observe two common beliefs about change leadership in higher education: the myth of visionary leadership and the telling-is-leading fallacy.

The Myth of Visionary Leadership

Make no mistake about it: visionary leaders do exist and institutions of higher education are better off for having them. In fact, we encountered a number of visionary leaders in chapter 7, and we'll meet several more in this chapter. All of these leaders played a vital role in bringing about truly transformative change at their schools. The myth of visionary leadership isn't that this sort of leader doesn't exist or isn't important but that a visionary leader can single-handedly bring about successful change. If you see most packages of executive compensation and read the public relations material generated by many colleges or universities, you might get the impression that all it takes to transform a school is to bring in the right CEO. He or she will arrive on campus, share a new vision for what the school should be in the future, overcome resistance with dogged determination, and carry the school "to the next level of excellence" that it could never have found on its own. Part of the reason that the myth of visionary leadership is so widely believed is that management books and MBA programs have been promoting this idea for years. For example, here's what Thomas Peters and Robert H. Waterman had to say in 1982 about the reason Delta Airlines led its industry: "One long-time student of the airline industry [explains Delta's success] this way: 'Braniff thought quality meant Alexander Calder paint jobs and [attractive flight attendants]. Delta knows it means planes that arrive on time'" (179).

A visionary leader knows what's important. He or she moves a company "from good to great" by practicing the "seven habits of highly effective people." And we can learn from their example. In fact, that is what the full title of Peters and Waterman's book told us: *In Search of Excellence: Lessons from America's Best-Run Companies*. In the case of Delta, the lesson we're supposed to learn is "stay close to the customer": don't get sidetracked by frills like painting aircraft in vivid colors or designing attractive uniforms for flight attendants. Since a visionary leader knows that the success of airlines depends on getting people where they need to go on time, he or she will get priorities into their proper order. That's how Delta became the world's largest airline: people could rely on it for on-time arrivals.

Unfortunately, management books and MBA programs have been notoriously poor predictors of which companies will have long-term success. Like stock analysts who can provide compelling reasons for why the market acted the way it did yesterday, they don't have a reliable track record in informing us how things will be tomorrow. The conclusion that Peters and Waterman made in 1982 seemed reasonable at the time, but it's harder to defend today. Delta may still be the largest airline in the world in terms of the number of passengers it carries, but it's not even in the top ten internationally for on-time performance (flightstats.com/company/flightstats-releases-april-2013-airlineairport-on-time-performance-report/), and in the summer of 2013, it didn't even make it into the top ten for US airlines (www.prweb.com/releases/2013/8/prweb10996328.htm). Its reputation for on-time arrival is so poor that Peter Sagal, host of the nationally syndicated NPR program *Wait, Wait ... Don't Tell Me!* joked that Diane Nyad, who successfully swam from Cuba to Florida without a shark cage, "first attempted this feat in 1978. That is thirty-five years of trying to get from Cuba to Florida. She is the only person on earth who would have gotten to her destination faster by flying Delta" (www.npr.org/templates/story/story.php?storyId= 219793534). And everyone got the joke.

Moreover, it's not just *In Search of Excellence* that relied on a notoriously clouded crystal ball. Probably the most influential leadership book of the late twentieth century was Stephen R. Covey's *The 7 Habits of Highly Effective People*. When Covey's book appeared in 1989, IBM was doing extremely well. The IBM PC, introduced in 1981, set the industry standard, and its mainframe computers were found in corporations all over the world. The name IBM seemed synonymous with modern, customer-oriented professionalism, and Covey traced both this tone and the company's success to visionary leadership:

> Time and time again, I see the leadership of the organization come into a group and say that IBM stands for three things: the dignity of the individual, excellence, and service. These things represent the belief system of IBM. Everything else will change, but these three things will not change. Almost like osmosis, this belief system has spread throughout the entire organization, providing a tremendous base of shared values. (Covey, 1989, 139)

That message is underscored by the various subtitles Covey used for his book. On the cover, the subtitle is usually given as *Powerful Lessons in Personal Change*. But on the title page, it becomes *Restoring the Character Ethic* in some editions. Either way the basic premise is clear: individuals can effect substantial change in their lives and in their organizations by developing certain habits and embodying certain values.

Of course, *The 7 Habits of Highly Effective People* was written before IBM sold off its entire PC business in 2004 and before Apple Computing's famous "Mac versus PC" ads began portraying IBM as stodgy, bumbling, and out of touch with the dignity of the individual, excellence, and service. (And, I might add, everyone got the joke.) In less than a decade after Covey drew his conclusions about leadership, writers commonly depicted IBM as the embodiment of Sloan Wilson's *Man in the Gray Flannel Suit* (1955), more *Mad Men* than Mac cool. As but one example, here is how Robert X. Cringely (the pen name of technology journalist Mark Stephens) described the company in an essay titled "The Decline and Fall of IBM":

> Internally IBM's culture is a lot like USA society in the 1950's and early 1960's. There was an implicit trust in the government back then and we accepted the answers we got from Washington. Most of the IBM community has been conditioned not to think and to

accept whatever they are told by management. If the server business is sold most will naively accept whatever explanation is offered. They won't know this is just one of many businesses that could be sold for the corporation to make its numbers. (www.cringely.com/2013 /04/22/the-decline-fall-of-ibm/)

That portrait is the antithesis of a highly effective corporation run by highly visionary leaders. If visionary leadership led to the company's greatest success throughout the 1960s, 1970s, and early 1980s, are we to conclude that IBM then suddenly stopped hiring visionary leaders and promoted managers who preferred stagnation?

There are countless other examples from the corporate world where faith in a visionary leader proved misguided, even destructive. Fred Silverman was a television executive who was hired by NBC because under his watch, CBS had developed successful schedules that included *M*A*S*H*, *The Mary Tyler Moore Show*, and *All in the Family*, and then led ABC to similar success with *Laverne & Shirley*, *Charlie's Angels*, and *The Love Boat*. But once Silverman arrived at NBC, his magic touch seemed to vanish. Even today, the shows he created—*Supertrain*, *Pink Lady*, and *Hello, Larry*—are cited as among the biggest disasters in broadcast history.

More recently, Ron Johnson was hired to serve as CEO of the JCPenney department store chain after his visionary leadership as senior vice president of retail operations at Apple led to such triumphs as Apple Stores and their Genius Bar. Johnson immediately began to rebrand JCPenney by offering daily low prices instead of coupons and periodic sales and by changing the look and feel of the shoppers' experience. Unfortunately, the demographic that proved to be the store's largest customer base hated these innovations. It preferred a more traditional store design and looked forward to periodic sales. Johnson's innovations ended up alienating the chain's existing client base without attracting a new one. He was fired only seventeen months after he began at JCPenney because, according to Steve Rosa in *Business Insider*, he failed to learn one fundamental lesson:

No matter how forward-thinking Johnson's changes were, they didn't work because his approach to rebuilding a brand was backwards. To truly change an external brand, you must change the internal company culture that is so critical in delivering the brand experience. In other words, brand and culture go hand in hand. (www.businessinsider.com /why-ron-johnson-failed-at-branding-jcp-2013–4#ixzz2kACozQpI)

What Rosa points to in his analysis is the secret of the myth of visionary leadership: in both the corporate and academic worlds, success doesn't occur simply because visionary leaders point the way; it can occur only when visionary leaders see their primary role as creating a culture of innovation. Once a leader stops believing, "We did it!" and starts believing, "I did it!" failure is almost guaranteed.

My point in providing these examples is not that Peters, Waterman, and Covey were entirely misguided or that Fred Silverman, Ron Johnson, C. E. Woolman, David Garrett, and Thomas Watson (both father and son) didn't play major roles in the success of, respectively, CBS, NBC, Apple, Delta, and IBM. They did. But we have to remember yet again the warning we constantly provide students about the difference between correlation and causality. To return to the example of stock analysts, there's an old principle in investing:

> Never confuse brilliance with a bull market.

When the price of almost every stock is rising, it doesn't take a great deal of skill to pick investments that will increase in value. A similar idea applies to visionary leadership in higher education: it may well be that the type of change proposed by the president or chancellor leads to an institution's success, but it also may be that a host of other factors—working with a talented staff committed to building something important, being on the receiving end of large government contracts, benefiting from a rising demographic, or even just happening to be in the right place at the right time—played a more important role. The real test of leadership comes when the CEO's visionary ideas continue to bring success even when all those other environmental factors change. In the highly dynamic world of higher education, the sands can shift very suddenly.

The Telling-Is-Leading Fallacy

Leaders tend to receive credit for the success of their organizations and blame for their failures in part because they're the most visible symbol of the organization. While visionary leadership can make an important contribution to institutional success—it may even be a prerequisite for prolonged success—we've seen how misguided it is to believe that all that's needed for effective change leadership is a visionary, forceful leader. In fact, visionary, forceful leaders who focus almost exclusively on their goals and their plans to achieve those goals, not on creating a culture of innovation, either fail entirely or institute changes that prove to be short-lived. Leadership isn't just deciding where to go and devising a strategy to get there. Many people don't understand that. Geoff Perry and Martin Wells vividly illustrated how common these misconceptions are by conducting a series of video interviews with people on the street and asking them if they could define leadership (www.youtube.com/watch?v=lagHU2Disso). Their answers generally associated good leadership with taking control, effective top-down management, having a strong personality, and keeping an organization well run. But Edgar Schein, whose work on organizational culture we considered in chapter 1 and whose learning culture theory we considered in chapter 4, concludes that effective leadership is actually something quite different. In *Humble Inquiry: The Gentle Art of Asking Instead of Telling* (2013), Schein notes that people who try to lead others this way—by imposing their ideas from above and telling them what to do—usually have an effect opposite to what they intend. Instead of motivating people, they immobilize them. People become filled with self-doubt, and rather than take action, they worry that the boss will blame them if they make a mistake. Leaders who try to impose their vision on an organization often tend to create strong opposition to that vision since people regard it as an indictment of whatever they were already doing:

> What is so wrong with telling? The short answer is a sociological one. *Telling* puts the other person down. It implies that the other person does not already know what I am telling and that the other person ought to know it. Often when I am told something that I did not ask about, I find that I already know that and wonder why the person assumes that I don't. When I am told things that I already know or have thought of, at the minimum I get impatient, and at the maximum I get offended. (Schein, 2013, 8)

The false belief that effective leadership is demonstrated by strong authoritarian guidance from supervisors is something I call the telling-is-leading fallacy, and it is found in higher education just as often as it is found in the corporate world.

Taken together, the myth of visionary leadership and the telling-is-leading fallacy help explain why strategic planning is so popular in higher education even though it's rarely been effective in bringing about positive transformational change. The legislatures and governing boards that select university presidents usually consist of people whose career in business, government, or the military have organizational cultures that, rightly or wrongly, have bought heavily into the notions that visionary leaders can single-handedly effect change and that telling is leading. In a typical search process, these groups don't spend much time interviewing each candidate and can readily mistake answers that are glib, facile, and close-minded with visions that are decisive, entrepreneurial, and tough. (See Buller, 2013a, 2013b.) Then once they are hired because they were viewed as strategic visionaries by the legislature or governing board, they embark on yet another strategic plan, understand their job to be remaining decisive and tough, and fall victim to the myth of visionary leadership and the telling-is-leading fallacy.

Schein encourages leaders to follow a very different model: to do more asking than telling, to get to know the people in the organization rather than making snap judgments about them, and to draw others out instead of shutting them down. This approach, which Schein calls *humble inquiry*, involves taking the same kind of systems approach to any type of leadership position that we found effective in creating a culture of innovation in higher education. In times of reactive change, leaders are under great pressure to abandon this approach. Crises seem to demand leadership by decree, with presidents and chancellors tempted to dictate the change rather than build the culture. But as we saw in the previous chapter, even reactive change leads to impressive results when leaders build systems instead of trying to orchestrate results. If that's the case for reactive change, how much truer will this principle be for proactive change?

We'll address this question by examining three case studies in proactive change where many people might expect to find strong authoritarian hierarchies: Arizona State University, the University of Notre Dame, and the Ministry of Higher Education in the Kingdom of Saudi Arabia.

Arizona State University

As was the case for Leo Lambert of Elon University and Nido Qubein of High Point University, it would be easy to attribute the transformation of Arizona State University (ASU) to a single charismatic individual: ASU's sixteenth president, Michael M. Crow. Crow is a dynamic, creative, and forceful personality who came to Arizona State in 2002 brimming with ideas about where the university needed to go next. He shares his vision freely in person, in print, and online (e.g., president.asu.edu). Even some of his most fervent supporters describe him as headstrong (Macilwain, 2007). Many politicians and governing boards look at Crow's success and want to hire a president exactly like him—someone who will come into the job with a visionary idea, advocate for it forcefully, brook no opposition, charge full speed ahead, and prove the naysayers wrong. But is that a fair assessment of what happened at ASU? No one will deny that Crow deserves a huge amount of credit for transforming his university. Not to put too fine a point on it, the ASU we see today wouldn't exist without him. But Michael Crow actually follows the same pattern for success that transformed Elon and High Point. Let's consider why.

When Crow arrived at ASU, its situation had obvious differences from what Fred Young faced at Elon or what Jacob Martinson dealt with at High Point. There was no imminent threat to the institution from an aggressive competitor or a sense that ASU was an undistinguished institution serving only a local market. From the 1960s through the 1980s, Arizona State had added academic programs, increased the rigor of its courses, and developed a reputation as a well-respected metropolitan research university. Nevertheless, long-term challenges were sitting on the horizon. ASU's academic reputation competed with its reputation as a place where students put their social life ahead of their school work. The university headed *Playboy*'s list of top party schools in 2002. And as Martin Van Der Werf and Grant Sabatier, the bloggers in the *Chronicle of Higher Education*'s The College of 2020 project (collegeof2020.com/), and others were predicting, the impact of online education and global for-profit universities meant that the future of higher education would soon be changing: name-brand schools with large endowments like Harvard, Princeton, Yale, and state flagship universities were likely to thrive; comprehensive universities, regional universities, and liberal arts colleges would eventually find their ability to attract students decreasing and their prestige diminishing. Indeed, a few years later, Sebastian Thrun, the cofounder of the online course provider Udacity, predicted that in fifty years, the world would have only ten institutions of higher education left (see, e.g., hackeducation.com/2013/10/15/minding -the-future-openva/ and www.forbes.com/sites/georgeanders/2013/04 /03/sebastian-thruns-online-goal-act-where-college-isnt-working/). Crow was not the sort of person who would let ASU lose its position in the coming marketplace, and he came to the job with specific ideas about what needed to be done.

In his inaugural address, "The New American University: A New Gold Standard," Crow outlined eight design imperatives (later more commonly referred to as design aspirations) that he believed to be necessary if the school wished to continue fulfilling its mission in the twenty-first century:

1. *ASU must embrace its cultural, socioeconomic, and physical setting:*
   One distinctive element that no other university could duplicate was the university's location in a beautiful metropolitan region of the

southwestern United States. For this reason, Crow encouraged the university to regard this unique environment as an increasingly valuable resource, incorporating issues related to the school's setting in class discussions and research projects and using cocurricular activities to celebrate the region's cultural, ethnic, and economic diversity.

2. *ASU must become a force, not only a place:* At the same time that it embraced its location, the university shouldn't be confined to that location. It should extend its mission as broadly as possible through its distance education programs and efforts like "ASU On the Move!" the university's educational outreach initiative. It should play a larger role as opinion leader in the legislature, cultural organizations, and civic groups. It should use the expertise of its faculty to guide public policy on behalf of all Arizona and the rest of the world.

3. *ASU as entrepreneur:* As state budgets experienced greater and greater constraints, public institutions needed to diversify their sources of revenue, using their discoveries as opportunities for investment, and funding their own future. Arizona State should thus take a number of calculated risks and seek commercial applications for the research it was already conducting. It should then reinvest the profits generated by these enterprises into improving the quality and impact of the institution for the future.

4. *Pasteur's principle:* Crow noted that although Louis Pasteur's research began in basic science, the principles he discovered were then applied to discoveries that had profound social benefits. Pasteur's principle, in Crow's view, could be summarized as a conviction that academic research should always be unfettered by vested interests, but guided by the needs of the university's stakeholders. He labeled this type of research *use inspired:* "Basic science that will lead to high social impact in a few short years" (president.asu.edu/node/1082).

5. *A focus on the individual:* Although ASU would always be a large institution, it could never lose sight of the needs of each individual student. In fact, as it grew, it would need to consider an increasingly broad range of student abilities. That principle meant that the university should focus not merely on the best and brightest, but on the full spectrum of students, meeting each person where he or she is and taking that student where he or she needed to go. Accomplishing that goal would require a complete reinterpretation of how programs should be delivered, with increased numbers of small classes where active learning was possible since not everyone learned well in large lecture halls.

There should be greater use of technology to make learning more effective. Opportunities for honors students should be increased, but not at the expense of developmental programs for at-risk students and those who faced other learning challenges. Students in a new ASU would graduate with the skills they needed to succeed in a global world, but also with a commitment to keep on learning throughout their lives.

6. *Intellectual fusion:* The key issues of the twenty-first century were not likely to be biological problems, sociological problems, questions of economics, or challenges in engineering; they were likely to be topics that would span all of these disciplines (and more) simultaneously. "The traditional disciplinary organization of universities may not be the optimal way to organize knowledge, or to organize the institution itself, or to teach students, or to solve the social, economic, and technological challenges confronting institutions in the regions in which they are located" (http://president.asu.edu/node/1085). For this reason, Crow encouraged faculty members and students to approach their scholarship from a problem-based perspective, adopting the knowledge and techniques of whichever disciplines they needed in order to find the answers to increasingly complex questions.

7. *Social embeddedness:* Just as the university needed to embrace its cultural, socioeconomic, and physical setting, it also had an obligation to serve that setting. Institutions of higher education could no longer remain insular by focusing on only their own needs or the interests of their most visible stakeholders. They had to recognize that everyone in the region was among the institution's stakeholders. (Compare Don Chu's open system versus closed system perspective as discussed in chapter 2.) For this reason, ASU had to become involved in such matters as high school retention and graduation rates, not merely the university's own retention and graduation rates, and the economic welfare of the underprivileged in the community, not merely the economic welfare of its own faculty and staff.

8. *Global engagement:* As committed as Arizona State must be to its local community, it couldn't ignore the fact that it operates in an interconnected world. Local issues easily become international concerns and vice versa, as the global impact of climate change, the flattening of the world marketplace through telecommunications and the Internet, and the international effect of local political conflicts have demonstrated. The university should work aggressively to develop an improved infrastructure that would allow it to play its proper role in this global marketplace. By becoming actively involved

in international issues, ASU would not be neglecting its commitment to its local community; it would be addressing the new reality of that commitment.

These eight principles, Crow says, could work together to create something he called the *New American University*, a type of institution that would meet the needs of students in the twenty-first century, honor the trust its stakeholders placed in it, and provide a model for other universities that wished to follow a similar path toward innovation.

If I limited this analysis to these facts alone, we might conclude that Crow disproved everything I've been saying. We would conclude that he was a visionary leader who dictated a new direction to his university and almost singlehandedly willed a new reality into place. But if we look more carefully into how his change leadership was demonstrated, we find that he guided Arizona State in asking the four questions associated with a strategic compass:

1. *What do we do best?* Crow's eight design imperatives weren't created out of nothing. He based them on the strengths that already existed at Arizona State. In his inaugural address, as well as in the many documents that followed, Crow consistently tied his eight themes to what the institution was already doing extremely well. For example, he related design imperatives 5 (a focus on the individual) and 6 (intellectual fusion) explicitly to the success of the university's New College of Interdisciplinary Arts and Sciences, founded in 1984, and on the Barrett Honors College, founded in 1988. He related design imperative 8 (global engagement) to partnerships already well established by the College of Business (www.asu.edu/president/inauguration/address/address.pdf). In so doing, Crow's vision wasn't to change the course of the university because it was moving in the wrong direction, but rather to do more of the things it was already doing with great success.

2. *What does that mean in terms of who we really are?* By emphasizing what Arizona State already did extremely well, Crow guided the institution to think about its identity in ways that went far beyond the traditional mission statement. By the time he arrived as president, ASU had a long history of success in educating students who came to the school with a broad range of academic abilities. To reinvent itself as a highly selective university or an institute for advanced studies, Crow (2010a) said, would mean betraying this past: "Private institutions seek Harvardization and public institutions attempt to replicate the patterns established by Berkeley and Michigan; each would do better to seek its own unique identity and situate itself in a synergistic network of collaboration" (37).

Crow argued that in ASU's case, that principle required a commitment to build academic programs and resources for the struggling student as well as the honors student, the undergraduate as well as the graduate.

3. *What does our identity tell us about where we should focus our resources?* As budget planning continued in the years following Crow's arrival, further investment was made in the type of programs that would improve ASU's ability to fulfill this mission. For example, investments in infrastructure would allow the university to provide access to a larger number of students. Investment in a new campus in downtown Phoenix that opened in 2006 provides access primarily to the university's professional programs. Investment in distance learning initiatives was designed to make an ASU education available to students regardless of their location. Each of ASU's campuses established a signature identity so as to avoid unnecessary duplication of services while making access to programs was more convenient for local students. Throughout all of these initiatives, Crow's goal was, as he said, not to imitate Harvard, Berkeley, and Michigan by becoming one of the top ten Research 1 universities in the world but to build on existing strengths and reinforce the school's well-established identity. While Crow emphasized the importance of interdisciplinary research, Colin Macilwain (2007) noted in *Nature* that that trend had already begun well before Crow's arrival. Using the school's actual identity to shape its budget led to a type of vision statement that is 180 degrees from the bland, generic mission statements in chapter 5:

> To establish ASU as the model for a New American University, measured not by who we exclude, but rather by who we include and how they succeed; pursuing research and discovery that benefits the public good; assuming major responsibility for the economic, social, and cultural vitality and health and well-being of the community. (president.asu.edu/about/asuvision)

In a proactive response to a long-term threat, the university began to distinguish itself from other comprehensive research universities in metropolitan areas. No matter how fierce competition in the higher education marketplace became, ASU now had a clear, widely recognized brand.

4. *How do we help our programs promote a culture of innovation that reinforces but doesn't alter our identity?* While Michael Crow certainly became a highly visible symbol of the New American University, much of his work was done off-stage, and he was generous in recognizing the role others played in the school's transformative change. For example,

in accordance with a policy he called *school-centrism*, Crow advocated for a distributed rather than highly centralized model of operation that would empower units by allowing entrepreneurial decisions to be made at the lowest organizational level possible (Crow, 2010b). He rejected a traditional hierarchical structure, which would have introduced a campus chancellor and provosts at each of ASU's physical locations, in favor of a more agile, interdisciplinary structure of deans who were charged with leading new colleges and schools. Faculty members and even students were given the freedom to innovate solutions to ongoing problems, with the most successful ideas providing new income streams for the academic areas that developed them. As Crow put it, "We want to engage all [academic areas], from the arts and humanities and social sciences to the natural sciences and engineering and the professional schools. Instead of just teaching courses in entrepreneurship that would reach all of the disciplines, we have decided to embed entrepreneurial opportunities and learning environments within each of them" (http:// president.asu.edu/sites/default/files/Building%20an%20Entrepreneurial %20University%20(Germany)%20060808%20Kauffman-Planck%20 Conference_0.pdf).

The result was to create a genuinely innovative culture and to unleash the power of ICE (see chapter 7) as a means of achieving ambitious goals.

University of Notre Dame

"That's all well and good," we can imagine an observer saying, "but you can't deny that Elon, High Point, and Arizona State all benefited from having visionary, dynamic, and forceful personalities as their presidents. Is it ever the case that less visible, more introverted presidents can bring about this type of innovative change? If not, doesn't that prove that visionary leadership rather than the development of an innovative culture is the key to effective change leadership in higher education?"

As a way of answering these questions, consider the dramatic transformation of the University of Notre Dame into a major research institution. Most people know about Notre Dame from its intercollegiate football program, its Catholic identity, iconic figures like Knute Rockne and George "the Gipper" Gipp, and alumni like Regis Philbin, Nicholas Sparks, and Condoleezza Rice. What people often don't know is how the university leveraged its public image to raise academic standards, intensify its research portfolio, and greatly expand its budget. From 1987 through 2005, the university added more than five hundred faculty positions (including nearly two hundred endowed positions), became one of the twenty most selective universities in the United States, increased the minority student population from 7 to 18 percent, added about forty state-of-the-art campus buildings, increased its endowment from less than $500,000 to over $3 billion, multiplied its research productivity, expanded the amount of financial aid available from $5 million to $136 million, and began a major international outreach initiative (www.nd .edu/about/history/pioneering-leadership/ and monkmalloy.nd.edu/).

While this transformation, like all other successful change processes, was an institution-wide effort, the university's president during this period provided effective leadership in creating the environment that made these achievements possible. As Notre Dame's website says, the CEO's "presidency was marked by the most impressive growth in the history of the University to date in facilities, endowment, faculty-student ratios, research funding, financial aid, and student diversity. (monkmalloy.nd.edu/)." *Well, of course, you may be thinking. Everyone knows who was president during that period. It was Notre Dame's charismatic, outspoken, and long-standing president, Father Theodore Hesburgh.* In fact, it wasn't. The president who witnessed "the most impressive growth in the history of the University" was actually Hesburgh's successor, Father Edward A. Malloy.

It's difficult to imagine two more different types of academic leader than Hesburgh and Malloy. Hesburgh was dynamic, endlessly enthusiastic, and a figure of immediate authority. Malloy was more commonly described as soft-spoken, unassuming, and content to work behind the scenes. His friends called him "Monk," and though there are conflicting stories about how that nickname came about, it suited his personality to a T. Whereas Hesburgh was an iconic figure, a lightning rod for media attention, Malloy shunned interviews. As one headline put it, "Soft-Spoken Leader Notre Dame's Rev. Malloy Doesn't Seek the Limelight" (http://news.nd.edu/news/3739-soft-spoken-leader-notre -dames-rev-malloy-doesnt-seek-the-limelight/). Hesburgh's achievements were certainly impressive. He was president when the university went coed, experienced a massive expansion in both students and faculty, witnessed the laity receiving a larger role in institutional governance, and amassed the $500,000 endowment that Malloy would multiply several times. But the Notre Dame a visitor sees today is a very different place, in both atmosphere and physical appearance, from the institution that existed in Hesburgh's day.

Today's Notre Dame is Malloy's creation. But he didn't build the university by imposing his vision on it; he did so by changing the culture. Malloy's contribution was to give stakeholders enough confidence in their ideas that they were able to build a university for the future. During Malloy's presidency, many of Notre Dame's most impressive changes, such as the dramatic rise in academic standards and the new emphasis on research productivity, were led by the faculty through initiatives that arose in academic departments, colleges, and the faculty senate. It was a perfect example of what Michael Crow would later call *school-centrism*.

In looking at the achievements of Theodore Hesburgh and Edward Malloy side-by-side, is it possible to call one a better president than the other? That's a difficult question to answer. What's easier to conclude is that the university underwent many changes under both of them despite their completely different styles of leadership. Many people associate effective change leadership with such figures as Leo Lambert, Nido Qubein, and Michael Crow because their drive, vision, and charisma caused them to become such visible symbols of leadership. They were the figures whose photos appeared in national magazines, and we tend to assume that they created the change. But what they actually did was to create the culture that created the change. To produce similar transformations at our own colleges and universities, we shouldn't imitate someone else's leadership style; we should do what Edward Malloy did and use our own individual styles to help our institutions create a more innovative culture.

The New Horizons Plan for Saudi Higher Education

One last example of leadership in a time of proactive change makes it clear that working to improve institutional culture can be effective even in an environment where hierarchical structures are a long-standing tradition. The Kingdom of Saudi Arabia is an absolute monarchy where many of the policies in place at universities are developed centrally by the Ministry of Higher Education. Although the culture itself has ancient roots, its university system was developed quite recently. The first school recognizable as a state university, the College of Islamic Law (*Shari'a*) in Mecca, was opened by King Abdulaziz in 1949. In 1981, the college was combined with several new units to form what is now Umm Al-Qura University. All other universities have even more modern origins: King Saud University in Riyadh was established in 1957, Islamic University in Medina in 1961, King Abdulaziz University in Jeddah in 1967, Imam Muhammad Ibn Saud Islamic University in Riyadh in 1974, King Fahd University of Petroleum and Minerals in Dhahran in 1975, and King Faisal University in Al-Hassa in 1975. For about twenty years, these seven universities, along with a handful of technical, vocational, and community colleges, provided almost all the postsecondary education that existed in Saudi Arabia. In fact, the Ministry of Higher Education itself was created only in 1975. But there were potential problems facing such a limited system:

○ It wasn't large enough to produce the number of faculty members needed to keep the system going. For this reason, a large number of professors at Saudi universities came from the United States, the United Kingdom, Australia, or New Zealand. Saudi professors usually earned their doctorates in those same countries.

○ A rapidly expanding population meant that many citizens who were qualified to attend a university had no opportunity to do so unless they left the country.

○ The number of women who wanted to pursue a college degree far exceeded the access women had to a university education.

○ The dependence of the Saudi economy on oil made the kingdom highly vulnerable if large petroleum deposits were discovered elsewhere or a clean, inexpensive alternative to fossil fuels was ever developed.

○ The hierarchical traditions of Saudi society meant that all schooling, even at the graduate level, was largely passive—the professor was regarded as an expert who taught and the students were regarded as subordinates who listened—even while other countries began to improve the quality of education through more student-centered active learning.

None of these threats posed an imminent danger to the system's existence in the way that Elon and High Point had been threatened. But those in charge of higher education throughout the kingdom were keenly aware of these issues and knew they needed to be proactive in leading change if they wished to avoid creating a serious crisis for their successors.

The approach the Saudis adopted progressed along three simultaneous tracks. First, the university system would invest heavily in higher education in order to create a number of new universities, expand the institutions that already existed, hire a large pool of faculty members (including more Saudi natives), and establish a scholarship fund for students to study abroad, particularly at the graduate level. As long as the petroleum economy could still fund the endeavor, the Saudis would devote roughly a quarter of their entire national budget to education. As a result, the number of universities tripled in less than a decade. Opportunities for women at existing schools increased, and new universities for women, like the massive Princess Nora bint Abdulrahman University in Riyadh (a vast "educational city" that was built in a single year and provided more than eight hundred new buildings and its own automated monorail system), were made national priorities. A new experimental research institution, King Abdullah University of Science and Technology, was built near Jeddah. Existing schools received new investments to build research centers, technology parks, and buildings for new academic programs. This first strategy, although the most costly, was the easiest for the kingdom to accomplish. Because the king could make decisions independently, policies could be developed and budgets allocated in an extremely short period of time. But the second track of the Saudi plan—having the universities adopt more active styles of learning and more independent ways of conducting research—would take far longer.

That task fell to Khalid Al-Anqari, a soft-spoken geographer with a commanding presence who became the kingdom's minister of higher education in 1991. Having received his doctorate from the University of Florida, Al-Anqari wanted to combine some of the best features of Western higher education with traditional elements that had long defined Saudi culture. For example, since he knew the practice of many Saudis was to go to the very top of any hierarchy to solve a problem, he held public sessions twice a day—at 8:00 a.m. and at 2:00 p.m.—throughout the work week at which anyone could bring any issue to his attention. Meeting hundreds of people in this way every week, Al-Anqari quickly discovered where the greatest needs were in his country's system of higher education. He decentralized as much decision making as possible, encouraging the universities themselves to make decisions that were once made for them by the government. Early in his tenure as minister, when oil prices plummeted and economic cutbacks became necessary, he developed a plan that encouraged universities to become more entrepreneurial. For example, a university could offer consultancies to industries operating in their regions, receive payment for their advice, and invest this money in their own programs. As a result, the seven universities that were then in existence all established business centers that could develop new ideas and increase income. Later, when oil prices rose and the national economy improved, he allocated new resources to institutions as block grants so that they had maximum flexibility to invest in whatever best served the needs of their stakeholders.

To decrease the country's dependence on the single commodity of oil further, the ministry began working with the universities to develop a comprehensive strategic plan, known as *Afaaq* ("Horizons"), which could serve as a blueprint for the future. But Al-Anqari chose not to engage in a traditional strategic planning process. The process he preferred had a far larger scope. Nearly eight hundred workshops, focus groups, and meetings were conducted to identify the major questions that the university system needed to answer. A peer group of university systems in five countries (the United States, Australia, Finland, Malaysia, and South Korea) was selected on the grounds that these nations pursued higher education in a manner similar enough to the Saudi system for comparisons to be made but with sufficiently better results to serve as aspirational examples. A close analysis of systemwide best practices was combined with scenario analysis, gap analysis, and the study of various strategic options to develop a full range of choices for the system, and the universities within it, to consider for the future. *Afaaq*, the result of this multiyear process, became a hybrid between a traditional strategic plan that proposes specific actions to be taken and a more versatile strategic compass that outlines possible directions for the future. Eight areas were identified as most important:

1. *Access to education:* Increasing institutional capacity and improving efficiency so as to meet the increasing demand for higher education

2. *Human resources:* Getting sufficient numbers of the right people into the right positions to improve both the quality of education and the public's access to it

3. *Curricula:* Moving from passive to active learning while modernizing pedagogical methods and course content for the twenty-first century

4. *Research:* Improving the quality and quantity of original research conducted by faculty and graduate students

5. *Governance:* Increasing flexibility and local decision making while improving quality through strict accountability measures

6. *Financing:* Increasing the resources available to higher education while making ongoing budgeting as predictable as possible

7. IT *infrastructure:* Ensuring that the entire university system has the technological resources needed to meet the goals of the plan

8. *Physical infrastructure:* Ensuring that the entire university system has the facilities and physical plant needed to meet the goals of the plan

This approach to planning, with its support for decision making at the lowest possible level and its encouragement of entrepreneurial activity, represents a significant cultural change for the Saudi university system. In order for this level of change to be possible, however, the Ministry of Higher Education had to precede it with more than two decades of preparation, making sure that university leaders and their faculty were ready to take full advantage of the system's culture of innovation when it arrived.

Conclusion

There is a school of thought that says that when it comes to success in life or at work, leadership requires people to be aggressive, assertive, and at times even abusive in order to achieve their goals. That philosophy, outlined in books like Donald Trump's *Think Big and Kick Ass in Business and in Life* (Trump and Sanker, 2008) and *Time to Get Tough: Making America #1 Again* (Trump, 2011) or Robert A. Glover's *No More Mr. Nice Guy!* (2003), stands in direct opposition to the idea, proposed in works like Edgar Schein's *Humble Inquiry* (2013) and Daniel Wheeler's *Servant Leadership for Higher Education* (2012), that more empathetic, stakeholder-focused leadership produces more lasting change. The failed leaders whom Stephen Trachtenberg studied in *Presidencies Derailed* (2013) didn't run aground because they weren't forceful, resolute, or confident enough. To the contrary, many of them failed because they were so committed to their own innovative visions of the future that they brooked no opposition, cut themselves off from dissident voices, and ultimately lost touch with the very people they claimed to be serving. A study of proactive change—the type of change that seeks to avoid problems before they arise—reinforces the notion that change leadership in higher education requires a commitment to creating cultures of innovation, that is, an environment in which new ideas flow from many sources simultaneously and alternative perspectives are valued and rewarded. While the forceful, dynamic, and charismatic leaders like Michael Crow and Theodore Hesburgh receive a great deal of attention because of their outgoing personalities, it's the time spent in building a new organizational culture, as understood by such different leaders as Edward Malloy and Khalid Al-Anqari, that produces the kind of change that can truly transform a university.

REFERENCES

Buller, J. L. (2013a). Are you tough enough? *Academic Leader*, 29(3), 1, 6.
Buller, J. L. (2013b). Bottom-line leadership. *Academic Leader*, 29(4), 1, 6.

Covey, S. R. (1989). *The 7 habits of highly effective people: Powerful lessons in personal change.* New York, NY: Fireside Press.

Crow, M. M. (2010a). Differentiating America's colleges and universities: A case study in institutional innovation in Arizona. *Change, 42*(5), 36–41.

Crow, M. M. (2010b). The research university as comprehensive knowledge enterprise: A prototype for a New American University. In L. E. Weber & J. D. Duderstadt (Eds.), *University research for innovation.* London, UK: Economica.

Glover, R. A. (2003). *No more Mr. Nice Guy! A proven plan for getting what you want in love, sex, and life.* Philadelphia: Running Press.

Macilwain, C. (2007). The Arizona experiment. *Nature, 46*(7139), 967–970.

Peters, T. J., & Waterman, R. H. (1982). *In search of excellence: Lessons from America's best-run companies.* New York, NY: Harper & Row.

Schein, E. H. (2013). *Humble inquiry: The gentle art of asking instead of telling.* San Francisco, CA: Barrett-Koehler.

Trachtenberg, S. J. (2013). *Presidencies derailed: Why university leaders fail and how to prevent it.* Baltimore, MA: Johns Hopkins University Press.

Trump, D. (2011). *Time to get tough: Making America #1 again.* Washington, DC: Regnery.

Trump, D., & Zanker, B. (2008). *Think big and kick ass in business and life.* New York, NY: Collins.

Wheeler, D. W. (2012). *Servant leadership for higher education: Principles and practices.* San Francisco, CA: Jossey-Bass.

Wilson, S. (1955). *The man in the gray flannel suit.* New York, NY: Simon & Schuster.

RESOURCES

Buller, J. L. (2014). Tellin' ain't leadin'. *Academic Leader, 30*(2), 1, 6.

Fullan, M. (2011). *Change leader: Learning to do what matters most.* San Francisco, CA: Jossey-Bass.

House, K. E. (2012). *On Saudi Arabia: Its people, past, religion, fault lines—and future.* New York, NY: Knopf.

Martinez, M., & Wolverton, M. (2009). *Innovative strategy making in higher education.* Charlotte, NC: Information Age.

Smith, L., & Abouammoh, A. (2013). *Higher education in Saudi Arabia: Achievements, challenges and opportunities.* Dordrecht, Netherlands: Springer.

9

LEADING INTERACTIVE CHANGE

THE VERY IDEA OF interactive change—changes that are needed but that we're not forced to make—can sound like an oxymoron. After all, if we're not compelled to make a change, how can we say that we have to make that change? This apparent contradiction wasn't an issue earlier in this book with the discussion of reactive and proactive changes. In both of those cases, I was addressing significant threats to institutions that were either imminent or at least predictable. But when we can't point to an obvious threat, how can we say that there's a need for change? Don't we have to rely on a comparative advantages case, a net benefits case, or any of those other types of arguments that, as we saw in chapter 3, tend not to be very effective in higher education?

Answering these questions starts by noting that alleging a threat exists when it actually doesn't is dishonest, manipulative, and likely to fail. The credibility of leaders can be destroyed if they're discovered to have intentionally misled stakeholders about their reasons for pursuing an objective. Yet we've seen repeatedly in this book why change is unlikely to be successful if it's mandated from the top in a distributed organization like a college or university. Since stakeholders throughout the institution are empowered to make decisions in their own spheres of authority, they have to be convinced that the time and energy needed to effect the change will be worth it. And without the common enemy of a perceived threat, that type of needs case may seem impossible to make. But in fact interactive change—change that is necessary for internal reasons—can and does occur in higher education. As a way of seeing how that type of change occurs, we're going to explore the change processes that took place at two very different types of institution: the University of Nebraska–Lincoln and Indian River State College in Florida.

University of Nebraska–Lincoln

We've already seen several examples of institutions that adopted the strategic compass approach without actually using that term. The University of Nebraska–Lincoln (UNL) did call its approach a strategic compass. Here, for instance, is a passage of the university's 2008 white paper that outlines how the university planned to set its goals for the future:

> This draft document ... is not a traditional strategic plan. Rather, it is a compass—confirming the direction initially set by a number of campus-wide reports and initiatives and subsequently refined by many of our academic units and faculty through their actions and their planning activities. Our underlying assumption is that a university advances faster if strategic plans emanate from units, departments and colleges, are the product of faculty deliberations, and are revised or confirmed through conversations with the campus administration ...
> In short, we did not want a restrictive University plan that limited opportunities or, worse, was too general to be ambitious. (http://www.unl.edu/ucomm/chancllr/compass/2008strategicplan.pdf)

In a way, the state of Nebraska found itself in a situation not unlike that which was unfolding in the Saudi Arabia example in chapter 9: too much of the economy was based on a single commodity. But there's an important difference between agriculture and oil. Oil can and probably will be replaced as a major source of energy within the foreseeable future. Agriculture, however, will become of increasing importance. People are always going to need food. And as more land is diverted from agriculture to urban development, research in agriculture will continue to be of crucial importance.

Nevertheless, there were important internal reasons for the state to diversify its economy. We might summarize the situation as follows.

- o It's not in Nebraska's long-term best interests for its economy to be based too exclusively on any one commodity. Agriculture, the state's primary commodity, will continue to be essential, but market-driven price fluctuations mean that the state's tax base is inherently unpredictable.

- o Just as diversifying one's portfolio is the key to financial regularity in the case of an individual's own investments, so should Nebraska diversify its financial base, particularly in the area of emerging technologies.

○ Certain demographic factors will affect the university system. Recent college graduates are leaving the state at higher rates than elsewhere in the country. Since the state's population is aging, the number of traditional-college-aged students who are Nebraska residents is likely to decrease.

○ Diversifying the economy can thus have a double benefit: more students graduating from the state's universities may remain in Nebraska because they are able to find attractive jobs there, and people from other states may relocate to Nebraska because of those same jobs.

○ By stemming the tide of emigration and increasing immigration, the trend of a shrinking pool of traditional-college-aged students may also be reversed. (For the data behind these assumptions, see www.unomaha.edu/cpar/conf2012/State-LocalTrends2012.pdf.)

In this way, although there wasn't a strong case that the state's universities were facing any imminent or long-term threat from external forces, there were compelling internal factors that made change necessary. In approaching this needed change, UNL decided that it would be guided by several principles. First, the institution would keep its options open by refusing to plan too specifically. As the university's chancellor, Harvey Perlman, likes to say, "The worst thing you can do with a strategic plan is to follow it—if a better opportunity comes along" (conversation with the author, November 21, 2013). Second, the institution would invert the typical academic planning process by developing strategies not at the top of the organizational chart and then aligning them downward, but among the faculty of the individual colleges or departments and then integrating them upward. We saw in chapter 5 that the strategic planning processes at most universities work down through various levels: level 1, strategic planning, occurs at the executive or board level; level 2, at the vice presidential or divisional level; and level 3, at the college or department level. What UNL would do would be to start its process at level 3 and then work backward until the plans of individual units could be integrated strategically at the institutional level.

Third, as a reflection of this philosophy, the institution wouldn't rely solely on the metrics conventionally gathered as part of strategic plans (student credit hours generated, retention and graduation rates, awards received, and the like) but would combine those metrics with others that demonstrated whether the university was successful in changing the culture and mind-set of its stakeholders. Perlman noted, for instance, that "among the most important contributions a president or chancellor can make at a university is to encourage people to think outside the box" (conversation with the author, November 21, 2013). He wanted people to feel free to see the future differently, and that meant they first had to see their role at the university in a different way.

In order to help accomplish this cultural transformation, the university began administering and tracking an employee engagement survey prepared by the Gallup Organization. The heart of this survey was a copyrighted instrument that Gallup dubs Twelve Questions That Matter—the Q12 (Buckingham and Coffman, 1999). The Q12 helps organizations determine the degree to which employees are satisfied with and committed to their work environment. In UNL's case, the instrument provided a comparison of its own campus climate to nationally normed data on employee engagement.

Approaching the change process from a campus climate perspective led to a very different outcome from what results from a typical university strategic plan. There was less fixation on the number of courses with high withdrawal rates, the amount of external funding raised from year to year, the percentage of the student body participating in study-abroad programs, six-year graduation rates, and the like. The Q12 encouraged the university's stakeholders to think not only of what they were contributing to the institution, but what they were gaining from it. What role could and did the university play in helping each person achieve his or her own goals, dreams, and aspirations? Moreover, the Q12 did not merely have a descriptive function. It was also prescriptive in that it suggested to supervisors that it was a good thing to explain their expectations to employees more clearly, recognize and praise the contributions of employees, demonstrate an interest in their development, and so on. By encouraging those who completed the survey to act in a way that would make other stakeholders feel more engaged in the welfare of the community, the Q12 didn't just measure; it also helped build a culture in which people could be more innovative and creative in their work.

While other schools simply tracked their freshman-to-sophomore retention rates, UNL also tracked its rates of employee engagement. In 2002, at the beginning of the process, 28 percent of the faculty, staff, and administration were actively engaged in their work at the university (identical to that of the US working population across all industries) according to standards set by the Gallup Organization. Nineteen percent were actively disengaged, a slightly larger percentage than the 15 percent found among the working population at large. By 2006, the actively engaged segment of the UNL workforce had increased to 33 percent, and the actively disengaged segment had decreased to 17 percent. The results seemed

Figure 9.1 Jim Collins's Hedgehog Concept

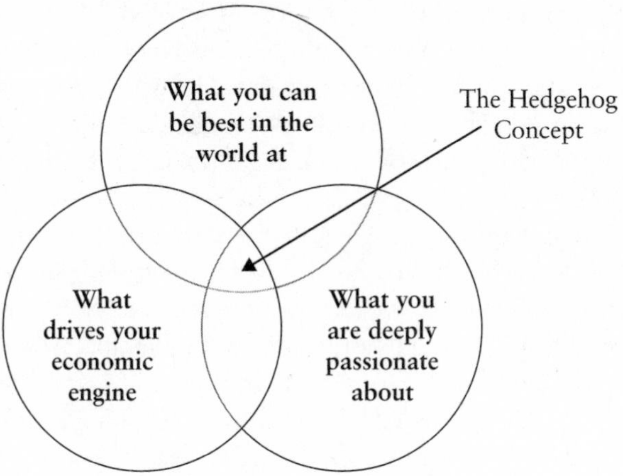

Source: Collins (2001, 95).

promising enough that Perlman coupled the Q12 with a second Gallup instrument, a ten-question survey that addressed the level of inclusivity found within a work environment (the I10). The I10, like the Q12, is a proprietary instrument of the Gallup Organization that offers those who administer it both a data-gathering mechanism and a guide on how to improve. The questions on the I10 make it clear that supervisors are expected to value diverse opinions and ideas, encourage people to use their diverse talents, and remain open to suggestions. (See, e.g., businessjournal .gallup.com/content/778/leverage-diversity-think-inclusively.aspx.)

As Perlman explored other ways of improving the culture of innovation that existed at the university, he discovered particularly useful advice in Jim Collins's *Good to Great* (2001). In Chapter 5 of that book, Collins presents his take on Archilochus's famous maxim that "the fox knows many tricks, the hedgehog only one. One really good trick." What Collins calls the hedgehog concept is "a simple, crystalline concept that flows from deep understanding about the intersection of the following three circles" (figure 9.1):

1. What can you be best in the world at?

2. What drives your economic engine?

3. What are you deeply passionate about?

If you can find an intersection among those three areas, Collins maintains, you have the capacity for greatness. That observation struck Perlman as an important insight into how to set UNL's strategic compass. He felt that most of the time at colleges and universities, people aren't given enough freedom to pursue what they feel deeply passionate about. They're too busy trying to "check all the boxes" they need in order to earn tenure, receive a promotion, have their grant funded, or reach whatever other metric the university sets for them. But if the faculty, staff, and administration at UNL were going to expand its culture of innovation—celebrating lateral thinking along with linear thinking, replacing innovation killers with innovation midwives, adopting a growth mind-set, practicing learned optimism, and engaging in all the other creativity-building activities explored in chapter 6—they first needed to feel engaged and included. They needed to feel passionate about something and understand that their passion was respected and valued. As a result, UNL's strategic compass became less about achieving some artificial goals and more about building a new type of university culture.

The Rules of the Red Rubber Ball

The idea that Perlman hit on in his search for constructive change at UNL is something that executive trainer Kevin Carroll (2005) calls the *rules of the red rubber ball*. Carroll derived that name from a lesson he learned while still very young. As a child, he had had little interest in his school-work but an obsession with sports. One day when Carroll was still in elementary school, a teacher pinned a note to his shirt that said, "Please encourage Kevin to think about something other than sports." The next day his grandmother sent him back to school with a reply pinned to his shirt in exactly the same place: "If that's what he loves—so be it!"

What his grandmother had done in this simple act of support was to give Carroll permission to pursue the things he cared about, not the things that other people thought he should care about. As he grew up, Carroll began to find ways in which his passion for sports could offer him a path to greater success. He joined the air force primarily so that he could play soccer in Germany. He became head trainer for the Philadelphia 76ers so that he could be exposed to sports on a daily basis. He took a job at Nike so that he could share his passion with others. As these opportunities unfolded, Carroll realized that there had been a symbol uniting all the athletic interests that motivated him: the inflatable red rubber ball commonly found on playgrounds all over the world. For Carroll, sports had been his "red rubber ball." But he also recognized that we all have our own red rubber ball. When we find it, work no longer remains work. It becomes play, a passion.

As a way of helping other people discover their own red rubber ball, Carroll developed six questions that are all attempts to reach the same answer from different perspectives.

1. What would you do for free?

2. What activities enthrall you?

3. What in life do you find irresistible, a source of inspiration, a reason to get out of bed?

4. What dream do you chase?

5. What topics do you love to discuss and ponder?

6. What's your primal source of joy? (Carroll, 2005, 37)

For individuals, the answers to these questions provide the key to creative and engaged productivity. When we're focused on our red rubber ball, we often find ourselves in the mental state that the psychologist Mihály Csíkszentmihályi (1990) calls *flow*: that highly absorbed or focused frame of mind in which we lose track of time, forget about our day-to-day concerns, and become almost blissfully engaged in what we're doing. For companies and universities, a collective red rubber ball is a function of the core mission and values of that organization. People become more creative and are willing to expend additional effort because the activity relates to something they regard as truly important and tied to their fundamental identity.

When Florida Atlantic University underwent its reaffirmation (i.e., reaccreditation) by the Southern Association of Colleges and Schools in 2012, much of the documentation and data generation was as arduous as is typical of any reaccreditation process. But when the institution adopted the promotion of undergraduate research as the topic of its required Quality Enhancement Plan, the level of engagement changed dramatically. People continually spoke about the topic with genuine excitement. They often worked long hours with little sense of exhaustion. Unlike most of the rest of the process, they actually enjoyed collecting data that dealt with undergraduate research. That topic served as what I call a spigot: an interest so dear to you that once you start talking about it (once you open the spigot), it's all but impossible to slow the stream (Buller, 2009). Individuals achieve Csíkszentmihályi's state of flow when they're engaged in the activity they really love, and departments, colleges, and universities achieve a state of maximum collegial flow when they're dedicated to a cause they really believe in. That spigot or red rubber ball is vital to them since it relates to how they see themselves and their contribution to the world (Buller, 2013). Organizations or units in a state of maximum collegial flow are like athletic teams or musical ensembles when their collective efforts seem to meld perfectly. Their results far exceed the sum of each member's individual contribution.

To Carroll, finding an object worthy of one's focused and ongoing dedication defines the difference between people who have a calling and people who merely work. The goal then is to maintain that level of dedication despite the obstacles we inevitably meet along the way. Among the biggest of these obstacles are the internal naysayers, those little voices inside our own heads that tell us we're not good enough to achieve the goal we've set for ourselves. "Once you find your red rubber ball," wrote Carroll (2005, 46), "may the source of your play become your life's work so much so that no one—not even you—will be able to tell the difference between the two." To reach that point, Carroll introduces seven rules that he believes make this type of commitment more meaningful and easier to sustain. Since the focus of Carroll's book is slightly different from this one, I'll reinterpret his seven rules of the red rubber ball in terms of how they might apply to colleges and universities:

1. *Commit to your red rubber ball and use it for guidance in both long-term decisions and everyday matters.* Remember step 3 of the strategic compass: What does our identity tell us about where we should focus our resources? Since your red rubber ball is something that truly matters to your institution, it should be your touchstone for every financial, curricular, and administrative decision you make. Of course, you will need to do things from time to time that don't directly help you achieve your goal, but you should always be aware that you're doing them, and they should be the exception, not the rule. Decisions define who you really are, not who you pretend to be. And that principle we saw in chapter 3 still applies: it's far preferable to be excellent at something you know you can do well than to be second-rate at something that someone else will always do better.

2. *Begin to hire people who can support your commitment to your red rubber ball and help you achieve your goals.* Just as all other choices should be guided by what your institution is passionate about, so should your decisions about whom to hire for the future. It's not that you want to reinforce groupthink by surrounding yourself only with people who will agree with you, but you don't want to hire those who will undermine these efforts either. A college where people truly become excited about fulfilling the school's liberal arts mission will probably not be happy with

a candidate whose sole focus is graduate-level research. Within a short time, that candidate probably won't be happy with the college either. Not every person you hire needs to be an ardent supporter of the school's mission and vision, but if that person can't support your mission at all, you're simply creating one more obstacle you don't need.

3. *Use the approaches explored in chapter 6—such as structured brainstorming, brainwriting, adopting a growth mind-set, experimenting with Seligman's ABC method, and replacing innovation killers with innovation midwives—to help you see familiar things in unfamiliar ways.* The way in which Carroll (2005) phrases this advice is, "Be creative, and you'll discover new opportunities" (45). But many people find a recommendation to "be creative" about as useful as advice to "be taller." It's one thing to say it and an entirely different thing to try doing it. In this book, I've given a lot of attention to ways in which we can jumpstart the creative elements of a change process. Part of creating a culture of innovation is preparing your existing culture for innovation. In many cases, we have to take specific steps toward helping people break out of current and familiar patterns before they can accept new and unfamiliar patterns. That takes time. It may not occur in a single year or even a single presidency. In fact, most of the case studies considered in this book consisted of a tag team of one administrator who laid the groundwork and two or more successors who helped design the new structure. If you attempt building too much too soon, the resulting framework will not be stable.

4. *Do the work behind the scenes, even if (or perhaps particularly if) others get credit for it.* Since change takes time, change leaders can't afford self-aggrandizement. Their focus has to be on the institution's mission and vision, not their own success as great leaders. As we saw in the myth of the visionary leader, the person in charge when a successful change takes place will frequently receive all the credit even though others carry out the real work. If leaders truly care about the mission of the institution more than their own egos, they have to do the spadework and be generous in sharing credit with others.

5. *Challenge commonly accepted boundaries, limitations, rules, regulations, and "the way things have to be done."* A few pages ago I mentioned the little voices in our heads that tell us we can't do something because we're not good enough to achieve such lofty goals. One of the ways in which this voice disguises itself is in this form: "We can't do this the A way because we've always done it the Z way," or even, "Our system requires us to do it the Z way." But the approaches considered in

chapter 6, along with the ten analytical lenses, can help break through these thought barriers. If someone tells you that the Z way is required by your accrediting body, call your institution's representative in that body to ask if that's true. (You'll be surprised how often you learn that it's not. Myths about accreditation requirements are even more common than sightings of Big Foot—and just as false.) Nevertheless, even if it does turn out to be true that the Z way is required, ask what sanctions would occur if you did things some other way. It may well be that as long as a similar result is obtained, it's perfectly possible to pursue that result by means of a different approach.

> Rules are wonderful as long as they make it easier for you to attain your ultimate goal. But once rules start hindering you from attaining that goal, they've outlived their usefulness. *Never let policies get in the way of progress.*

6. *Take full advantage of the unexpected.* As we've seen repeatedly, one of the challenges of strategic planning is the unavoidable influence of factors we can't possibly plan for. When a major opportunity arises that couldn't have been foreseen, institutions that are strongly committed to their strategic plans have a difficult choice to make: reject the opportunity because it doesn't fit in with their plans (thus missing out on something that could have been very beneficial to their stakeholders) or pursue the opportunity even if it means abandoning the plan (which calls into question how sensible it was to devote all those resources to planning). Harvey Perlman's philosophy at UNL was, "If you see an opportunity, take it." The advantage of the strategic compass over a strategic plan was that it provided the university with general guidance about what its priorities should be without locking it into a specific set of goals and tactics. If a chance arose to pursue the state's red rubber ball by diversifying the economy and staunching the flow of college graduates from the area, the institution was committed to taking that chance regardless of whether it was part of its written plan.

7. *Focus on the moment as the best way of preparing for the future.* Much of the mission creep found throughout American higher education is the result of a cultural phenomenon that Dalton Conley describes in *Elsewhere U.S.A.* (2009). As a people, Americans rarely focus on what they're doing at the moment; rather, they're always focusing on what comes next. Life lived in this way becomes an endless series of preparations for an end result that people somehow never reach. While our

tendency to act in this way as individuals helps explain the amount of stress, anxiety, and burnout we experience, there's also an institutional tendency to adopt a similar mind-set. If you can't demonstrate that you're going somewhere, many people will assume that you're not going anywhere. As a result, the needs of current students become overlooked as we plan to serve the next generation of students—whose needs will then be overlooked as we plan to serve the following generation of students, and so on. The most effective preparation for the future is to be the very best at what you currently do, not to regard the present as little more than a springboard for a new identity.

At this point, someone might object:

> Don't the rules of the red rubber ball contradict much of what you've said before? According to the myth of visionary leadership and the telling-is-leading fallacy, it's a mistake for administrators to insist on their vision in the face of naysayers and faculty resistance. But according to the rules you've just outlined, we should commit to that vision and refuse to give it up despite any opposition we encounter. How do you reconcile your former notion that the academic leader's job is to tend the system, not announce the dream, with this new idea of "damn the torpedoes, full speed ahead"?

It's a fair question, and its answer lies at the heart of what distinguishes successful from unsuccessful change leadership. The difference is that academic leaders who insist on the primacy of their own red rubber ball are almost certainly doomed to failure. They're putting themselves ahead of the needs of their stakeholders. They're becoming so preoccupied with their own visions of the future that they lose sight of the mission and identity of the institution. Presidents of teaching colleges who wish they were presidents of research universities or deans of service programs who wish they were deans of programs that enrolled large numbers of majors can do a lot of damage by trying to insist that their units become something they're not. They mistake what they're passionate about with what the people they serve are passionate about.

But academic leaders who can tap into the energy that results from how members of the faculty, staff, administration, and student body view their mission and identity have access to a powerful force for positive change. People become very excited about better and more effective ways of doing something they truly care about. What they tend to resist is being expected to fulfill someone else's dream or vision. For this reason, Perlman didn't want UNL to abandon the mission that had brought it so far already, and he wanted people to have an opportunity to pursue the goals that they themselves were passionate about. As he spoke to people throughout the institution, he realized that the three questions posed by Collins's hedgehog concept could be answered as follows.

1. What needs drive the state's economic engine?
   - Attracting and retaining young, highly educated, talented people
   - A more diversified economy
2. What are people at UNL passionate about?
   - Teaching
   - Research
3. What can UNL be the best at in the world?
   - Undergraduate education
   - Research in specific, focused areas

In other words, it would not be the university's mission to become another Berkeley, Michigan, or Harvard. What people cared about at UNL was teaching (particularly at the undergraduate level) and research (particularly in a few key areas). In keeping with the principles of appreciative inquiry, Perlman sought to emphasize what the university did best and then do more of it.

The results were impressive. Six-year graduation rates rose from 50.5 percent for the class that entered in 1994 to 66.8 percent for the class that entered in 2007. Total research expenditures increased 93 percent from $131,046,000 in 1998–1999 to $253,320,561 in 2011–2012. And freshman-to-sophomore retention rates improved from 59.4 percent for the class that entered in 1994 to 72.7 percent for the class that entered in 2007 (available at irp.unl.edu/fb13_14_21.pdf). The lesson to be drawn from these results is clear: if you focus only on the metrics, you may see some temporary improvements, but those increases are not likely to be sustainable. If you focus on people and building a culture of innovation, the metrics will follow. Put more colloquially, if you want more golden eggs, don't become preoccupied with golden eggs. Tend the goose instead.

Indian River State College

Perhaps the most important lesson to be learned from the rules of the red rubber ball and the hedgehog concept is that your school doesn't have to be a flagship university to use these ideas and create meaningful, lasting change. Indian River State College (IRSC) in Florida is a multi-campus institution with an open-admissions policy for its associate, certificate, and vocational programs that also offers baccalaureate degrees in workforce-related areas like organizational management, nursing, biology, and education. The school began as Indian River Junior College in 1959, became a community college in 1970, and was authorized to issue four-year degrees as a state college in 2008. Its main campus today was once a landfill that now boasts three hundred acres of breathtaking, state-of-the-art buildings. Many of its classrooms and facilities are specially designed with student learning style preferences in mind since the college serves as a member and center within the International Learning Styles Network (see www.learningstyles.net). Other facilities provide a smooth transition from college to the workforce by imitating the professional environments in which its graduates will work. For example, health care courses are offered in a building that resembles a hospital, power plant maintenance is studied in a mock nuclear facility, nanotechnology is taught in a classroom that mimics a modern "clean room," and so on. The entire learning environment radiates positive energy. As you walk across campus, you notice people readily greeting one another. Visitors are not just directed to their destination; they're escorted there personally by staff members regardless of their job assignments. Faculty members eagerly and excitedly invite visitors into their training labs and classrooms. As at Elon University, there's a surprising lack of faculty conflict and intrigues. In terms of both its physical plant and interpersonal relations, IRSC has achieved a goal that many larger, wealthier, and more prestigious institutions would envy.

IRSC wasn't always this way. In its early years, it resembled a typical junior or community college with good programs that resulted in solid conventional indicators (graduation rates, transfer rates, job placement rates, and the like) and a faculty and staff who were dedicated but without the high level of ownership, morale, and passionate spirit that exists today. What happened to create this transformation? The college's change process bears such a close resemblance to what UNL did that it almost seems as though they were following the same rule book. IRSC's president, Edwin R. Massey, admits that for a long period after entering his position in 1988, he led the college in a strong procedural way, correcting policies so as to make them clearer and more effective and expecting people to follow the rules:

> The new president inherited several challenges including a state audit, erroneous enrollment records, fiscal insecurity, and impaired local

and state relationships. For the next 13 years, this administration focused on corrective actions to strengthen the policies, procedures, and specific components of the college that needed improvement. To accomplish these enhancements the president practiced a no-nonsense, top-down leadership approach. (Massey and Hart, 2010b, 2; see also Nevarez and Wood, 2010)

By means of this approach, the issues were resolved, and by 2000, the reputation of the college had greatly improved. But there was a price to pay for these successes. "After a certain point, we seemed to be stuck in the status quo," Massey says. "I knew there was more potential in our people and in our college, and I wasn't sure how to release it." (All quotations from Edwin Massey, unless otherwise indicated, are from my interview with him on January 22, 2014.)

While participating in Leadership Florida, a statewide leadership training program created by the Florida Chamber of Commerce in 1982, Massey heard a presentation by the organizational psychologist Olaf Isachsen, author of *Working Together: A Personality-Centered Approach to Management* (Isachsen and Berens, 1995) and *Joining the Entrepreneurial Elite: Four Styles to Business Success* (1996). Isachsen's mantra was, "If *you* change, everything around you will change." That idea and the principles Isachsen espoused struck a chord with Massey. The president invited Isachsen to visit IRSC to conduct a leadership workshop for college supervisors. That initial visit evolved into an ongoing consultant relationship that influenced numerous activities over more than twelve years. Those activities collectively became the foundation of what resulted in an enhanced college culture. Working with Isachsen, Massey began to realize the lesson we've seen repeatedly throughout this book: an autocratic or authoritarian leadership style may produce change in the short term, but that change will be superficial and not sustainable over the long term. "You leave too much potential on the table," Massey says. "You inhibit the creative side of your employees whose knowledge and energy you need to advance and reinvent the college. Prior to our cultural change, employees were afraid or reluctant to bring forward new ideas because they thought the administration was not interested or would get angry with them for disagreeing with it. A strict authoritative leadership style can be really valuable if you need to fix a problem. But that style will not tap potential and lead people to be more innovative. It will not lead you to greatness."

Over time Massey realized he needed to explore ways to enhance the college culture and change his approach to leadership. To initiate this process, he took a step similar to Perlman's use of the Q12 and I10. He agreed to have Isachsen meet in small focus groups with more than two hundred employees over two days. During these sessions, Isachsen engaged employees in conversations about their experiences working at IRSC. He took extensive notes and later summarized all of the feedback into a thirty-page climate survey. The results were dramatic. "I thought we were doing pretty well, but what the climate survey told me was devastating," Massey concluded:

> It became apparent that some employees had strong feelings about certain issues created during the "clean-up" years of the current administration, yet they kept these topics under the radar rather than "rock the boat." These issues included: communication; top-down chain of command; internal technical support; adjunct faculty; staffing levels; training for supervisors; career development and compensation; cross training; and rewards and recognition. (Massey and Hart, 2010b, 3)

The faculty and staff increasingly trusted Isachsen since his long-term association with the college made him come to be accepted as "a member of the family." People knew their candid remarks on the climate survey wouldn't lead to retribution but would be interpreted as their desire to make things better. As Isachsen's work at IRSC continued, each new step in the change process emerged after careful review and analysis of the previous activity. Work groups made up of faculty and staff were created to explore solutions for each issue noted in the climate survey. "Students are the most important people on campus" emerged as a core value, yet in time faculty and staff wanted to know that they too were important. They asked questions like, "What difference do our efforts make?"

Throughout these years, it became clear to Massey that "if we were going to change the college, it had to begin at the top. I had to change." He knew he had to demonstrate a new philosophy to build trust over time. He began to see his role as more than the CEO of an institution; he had to act as a mentor to people as well. The value that said, "Students are the most important people on campus," was rephrased as, "Student *success* is what matters most," so as to emphasize how every member of the faculty and staff also made a unique and important contribution toward that goal.

Working with Isachsen and IRSC's vice president of institutional effectiveness, Tina Hart, Massey began taking steps to create a new culture of empowerment. When new buildings were planned, faculty and staff members now participated in their design, making decisions both great and small about each structure. That initiative was what put IRSC on the path to creating campuses with such stunning facilities that the people who work in them display genuine excitement about their work space. Classrooms were designed with insights from the faculty and staff about students' learning style preferences. Workrooms were designed with significant input from the staff members about what they needed to do their jobs.

Like Perlman, Massey became a great believer in the principles of Collins's *Good to Great* (2001). The book resonated as he observed the principles in action. The IRSC employees were freed to do the work they were passionate about, resulting in a profound expansion of innovation and creativity. Massey discovered that the administrators had the most difficulty changing their approach for fear of giving up their authority and control. Yet by being encouraged to see their role more as mentor than director, they began to experience progress. "A business doesn't develop great customer service by having the boss order the employees to treat people better," Massey says. "It develops it when employees are genuinely engaged in their purpose and passionate about their organization, wanting their customers to be happy and satisfied as well. We wanted the faculty and staff to have a voice in what they were doing so they would take pride in and ownership of their jobs, their facilities, and the college's mission. They would want students and visitors to experience the same."

In 2010 IRSC decided to participate in the *Chronicle of Higher Education*'s "Great Colleges to Work For" survey. The *Chronicle* sent the survey directly to college employees, posing questions related to their work environment. The results of this survey qualified IRSC for the Top Ten Honor Roll for large colleges, in the company of Georgia Tech, Notre Dame, the University of Southern California, the University of Michigan, the University of Mississippi, and others. The ranking also reflected an unbelievable voluntary turnover rate of only 0.5 percent for faculty and 0.4 percent for staff. In summing up the atmosphere at IRSC, the *Chronicle* noted,

> Employees are encouraged to feel that the college will help them succeed both on the campus and beyond. Indian River's institutional effectiveness department helps them find advancement opportunities, both within the college and [at] other institutions. (chronicle.com /article/Great-Colleges-to-Work-For/65724/)

Notice what that summary reveals: instead of a traditional office of institutional effectiveness concentrating only on traditional growth metrics like student credit hour production, retention, and graduation rates,

IRSC's institutional effectiveness office also includes a major focus on employee development. This focus is intended to foster *institutional* success by promoting and supporting *individual* success, to make the office a place where people find tools that can help them grow, learn, and become more effective.

Like UNL, IRSC didn't have any external forces that compelled it to make these changes. It could have simply continued to exist as a pretty good community college, with solid conventional indicators yet not particularly distinguished from its peers. But its leadership realized that internal factors were getting in the way of the institution's success. Yet before they could change the college, they first had to change the culture. Massey and Hart learned that "layering initiatives onto an old, tired, stale culture creates a 'project' mentality. When you begin with the culture you begin at the core creating a foundation through which unleashed potential will flourish beyond your expectations."

In its designation of IRSC as one of the "Great Colleges to Work For," the *Chronicle of Higher Education* cited the school's high ratings for collaborative governance, professional development programs, teaching environment, facilities, job satisfaction, work/life balance, confidence in senior leadership, supervisor relationships, and respect and appreciation. Those achievements didn't arise spontaneously. As Massey noted, "If you take time to work with and listen to your people, everything else follows. They'll be the ones who will change the culture. But first you have to work on yourself. Words are words. People needed to see me change the way I did things so that they could feel empowered to change the way they did things. My job was to help them so that they could more effectively do their job of helping our students succeed." The lesson Massey and Hart drew from their own change process was that

> *the culture of a college is what matters most.* If left alone the value of
> an organization's culture is always depreciating. Change is inevitable
> but it's much better to change from a position of strength when you're
> able to *choose* to change vs. changing from a position of weakness
> when forced to change. Change that is not anchored in *cultural change*
> will prove to be just another "project" and will fail to provide sustainable, long-lasting change. Cultural change requires a long-term
> commitment to altering internal working relationships, attitudes, and
> approaches to leverage organizational potential. (Massey and Hart,
> 2010a, 2–3)

Types of Change Leaders

What makes what happened at IRSC different from what occurs at many other colleges and universities isn't just that Edwin Massey began his presidency with an autocratic, top-down style of leadership, saw the limitations of this approach, and then adopted a more positive, systems-oriented approach, but that he did so in the same job. For many presidents, it takes them until their second or third presidency before they get things right. As Stephen Trachtenberg argues in *Presidencies Derailed* (2013), it's not uncommon for people to try leading universities in an authoritarian manner, only to run aground with the faculty, governing board, or other constituencies. Sometimes those presidents learn from their mistakes and adopt a more effective approach in later jobs. But learning what doesn't work while you're still in office and then taking corrective action isn't common. It requires a change leader who understands that it doesn't detract from his or her authority—it may even enhance it—to admit, "I've got to change the way I do things before I expect changes to occur throughout the institution."

The common characteristic of the successful change leaders we've seen in this and the previous two chapters is that they understood the importance of creating a culture of innovation. They were different from each other in many other ways. Some were outgoing charismatic personalities. Others were more introverted and preferred to work behind the scenes. But they all recognized the futility of imposing an idea on an organization that wasn't ready for it and that was thus likely to resist the new idea as though it were some kind of invasive species. There are also other types of change leaders who are different from the examples studied thus far. Admittedly the examples I chose were those who brought about large-scale changes at their colleges or universities; they proved easier to consider because the impact of their decisions was so noticeable. But transformational change isn't the only way in which effective leaders help improve their institutions. We might think of change leaders as falling into five sometimes overlapping categories:

1. *Renovators* make incremental changes through minor improvements in existing structures or policies. Regardless of how they themselves see their roles at their institutions, most administrators act as renovators all the time, doing what they can to make what's already in place function more effectively.

2. *Borrowers* discover best practices at other institutions and introduce them to their own colleges or universities. While it can initially seem

as though there's very little innovation involved in being a borrower, not every improvement calls for a completely new idea. Instead of reinventing the wheel, borrowers observe what's already working somewhere else and adapt it to their own environment. Frequently they have the advantage of learning from others' mistakes as well as from their creative ideas.

3. *Combiners* take borrowing one step further by fusing two or more ideas from other institutions into a new synthesis. The innovative contribution of combiners comes from their ability to see similarities where others see only differences and thus gain from a synergy that others have overlooked. We can think of combiners as engaging in something similar to Ernest Boyer's (1990) scholarship of integration, but on an administrative, pedagogical, or structural level. At one time, such ideas as the research college (a liberal arts college that has the degree of research focus more commonly found at research universities), the public liberal arts university, and Michael Crow's New American University were the innovations of combiners.

4. *Planners* try to effect a greater degree of change than do renovators and thus design a long series of incremental changes that will eventually yield a more significant benefit. While planners may also be borrowers or combiners, they often rely on their own inspiration. The work of planners may fail because of unforeseen factors that complicate the change process, and so planners rarely see more than a small fraction of what they envision. Successful planning often takes place behind the scenes by leaders who lay a solid foundation that later administrators can build upon.

5. *Redefiners* are the leaders who bring about a complete transformation of their institutions. This group includes such leaders as Fred Young and Leo Lambert at Elon, Jacob Martinson and Nido Qubein at High Point, Michael Crow at Arizona State, and Edward Malloy at Notre Dame. While other types of change tend to be evolutionary, redefiners usually bring about revolutionary change, and their institutions are utterly transformed as a result.

The truth is that almost all academic leaders view themselves as redefiners, at least initially, but not every institution of higher education really needs redefining. Remember the situations in which Elon and High Point found themselves: unless they did something dramatically different, their very existence was threatened. That isn't the case for most colleges or universities. They may not be growing as quickly as they'd like. They may be challenged by new competition. They may even have inconsistent or declining enrollments because of demographic factors and all the other drivers of change considered in chapter 3. But they don't need transformation. If they try to implement that degree of change without there being a legitimate needs case, they can succumb to mission drift, a muddled vision for the future that we might call next-rung envy: the tendency of an institution to covet the status of whichever institution stands right above it on its perceived ladder of prestige. In order for change leadership to occur with integrity, change leaders must ask, "What sort of improvement does this school really need?" rather than, "What sort of improvement will make me look the most visionary?"

Conclusion

Sustainable change in higher education often occurs in a very different way from what we might suspect. The examples of the University of Nebraska–Lincoln and Indian River Community College demonstrate that significant change can begin not with establishing a sense of urgency, developing a change vision, and then communicating that vision for buy-in (as described by the Kotter model in chapter 1) but with something as simple as a morale survey. These examples also illustrate that the most important change that can occur at a college or university is often not transformational change. In fact, trying to impose an entire redefinition of an institution's mission on a culture that isn't ready for it or doesn't need it can lead to a derailed presidency (to borrow Trachtenberg's term) or an administrative career shortened. Change leadership requires the skills of the surgeon, not the car salesman: the question isn't, "How can I make this transaction as large as possible?" but, "What is the minimum level of treatment that will produce the results needed in this case?"

REFERENCES

Boyer, E. L. (1990). *Scholarship reconsidered: Priorities of the professoriate.* Princeton, NJ: Carnegie Foundation for the Advancement of Teaching.
Buckingham, M., & Coffman, C. (1999). *First, break all the rules: What the world's greatest managers do differently.* New York, NY: Simon & Schuster.
Buller, J. L. (2009). Finding the spigot. *Academic Leader, 25*(10), 1, 6.
Buller, J. L. (2013). *Positive academic leadership: How to stop putting out fires and start making a difference.* San Francisco, CA: Jossey-Bass.
Carroll, K. (2005). *Rules of the red rubber ball: Find and sustain your life's work.* New York, NY: ESPN Books.

Collins, J. C. (2001). *Good to great: Why some companies make the leap—and others don't*. New York, NY: HarperBusiness.

Conley, D. (2009). *Elsewhere, U.S.A.* New York, NY: Pantheon Books.

Csíkszentmihályi, M. (1990). *Flow: The psychology of optimal experience*. New York, NY: Harper & Row.

Isachsen, O. (1996). *Joining the entrepreneurial elite: Four styles to business success*. Palo Alto, CA: Davies-Black.

Isachsen, O., & Berens, L. V. (1995). *Working together: A personality-centered approach to management* (3rd ed.). San Juan Capistrano, CA: Institute for Management Development.

Massey, W. R., & Hart, C. T. (2010a). *Realizing potential—it's about the culture*. White paper for Indian River State College.

Massey, W. R., & Hart, C. T. (2010b). *Sustainable change—it's about the culture*. White paper for Indian River State College.

Nevarez, C., & Wood, J. L. (2010). *Community college leadership and administration: Theory, practice, and change*. New York, NY: Peter Lang.

Trachtenberg, S. J. (2013). *Presidencies derailed: Why university leaders fail and how to prevent it*. Baltimore, MD: John Hopkins University Press.

RESOURCES

Buller, J. L. (2014). Tellin' ain't leadin'. *Academic Leader, 30*(2), 1, 6.

Carroll, K. (2008). *What's your red rubber ball?* New York, NY: Disney Press.

Carroll, K. (2009). *The red rubber ball at work: Elevate your game through the hidden power of play*. New York, NY: McGraw-Hill.

ORGANIC ACADEMIC LEADERSHIP

BY THIS POINT, you're probably aware that the title of this book is meant to be taken in two different but complementary ways. That is, if we read *change* in the title as an adjective (or, technically, a noun modifier), change leadership in higher education describes what the subject of this study has been: How do we find the best way to lead meaningful change in a department, college, or university? But if we read the word *change* as a verb, change leadership in higher education becomes a command: if you want to bring about lasting, effective change in a department, college, or university, change the way you lead. Change how you approach issues, interact with your stakeholders, and set your strategic compass for the future. Refocus your energy toward people and processes rather than outcomes and metrics. Although that conclusion may be counterintuitive, and contradicts everything you've heard at higher education conferences for decades, you have to unlearn what you think you know about managing change at a college or university. I might summarize the theme of this book as follows:

> If you want to improve an outcome, don't spend your time thinking about the outcome itself. Spend your time improving the culture that produces the outcome.

Successful change leaders understand that change is produced by people. In order for change leadership to be effective, they have to help people come to grips with the idea of change, see the benefits in it, and embrace a culture of innovation, not just a culture that endures innovation. A university is not a machine that produces student credit hours or degrees. Change leadership is more like gardening: you can't just order plants to grow; you have to put in the necessary effort preparing the soil.

○ Like gardening, change leadership requires a sustained investment of time. Some results may occur very quickly. But some of the things that grow very quickly (weeds, flawed strategic plans) aren't useful for the long haul. While you (the gardener, the academic leader) may get a lot of the credit, it'll be others (the plants, the faculty and staff) who do most of the work.

○ Both gardening and change leadership in higher education require people to adopt systems thinking. You can't just introduce a fertilizer or pesticide for one plant in a garden without considering how it might affect all the others. All the plants in a garden affect and are affected by one another. If you group the right plants together, they can protect and nourish one another. But if you group them incorrectly, the result could be toxic. That same kind of thinking is required for change leadership in higher education: a change in one area can be beneficial or harmful to other areas, and it's careless to proceed without examining the possible consequences of each change.

While a computer network or a manufacturing facility is a mechanical system, a garden is an organic system. Organic systems usually function far more slowly and unpredictably than mechanical systems. If you over-fertilize a garden, you may initially think that you've done something good: growth seems to speed up and the plants appear healthy and green. It's only in time that the damage you've done becomes apparent. Moreover, gardens are less predictable than machines. If you set up a computer system properly, it'll work. But no matter how carefully you garden, you can never quite be sure which tomato plant will yield the most fruit.

Change in higher education has this same extended timetable and unpredictability. As we've already seen, forceful top-down managers can impose ideas that initially appear to be working. Enrollments increase, student credit hour production rises, and everything appears to be moving forward. Only years later may people realize how much damage was done by driving away some of the most capable members of the faculty and staff, spreading resources too thin, and alienating the constituents who could've been strong allies.

Change in higher education is not an exact science. Innovations that seem perfectly logical now because of current demographic trends and market demands can seem wildly inappropriate five years from now when they're fully implemented. At that time, there may be completely different demographic patterns and the impact of a new technology that hasn't yet been introduced. Does that mean we should never try to work for changes that will improve our institutions? Of course not. But like thoughtful gardeners, we should remain circumspect, be prepared to react suddenly in case conditions change, and remember that we won't be able to foresee the consequences of every choice we make.

We've been moving throughout this book toward an understanding that successful change leadership in higher education requires something I might call *organic academic leadership*: an understanding that colleges and universities are organic systems that have to be approached in ways most suited to their organizational culture. Like Edwin Massey at the beginning of the change process at Indian River State College, we have to realize, "If I want the culture to change, then first *I* have to change." I have to change the way I interact with people, change the way I develop new visions of the future, and change the way I measure success. I have to stop trying to plan everything strategically and start setting a strategic compass, a general guide for the future that allows me to change course or indulge in occasional side trips as necessary. I have to examine my institution through our ten analytical lenses, construct a solid needs case for the changes that are truly justified, replace innovation killers with innovation midwives, and spend less time planning and more time preparing. If it seems useful to do so, I can borrow insights from such approaches as learning culture theory, the change journey, mindfulness-based leadership, and creative leadership so as to adopt a new alternative to the all-too-common view that students are customers and colleges are businesses. Although most of the successful change leaders we met in this book didn't use the same terminology, they did these very things, and we can learn a lot from their example.

Organic Academic Leadership and the Type Z Organization

In chapter 4 we encountered the distinction that Douglas McGregor (1960) made between theory X organizations (where people are assumed to be basically lazy and motivated only by rewards or punishments) and theory Y organizations (where people are assumed to be doing their best, at least most of the time). In 1981, William Ouchi, Distinguished Professor of Management and Organizations in UCLA's Anderson School of Management, published *Theory Z: How American Business Can Meet the Japanese Challenge*, in which he argued that there was a third important type of organizational culture. Theory Z organizations, according to Ouchi, are those in which managers promote strong loyalty of employees to the company by taking a general interest in employee welfare, at both work and home. He contrasted bottom-line-oriented

American businesses that retrenched during economic downturns to Japanese businesses in which the perspectives of workers are respected and care is taken to protect them even during difficult financial times. Whereas most Japanese workers remained with a single company throughout their careers and regarded their association with the company as an important part of their identity, American workers, Ouchi argued, changed jobs frequently. While Americans may derive part of their identity from their profession, they rarely do so in terms of the company that happens to employ them. The result was that American companies lost a bit of their institutional history and skill base every time an employee left, while Japanese companies tended to retain these resources. In addition, since Japanese managers respected their employees, they consulted with them more often and benefited from the insights employees had at their specific level of the corporation.

For all their differences, theory X and theory Y organizations focused managers' attention on the bottom line—the quality of the results that the company produced. By contrast, Ouchi's theory Z organizations expected managers to adopt a different focus: the employees themselves. This structure enabled employees to be much more creative and effective in producing successful results. By knowing their boss had their best interests in mind, they were freed to devote all their energy toward serving the customer. They were aware that management "had their backs," and they could share their concerns and ideas with their supervisors openly. If theory X and theory Y managers see it as their responsibility to be results oriented, theory Z managers see it as theirs to be process and people oriented. By removing a corporate fixation on the bottom line, the bottom line tended to take care of itself. For this reason, Ouchi urged more American corporate leaders to adopt a theory Z management style in these ways:

o Make employee welfare a high priority.
o Evaluate the performance of workers not just on quantitative measures (how much they produced) but also on qualitative measures (how well they worked, progressed in their jobs, and interacted constructively with colleagues).
o Avoid excessive specialization so that they could better see the big picture and relate to the needs of employees in different roles.
o Make as many decisions as possible collectively, with the insights of workers genuinely respected, not simply given lip-service.
o Trust workers to know their own jobs better than anyone else.

○ Empower workers so that they didn't just have responsibility, but also authority in appropriate areas.

○ Demonstrate authentic concern for people.

Much in the world has changed, of course, since Ouchi's book first appeared, and the "Japanese economic miracle" of the 1970s and 1980s has been tarnished by long periods of economic decline and stagnation in the 1990s and after. But if theory Z may be said to have limitations when applied to hierarchical or decentralized organizations, it remains a powerful approach in distributed organizations like a college or university. As Harvey Perlman and Edwin Massey learned, they didn't get the results they wanted when they spent their time tracking traditional academic metrics, but they did get those results when they set about improving areas of weakness they noticed on their morale surveys. When the workplace stops feeling to employees like a battlefield where they have to watch out for their own survival and starts feeling like a supportive environment, they can spend their time focusing on the people they were hired to serve.

A common mistake made in higher education is to adopt a bottom-line approach to academic leadership without even recognizing it as such. In business, we might imagine the corporate mind-set as looking something like Figure 10.1a: the whole concern is for profit or shareholder value, and so managers, manufacturing staff, and sales personnel are all expected to be continually mindful of how their work affects that all-important concern. The mind-set that is common in higher education translates this focus into something we might visualize as Figure 10.1b: instead of profit, administration, faculty, and staff are all expected to focus their attention on the students. Metrics like student credit hour production, retention and graduation rates, and national rankings assume importance as indirect indicators of student success. Just as the numbers on a balance sheet represent profit to a corporation, so do these metrics represent achievement to most universities. But that common mind-set comes at a very high cost. Institutions begin to adopt, consciously or subconsciously, a mechanistic self-image: administrators treat members of the faulty and staff as though they were machines for producing student credit hours and graduates instead of treating them as valued colleagues in a common enterprise.

What a more organic theory Z style of leadership brings to higher education is a positive shift in this focus. Instead of saying, "We're here only for the students," academic leaders say to the faculty and staff, "I'm only here for you, so that you can be here 100 percent of the time for student success" (figure 10.2). The result is that everyone at the institution

Figure 10.1 Bottom-Line Leadership: (a) Business and (b) Higher Education

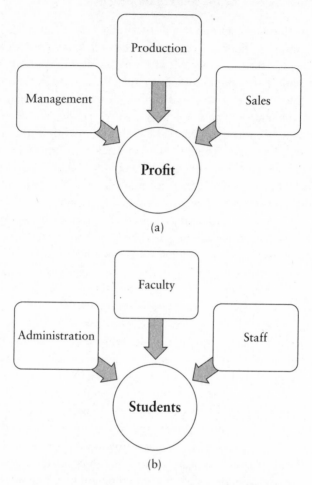

Figure 10.2 Organic Theory Z Academic Leadership

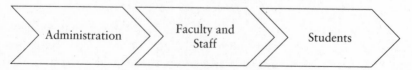

begins moving in the same direction, and everyone has someone to turn to for support. If the system is working well, even the president or chancellor receives this type of support from the governing board. Members of the faculty and staff stop regarding the administration as a group of efficiency experts always demanding that they do more and more with less and less, and start regarding them as colleagues, advocates, and allies.

An Exercise in Organic Leadership

How does the approach I'm recommending contribute to a more effective change process in higher education? In order to answer this question, let's engage in one of those exercises in creativity we considered in chapter 6, starting with a concept that political scientists often call the iron triangle—the tension among the three powerful forces, only two of which can ever have their way. In national politics, those three forces are usually Congress (or congressional committees), the federal bureaucracy, and special interest groups. At any one time, it may be possible to satisfy two of these forces simultaneously, but it's nearly impossible to satisfy all three.

Economists and project managers have adapted this concept and applied it to three other forces that are very difficult to address simultaneously: cost, quality, and access (figure 10.3). For example, in higher education, we can keep cost low and grant students a high degree of access by eliminating admissions offices, enrolling every student who applies, and lifting caps on the size of courses. In that scenario, quality would almost certainly suffer. Of course, we could maintain quality by keeping section size small and hiring only faculty members with highly distinguished records of teaching

Figure 10.3 The Iron Triangle in
Higher Education

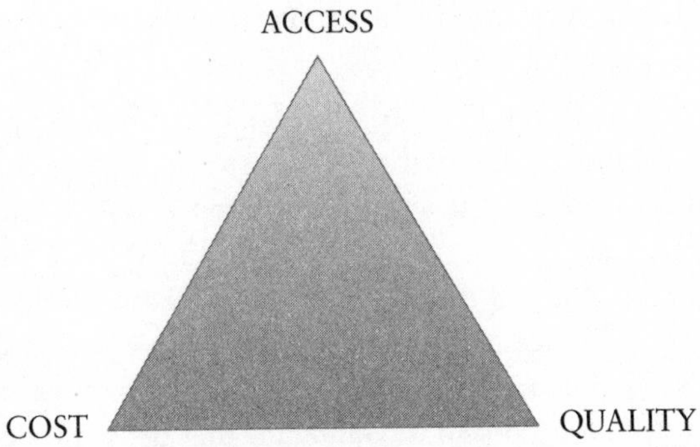

ACCESS

COST

QUALITY

and research, but then we wouldn't be able to contain costs. Or we could keep tuition low and maintain high quality by offering only a very few programs in select areas, but then we'd have to reduce students' access to higher education, at least at our own college or university. Attempting to find a solution to the iron triangle is what a lot of institutional change processes are all about.

As an exercise in organic leadership, imagine that you've been hired as a consultant to five institutions, each grappling with this problem in its own way. At each institution, a particular person or group has a visionary idea. Your job isn't to critique the idea; you may think of dozens of reasons that the proposal is bad or impractical, but that isn't the point of this exercise. You've been hired to advise the institution how its change process should proceed in order to give the proposal the greatest chance of succeeding. What do you recommend the institution do first? What steps in an effective change process has the school already omitted that it now needs to back up and accomplish?

○ *Institution A* has decided to deal with the iron triangle by focusing entirely on access and cost, while relegating quality to a subordinating role. A new president arrived four years ago and has been devoting time to working with various focus groups on how the institution can reverse a pattern of severely declining enrollment. Studies conducted by a joint committee of administrators and faculty members indicate that students in the institution's highly impoverished service area cannot afford even the relatively modest tuition the school charges. As a result, the committee recommends to the president a new vision in which the institution would peg what it charged for tuition and fees for thirty credits a year to that year's federal limit on Pell Grants. (At the time of publication, that limit is $5,645. Since this rate fluctuates, be sure to check the current limit when you conduct this exercise.) The institution's governing board opposes this idea because they believe that the school's quality of education will suffer so much that its reputation will decline. The faculty and staff largely support the concept, but the president remains uncommitted.

○ *Institution B* is a relatively new school that hasn't yet established a clear image for itself in the marketplace. As a way of creating a distinctive identity, the academic affairs committee of its governing board (which includes a number of faculty representatives) recommends a radical approach: the school will address only the quality component of the iron triangle, greatly sacrificing concessions to cost and access in order to do so. Inspired by the example of High Point University, the academic affairs committee of the board recommends that the school carry the

concierge concept of education to an extreme. It proposes what it calls
the Million Dollar Degree. For $250,000 a year (which will cover tuition,
fees, room, and board), the institution would offer the most luxurious
educational experience available anywhere, tailor each program to the
needs and interests of each individual student, and guarantee that the
student will graduate in four years provided that he or she remains in
good standing. The campus will be transformed into what the governing board calls "a cross between a country club and a beach resort." All
students will have private, fully furnished apartments that include maid
service. Meals will be cooked to order, and feature films will be available
on demand. Courses will be offered whenever and in whatever format
the student desires, with a full staff of tutors and academic coaches to
increase the likelihood of student success. The school's faculty generally
seems intrigued (and a bit amused) by this idea, but many members of the
administration and staff are having trouble visualizing how to make the
transition between what currently exists and this new vision. The president, provost, and board chair have enthusiastically endorsed the idea.

○ *Institution C* has an administration that believes the iron triangle,
as it is traditionally presented, overlooks an important element. It has
rephrased the challenge as an "iron rectangle" and suggests that issues
of access, cost, and quality are all manageable if schools simply sacrifice a fourth element: student choice. The administration of the school
believes that the reason so many colleges and universities become caught
in the iron triangle is that they are inefficient. Offering numerous electives and too many different degree programs means that many sections
end up running with less than full classrooms. As a result, personnel costs
are high and space use is far from economical at these colleges and universities. To reverse this trend, the administration unanimously supports
the idea of offering only a single program: a lockstep cohort program in
which all students will take the same courses and from which students
will all receive the same degree. The new curriculum will consist of four
years of English, mathematics, history, science, and a foreign language.
Students who maintain a cumulative B average or better will be permitted to take a single elective with only three options: psychology, business
administration, or studio art. The administration argues that the new curriculum will serve students' needs far better than the current system. For
example, those interested in applying to medical school will all have taken
biology, physical and organic chemistry, and physics in time for them to
take the MCAT at the end of their junior year. The students' attractiveness to employers and graduate or professional schools will be enhanced
because after four years of studying a single language, they will all have

achieved a high degree of proficiency in speaking Spanish, Mandarin Chinese, or Arabic (the only languages offered); once a student begins one of these languages, he or she will not be permitted to switch to any other. Written and oral communication, critical thinking, and cultural literacy will all be improved through a highly scaffolded series of required literature and history courses. Finally, students with a strong interest in psychology, business, or art will have an added incentive to work hard in their other courses. Best of all, each student will receive all of these benefits because everyone will be taking the same courses. To ensure a high four-year graduate rate, only full-time students would be accepted once the new curriculum is adopted. (Part-time students were not a large contingent of the institution's enrollment anyway.) While the staff supports the new vision wholeheartedly, there is strong faculty opposition, particularly from those whose favorite courses or even their entire program will be eliminated under the new system.

   o *Institution D* has a governing board that believes it has discovered a completely different kind of iron rectangle. In its view, the factor that is commonly overlooked when only cost, quality, and access are considered is the outdated instructional model that colleges and universities still use. Although institutions of higher education have come to realize that online courses are often a viable alternative to traditional classroom-based courses, they still haven't taken into consideration all the different ways in which students can acquire university-level knowledge and skills: life experience, private vendors like Rosetta Stone Language Programs and the Teaching Company, independent learning, massive open online courses, and the many other sources of information and training available in a highly technological society. As one member of the board said, "Why should we care how a student learns something? Our sole concern should be that he or she has learned it." The board then decides that the school will reinvent itself as a "credentialing university." Its sole purpose will be to validate and certify what students have learned, regardless of how they learned it. While it will continue to offer courses on a variety of platforms, none of its courses will be required for a degree. The institution will replace credit hour requirements with carefully developed outcome requirements. As long as students can demonstrate a certain level of competence in an area through exams, internships, or capstone projects, they will have fulfilled their requirement for that area. When the proposal is announced, there's an immediate backlash from the faculty who see their jobs in jeopardy. "We'll lose our accreditation!" one member of the faculty senate declares. In response, the trustees make the matter even worse by accusing the faculty of merely looking out for their own self-interest and using "high academic standards" as a screen for featherbedding. Tensions at the school are running high.

o *Institution E* has a faculty senate that observes the way in which institution D has proposed to reinvent itself and while it's intrigued by that idea, decides to take an equally radical but somewhat different approach: it suggests that the school do away with academic degrees entirely. Since institution D and its imitators will serve as "credentialing universities," institution E can fill a new need by becoming a "pedagogical university." The theory is that the sole mission of the school will be to convey knowledge and develop skills. It will continue to offer courses, but there will no longer be any requirement for those courses to last any minimum length of time. For example, a module on the use of a particular scientific instrument might last anywhere from three hours to two weeks. A program on piano proficiency might last three years. Since the entire concept of the four-year degree will be abandoned, students will be free to come to the university, take whatever modules or courses they want or need, and leave whenever they believe it's appropriate. They will pay only for the units of instruction they want. Grades will still be given for assignments, papers, and exams, but those grades will be only formative indicators of progress, not summative indicators of achievement. If students decide they need a degree, they will simply demonstrate their competence at a "credentialing university." The faculty senate argues that because the school will no longer offer degrees, it no longer needs either regional or specialized accreditation. It can close administrative offices devoted to accreditation, assessment, and institutional effectiveness and redirect the resulting savings into pedagogy so that more disciplines can be covered in more different ways on more instructional platforms. Administrators at the university reject the proposal out of hand, and communication between the faculty, students, and alumni is so intense that it eventually breaks down entirely.

Certainly the solutions proposed at each institution are creative and guaranteed to result in substantive change if adopted. And certainly there is a leadership group at each school that supports the idea that has been proposed. But where can each institution go from here in order to adopt, adapt, or reject the suggested innovation? What can you recommend not about the change itself but rather about the change process? Spend some time considering what your response would be before continuing to the next section.

Discussion of the Exercise

The five institutions described in the exercise vary widely in the extent to which they have practiced organic leadership. Institution A, for example, has a president who has spent his or her first four years working with focus groups on the school's enrollment problems. In none of the other institutions does there appear to have been that level of consultation and preparation for a change process. In fact, conflict or tension is specifically mentioned at institutions C, D, and E because one group or another got too far ahead of other stakeholders and began developing the substance of a proposed change without thinking through the most effective process to produce that change. As a result, at least one faction at each of those schools now actively opposes the initiative, perhaps even strongly enough to scuttle it. But these problems don't necessarily mean that each proposal is doomed. At institution D, for instance, if the faculty become properly engaged in developing the idea further, people may find a way in which becoming a "credentialing university" frees them from certain obligations that are currently unproductive and allows them to engage more extensively in activities that are more productive. For example, as a consultant, you could point out to faculty members that under the new system, they could reduce the number of introductory and survey courses they teach, allowing them more time for research. Administrators (except perhaps those directly involved in accreditation, assessment, and institutional effectiveness) at institution E might still be brought onboard the project if you can demonstrate to them that tuition revenue won't suffer, cost savings will increase, and the process is still early enough in its evolution that they'll have plenty of opportunities to help shape this radically innovative approach. Nevertheless, you would want to encourage them to engage in those discussions as soon as possible because the best time for them to have occurred is already past.

Institution B appears to fall somewhere between the (at least rudimentary) organic leadership found at institution A and the complete lack of it present at the other three schools. Its faculty is intrigued by the proposed concept, even though the idea was developed by the academic affairs committee of the governing board. That reaction would seem to suggest a somewhat amicable relationship between the board and the faculty, perhaps because there is direct faculty representation on that committee or perhaps because the two groups have worked together enough on previous projects that a level of trust has grown between them. In any case, if the idea is to have any chance of success, it'll be necessary for the faculty to be engaged even more directly, developing policies to ensure that suitable academic standards are preserved and providing practical advice on how to handle the difficult transition between the institution's current focus and the board's proposal.

Perhaps the biggest problem for you as a consultant is the absence of a compelling needs case at most of these schools. Institution A clearly has a pressing need: it has experienced severely declining enrollments, and its ongoing viability is being challenged. Institution B could certainly develop a compelling needs case on the basis that it doesn't yet have a clearly defined image in the marketplace and that challenges will inevitably arise if the school can't adequately establish its identity. In fact, it was that very need that drove the governing board to develop its proposal. But what's more uncertain is whether that need has been adequately conveyed to other stakeholders. The faculty doesn't appear to be aware of it, and there's no indication that current students understand why the school will be changing so drastically either. As part of your recommendations as a consultant, therefore, you may want the school not only to expand its emphasis on organic leadership but also to backfill the communication of a compelling needs case related to the proposed change.

Institutions C, D, and E are in an even worse situation. We have no idea at all why they've decided to embark on a change process at this particular moment in their history. All we know is that they feel they've found a solution to the iron triangle dilemma, but what requires them to implement that solution right now? The lack of an answer to this question may explain why the proposed idea is encountering so much opposition. The stakeholder groups resisting the initiative may be less likely to work against it if they understand why the change has to occur. One receives the idea in institutions C, D, and E that the body advocating for the change began to pursue it not because it believed the institution would be weakened if no action was taken, but because it was attracted by the novelty of the concept.

One final area that should trouble you as a consultant is how little attention has been paid at most of the institutions to their own mission and values. Institution B can be excused from this criticism because it's a new college that is currently grappling with precisely what its mission and values should be. But the lack of attention at the other schools to what they really are and what they're trying to accomplish should be a cause of concern. At institution A, the joint committee implies that the school has a mission to provide access to education for residents of its highly impoverished service area, but there's no direct reference to the school's mission and vision to support this assumption. The committee's recommendation to lower the cost of tuition seems laudable—unless the long-standing purpose of the school has been to conduct advanced research and few if any of its students have traditionally come from the impoverished area in which the school is located. Perhaps, like Elon and High Point, a very affordable community college is already meeting the needs of local students. In that case, lowering tuition rates would merely create destructive competition with a school that's already fulfilling institution A's proposed new mission. In a similar way, institution C's proposal might be appropriate if its mission is to prepare students for certain graduate, professional, and law schools but not if it's a land grant university that has a mission to provide a widely comprehensive range of programs. Institution D's proposal might be appropriate if it's a state or community college, but not if it's been functioning effectively as a highly selective liberal arts college. And institution E's plan might be suitable at a liberal arts college, but not at a vocational or training school.

In sum, what you're encountering as a consultant is largely a group of schools where the excitement of a novel idea has outstripped need, identity, and political reality. The schools you're advising haven't adequately answered the question of what type of change is really appropriate for them: direction, personnel, tactics, structure, or procedures (see chapter 7) and why that particular type of change is needed. The most ethical—and ultimately the most effective—thing you can do as an advisor will be to try to slow down these change processes, not speed them up. Guide the various constituent groups at the schools to set aside for a moment their strong feelings for or against the particular plan under discussion and reconsider why they're interested in change in the first place. As I've noted from the beginning of this study, change is pervasive in higher education today. But we can't conclude from this observation that all change is either good or necessary. While the changes under consideration at many colleges or universities today may not be nearly as sweeping as those under consideration in our thought experiment, they often share with them the tendency to want to begin fixing a problem before it's been clearly articulated. At times, these processes are already well under way before it's even established that a problem exists.

Measuring the Unmeasurable

Since I've spent much of this book criticizing what doesn't work—traditional strategic planning, change models designed for the corporate rather than academic world, top-down change processes imposed by "visionary" leaders, metrics commonly used to document institutional success, and all the other failed ways in which people usually try to change higher education—it seems only fair that as we draw near the end of this study, I lay out what I believe *does* work. For example, in chapter 5 I mentioned the limited value that was gained by tracking most of the metrics usually gathered as part of strategic planning processes. Those metrics, you'll recall, are frequently overinterpreted, predetermined by input metrics (such as how selective the institution is in admitting students), and measured largely because they happen to be the type of information that schools have on hand. But if such commonly tracked data as retention and graduation rates are not the best indicators of a school's success, what are? How do you measure such seemingly unmeasurable phenomena as the improvement a university brings to a student's life, the increase in wisdom and understanding that results from a general education program, and the positive impact on society made by any one academic department? Certainly there's an abundance of data available on how higher education in general improves lives (see Buller, 2013), but how can we demonstrate how much of that impact comes from any particular school, program, course, or professor?

A good way to begin to answer this question is to admit that we can't measure it—at least not directly. But what we can measure are things that play a more important role in what colleges and universities do than we can gather from the metrics commonly found in strategic plans and annual reports. As we saw in chapter 9, Harvey Perlman at the University of Nebraska–Lincoln and Edwin Massey at Indian River Community College did exactly that by studying the climate and culture of their schools and then making improvements to that climate and culture wherever they could. For instance, IRSC began to pay less attention to *US News and World Report* rankings and more attention to these components considered by the *Chronicle of Higher Education* when compiling its "Great Colleges to Work For" issue:

1. Collaborative Governance: Faculty members play significant roles in decisions on academic programs.

2. Compensation & Benefits: Pay is fair, and benefits are satisfactory.

3. Confidence in Senior Leadership: Leaders have the knowledge, skills, and experience necessary for the success of the college.

4. Diversity: The college makes a concerted effort to create a welcoming and fair environment for all employees.

5. Facilities, Workspace & Security: Facilities meet employees' needs, and the campus looks good.

6. Job Satisfaction: There is an overall sense that the job is meaning-ful to the employee and to the college.

7. Professional/Career-Development Programs: Employees get chances to develop skills and understand requirements for career advancement.

8. Respect & Appreciation: Employees are regularly recognized for their contributions.

9. Supervisor or Department-Chair Relationship: Supervisors or chairs solicit ideas and make expectations clear.

10. Teaching Environment: Faculty say the institution recognizes innovative and high-quality teaching.

11. Tenure Clarity & Process: Requirements for tenure are clear.

12. Work/Life Balance: Policies give employees flexibility to man-age their lives on the job and at home. (How the Survey Was Conducted, 2013)

Making improvements in these areas had a far greater impact on the students' experience, the faculty's productivity, and the institution's community engagement than trying to increase retention rates and the number of research grants submitted. Counterintuitively, by not becoming preoccupied with *US News and World Report* rankings, IRSC actually improved its *US News and World Report* rankings, rising to become number 12 among all the public regional colleges in the southern United States (http://www.irsc.edu/uploadedFiles/AboutIRSC/USNewsRankingTop12 .pdf). Expanding collaborative governance, making a concerted effort to recognize individual contributions, changing reward structures to emphasize innovation in teaching, and improving the work/life balance of the faculty and staff may not initially seem likely to improve the overall student experience and the institution's engagement with its community, but they do. Similarly at UNL, efforts to improve the institution's scores on the Gallup Organization's Twelve Questions That Matter (Q12) and ten-question inclusivity inventory (I10; see chapter 9) ended up yielding improvements in areas that you might not immediately believe to be related to campus climate and inclusivity.

When measuring the effect of organic change leadership, therefore, we have to remember its proper focus: this type of leadership seeks to improve a culture, not merely move the needle on a gauge that's ultimately not particularly informative. Climate or morale surveys can be valuable resources in gaining a sense of where your institution is with regard to creating its culture of innovation. Best of all, you don't have to start from scratch. Many colleges and universities have already developed instruments to help take the pulse of your institution. These are particularly good examples:

- o The University of California, Riverside's Survey of Staff Views and Ideas: morale.ucr.edu/pdf/staff_survey.pdf
- o The One Minute Climate Assessment, as developed by the University of Wisconsin-Stout and adapted by the University of Wisconsin-Madison: www.provost.wisc.edu/deptChairs /images/ImprovingClimate.pdf
- o Radford University's Faculty Morale Survey: http://senate.asp .radford.edu/current/reports/campusenvironment/120424_CEC _MoraleSurveyReport_GeneralRelease.pdf

Many climate surveys deal almost exclusively with issues of diversity and inclusiveness. While those issues are certainly an important part of any study of institutional climate, for the purposes of monitoring the overall culture of an institution, it's better to examine a broader range of issues. The Campus Climate and Morale Survey in exhibit 10.1 might serve as an initial template until you develop an instrument better tailored to your own specific purposes.

Exhibit 10.1 Campus Climate and Morale Survey

Instructions: After entering some demographic data that will help us determine whether the climate and morale of the institution are perceived differently by different stakeholder groups, indicate the degree to which you agree or disagree with each of the twenty-five items on the inventory. Use the right-most column (N/A or N/R) for any question that you feel doesn't apply to you or that you'd prefer not to answer.

Relationship to the Institution

- ▢ Administrator
- ▢ Full-time faculty
- ▢ Part-time faculty
- ▢ Staff
- ▢ Student
- ▢ Prefer not to say

Gender

- ❏ Male
- ❏ Female
- ❏ Prefer not to say

Ethnicity

- ❏ White/Caucasian/European American
- ❏ Black/African/African American
- ❏ Latino/Chicano/Hispanic
- ❏ Asian
- ❏ Native American/American Indian
- ❏ Multicultural/blended heritage
- ❏ Other
- ❏ Prefer not to say

How many years have you been associated with this institution? _____ year(s)

Please place an X in the column for each item that best fits your response:

	Strongly Agree	Agree	Neither Agree nor Disagree	Disagree	Strongly Disagree	N/A or N/R
1. I receive the information I need in order to do my work effectively.						
2. I am able to manage the stress associated with my work.						
3. I feel physically safe on campus.						
4. I feel that my work is appreciated.						
5. I feel that diversity is valued at this institution.						
6. I feel that creativity and new ideas are appreciated at this institution.						
7. I feel that my opinion is respected at this institution.						
8. I feel at home at this institution.						

	Strongly Agree	Agree	Neither Agree nor Disagree	Disagree	Strongly Disagree	N/A or N/R
9. There are people at this institution to whom I can express my concerns openly and without fear of reprisal.						
10. I have received at least one thorough appraisal of my work within the last year.						
11. The central administration of the institution acts ethically.						
12. The administration of my college acts ethically.						
13. The administration of my department acts ethically.						
14. On the whole, my peers interact with me in a collegial manner.						
15. I am regularly offered opportunities that allow me to grow or improve in my work.						
16. I believe that my performance is evaluated fairly.						
17. I believe that the institution is following the right priorities.						
18. I believe that the institution genuinely cares about the faculty.						
19. I believe that the institution genuinely cares about the staff.						
20. I believe that the institution genuinely cares about the students.						
21. I feel that the institution has a positive reputation with the public at large.						
22. I am proud to be associated with this institution.						
23. I am optimistic about my future relationship with this institution.						
24. I could honestly recommend this institution for a student to attend.						
25. I could honestly recommend this institution as a place for someone to work.						

Some of the information you'd gain from this type of survey lets you know immediately what you should do. For example, if you observe relatively low scores on such items as "I receive the information I need in order to do my work effectively" or "I feel physically safe on campus," obvious responses seem called for. You can work on improving internal systems of communication, strengthen security through a more visible presence of the campus safety office, install more emergency call boxes, and the like. But what do you do if many people say that they don't feel at home at the institution or wouldn't recommend it to a prospective student? These are matters that you can't change by introducing a new policy or merely telling people to be nicer to one another. It may require a complete transformation of the institution's operating procedures. Discovering what you should do begins with a candid self-reflection of what message you yourself are sending your stakeholders by your words and actions. Are you demonstrating that you truly care about the people who work or study at the school? Do you publicly recognize exceptional performance, creativity, and the willingness to take calculated risks? Do you encourage the people who report to you to do the same? Have you ever made it clear in your public statements and annual reports that progress in these areas is an important goal for you?

The demographic information collected at the beginning of the inventory is a crucial part of what you need to know. If you discover that a particular population at your college or university differs in its responses to the aggregated scores of everyone at the institution or from some other particular population, you'll then have some additional questions to ask. For example, why might the faculty feel less optimistic about the school's future than the administration, staff, and students? Why might women feel that the campus is less safe than the men? Why might Asian students feel more at home at the school than other ethnicities do? What are you to make of the fact that pride in the institution increases or decreases over time? Identifying differences among various stakeholder groups or other populations at the institution can be highly revealing for how the same message or policy is perceived in ways that are poles apart by different constituencies. It can often be helpful to drill down into answers that are completely unexpected by holding meetings with focus groups where people feel safe to voice their opinions without any fear of reprisal. You may learn things that are painful to hear but ultimately beneficial for the type of leadership you provide.

How does this type of morale survey help you bring about positive change? Remember that effective change leaders are those who create a culture of innovation, not those who track metrics as though they were recording league statistics. All the rhetoric of "keeping our eyes on the prize" only obscures the fact that in order to win that prize, there are a lot of other things we need to keep our eyes on. As we saw in chapter 6, creative change tends to be produced by creative people. And people are at their most creative when they feel safe and valued, when they have trust in the people they work for. (For studies documenting the effect of safety and trust on employee creativity, see Gong, Cheung, Wang, and Huang, 2012, and Lovelace, 1986.) Creative thinking also tends to emerge in work groups where diversity is both visibly present and highly valued (Milliken, Bartel, and Kurtzburg, 2003). In other words, although the issues addressed in the sample morale survey in exhibit 10.1 may initially appear somewhat removed from the topic of change leadership in higher education, it turns out that they are exactly the factors that make innovative and substantive change possible. They also indicate why so many traditional strategic planning processes either fail entirely or produce only limited results: tying rewards like job security and salary increases to performance metrics results in stress, fear, and distrust between supervisors and employees; stress, fear, and distrust inhibit creativity and willingness to change. So as paradoxical as it may seem, obsession with the kind of metrics usually associated with strategic planning can actually prevent colleges and universities from improving in those areas. People become entrenched in their positions because changing their approach brings risk. Time, which could be spent in exploring creative new solutions, becomes devoted to justifying why progress isn't possible rather than making it possible. It's time for academic leaders to stop confusing metrics with goals. Our goal should be to improve student learning and produce research of a very high quality, not gathering data that demonstrate we're doing so.

Conclusion

We are now in a position to answer the question I asked at the beginning of this study: If change is all around us, why do we handle it so poorly at colleges and universities today? It's because we rely on change models unsuited to the organizational culture that exists in higher education—models that encourage us to act in ways that are actually counterproductive to bringing about positive, meaningful change. If we want change processes to be more effective, we have to progress from many of the common and traditional ways of looking at change. We have to reexamine the possibilities at our institutions in light of approaches that force us to shift our perspective, like Bolman and Deal's four frames,

Edward de Bono's six thinking hats, or our ten analytical lenses. We need to keep in mind how the drivers of change we encounter in a STEEPLED analysis can help us prepare better for whatever scenarios may arise. We have to ground our arguments for change in terms of a needs case, not a mere summary of the change's comparative advantages or net benefits. We need to phase out traditional strategic planning in favor of setting a more flexible strategic compass. We need to devote energy toward creating a culture of innovation, not to tracking metrics we can't easily control and don't really reflect what's most important to us. We need to create that culture of innovation by focusing on people and processes, not by overemphasizing outcomes. And if we do all that, we'll be engaging in a new kind of change leadership—one that takes an organic approach to "grow" change, not a mechanical approach to "manufacture" change—which draws on the best practices found at institutions that have truly been transformed by the changes that academic leaders have recommended. The best news of all is that in order to practice this new kind of organic change leadership, we don't have to be the president or chancellor or chair of the governing board. As the name of Mark Sanborn's book on positive leadership puts it, *You Don't Need a Title to Be a Leader* (2006). You can begin to affect the culture of your institution no matter what your job description may be. All it takes is a recognition that meaningful change is all about the culture and that the culture is all about the people. Trust the people you work with, empower them, and recognize their efforts to be creative, and the change that will result will be far more spectacular than can be possible with even the most well-developed strategic plan.

REFERENCES

Buller, J. L. (2013). *Positive academic leadership: How to stop putting out fires and start making a difference.* San Francisco, CA: Jossey-Bass.

Gong, Y., Cheung, S.-Y., Wang, M., & Huang, J.-C. (2012). Unfolding the proactive process for creativity: Integration of the employee proactivity, information exchange, and psychological safety perspectives. *Journal of Management, 38*(5), 1611–1633.

How the survey was conducted. (2013, July 26). *Chronicle of Higher Education,* A4.

Lovelace, R. F. (1986). Stimulating creativity through managerial intervention. *R&D Management, 16*(2), 161–174.

McGregor, D. (1960). *The human side of enterprise.* New York, NY: McGraw Hill.

Milliken, F. J., Bartel, C. A., & Kurtzburg, T. R. (2003). Diversity and creativity in work groups: A dynamic perspective on the affective and cognitive processes that link diversity and performance. In P. B. Paulus & B. A. Nijstad (Eds.), *Group creativity: Innovation through collaboration*. New York, NY: Oxford University Press.

Ouchi, W. G. (1981). *Theory Z: How American business can meet the Japanese challenge*. Reading, MA: Addison-Wesley.

Sanborn, M. (2006). *You don't need a title to be a leader: How anyone, anywhere, can make a positive difference*. New York, NY: Currency Doubleday.

RESOURCES

Buller, J. L. (2014). Change leadership for chairs. *Department Chair, 24*(3), 3–5.

Buller, J. L. (2014). Tellin' ain't leadin'. *Academic Leader, 30*(2), 1, 6.

ATLAS: Academic Training, Leadership, & Assessment Services offers training programs, books, and materials dealing with collegiality and positive academic leadership. Its programs include:

- Time Management
- Work-Life Balance
- Conflict Management
- Promoting Teamwork
- Promoting Collegiality
- Communicating Effectively
- Mentoring Faculty Members
- Positive Academic Leadership
- The Essential Academic Dean
- The Essential Department Chair
- Best Practices in Faculty Evaluation
- Change Leadership in Higher Education

These programs are offered in half-day, full-day, and multiday formats. ATLAS also offers reduced prices on leadership books and distributes the Collegiality Assessment Matrix and Self-Assessment Matrix, which allow academic programs to evaluate the collegiality and civility of their faculty members in a consistent, objective, and reliable manner. The free *ATLAS E-Newsletter* addresses a variety of issues related to academic leadership and is sent free to subscribers.

For more information, contact:

ATLAS: Academic Training, Leadership, & Assessment Services
4521 PGA Boulevard, PMB 186
Palm Beach Gardens FL 33418
800–355–6742; www.atlasleadership.com
E-mail: questions@atlasleadership.com

INDEX

If you enjoyed this book, you may also like these:

ositive Academic Leadership: How to Stop
ting Out Fires and Start Making a Difference
by Jeffrey L. Buller
ISBN: 9781118531921

Best Practices in Faculty Evaluation: A
Practical Guide for Academic Leaders
by Jeffrey L. Buller
ISBN: 9781118118436

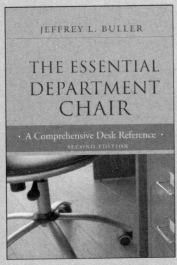

The Essential Department Chair: A
omprehensive Desk Reference, 2nd Edition
by Jeffrey L. Buller
ISBN: 9781118123744

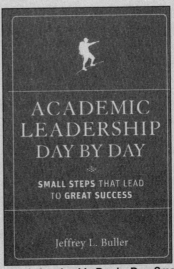

Academic Leadership Day by Day: Small
Steps That Lead to Great Success
by Jeffrey L. Buller
ISBN: 9780470903001

WILEY